CHARACTER DEVELOPMENT IN COLLEGE STUDENTS

Volume I: The Freshman Year

by

John M. Whiteley

International Standard Book Number 0-915744-30-9 (hard cover)
International Standard Book Number 0-915744-22-8 (paperback)
Library of Congress Catalog Card No. LC 82-071329
First Printing

Typesetting
by
Helen C. Cernik

CHARACTER DEVELOPMENT IN COLLEGE STUDENTS

Volume I: The Freshman Year

By John M. Whiteley
University of California, Irvine
and Associates:

Barbara D. Bertin
University of California, Irvine

J. Steven Jennings
Pennsylvania State University

Loren Lee
University of California, Los Angeles

Holly A. Magaña
Centro Interdisciplinario de Investigacion
y Docencia en Educacion Tecnica,
Queretaro, Mexico

Arthur Resnikoff
University of California, Irvine
with the editorial assistance of
Karen Kao

Published by:

Character Research Press
207 State Street
Schenectady, New York 12305
in association with:
American College Personnel
Association

Distributed by:

American Personnel and
Guidance Association
Two Skyline Place, Suite 400
5203 Leesburg Pike
Falls Church, VA 22041

ABOUT THE FRONT COVER

The cover design, featuring the Chambered Nautilus (N. Pompilius, Linn.), is the inspiration of Vivian Chang of the Publications Office at the University of California, Irvine. She read portions of this book in its manuscript form and subsequently prepared a series of sketches from which this cover was selected. Apart from the subtlety and attractiveness of what Vivian has developed, the metaphor itself is highly appropriate, for it symbolically illustrates the growth process which occurs in the development of character.

The Chambered Nautilus is a member of the class Cephalopoda which contains the nautili, octopods, squids, and cuttlefish. Cephalopoda are the most highly organized of all mollusks and have attained the largest size of any invertebrates. In contrast to the occupants of "ordinary shells" whose bodies fill the entire shell cavity,

> the animal of the nautilus uses only a small portion of the shell or outer chamber, and builds pearly partitions behind its body as it increases in size, although a slender fleshy cord extends from the body through all the partitions, thus forming an anchor or mooring to the shell (Verrill, 1936, p. 150).

Several stanzas of a poem by Oliver Wendell Holmes on the Chambered Nautilus describe the growth of the Nautilus and parallel the growth which we have hoped to inspire in the character development of college students.

Year after year beheld the silent toil
That spread his lustrous coil;

Still, as the spiral grew,
He left the past year's dwelling for the new,
Stole with soft step its shining archway through,

Built up its idle door,
Stretched in his last-found home, and knew the old no more....

"Build thee more stately mansions, O my soul,
As the swift seasons roll!

Leave thy low-vaulted past!
Let each new temple, nobler than the last,
Shut thee from heaven with a dome more vast,

Till thou at length are free,
Leaving thine outgrown shell by life's unresting sea!"*

References

Verrill, A. H. *Strange sea shells and their stories*. Boston: L. C. Page & Co., 1936.

The works of Oliver Wendell Holmes (Vol. I). New York: Houghton, Mifflin, 1950.

*From *The works of Oliver Wendell Holmes, Volume 1* pp. 97-98. The Chambered Nautilus. Boston: Houghton, Mifflin, 1892.

APPRECIATIONS

The Sierra Project and this report of it could not have happened without the contributions of many different individuals — without the colleagueship and support of students and staff at the University of California, Irvine, the invaluable advice and encouragement of pioneers in the fields of developmental psychology and psychological education programs, and the continuing commitment to the goals of the Sierra Project of its participants, teachers, evaluators, and administrators. I would like to express at least a part of my appreciation to the following individuals:

Janet Clark Loxley, our principal classroom instructor who brought a high level of creativity and sensitivity as teacher and psychologist to the task of building and delivering the curriculum;

James B. Craig, our principal contact with the Housing Office, who facilitated all housing related aspects of the Sierra Project and who has assured that subsequent freshman classes have also benefited from the Sierra psychological intervention;

Barbara D. Bertin, who assured us a dependable administrative structure for collecting and scoring our data and who made valuable contributions to both the curriculum development and the evaluation portions of the project;

Karen H. Nelson, the initial project evaluator, who helped plan our evaluation and brought my attention to recent advances in developmental psychology and life-span developmental research;

Holly Magaña, principal data analyst for the Sierra Project, who established the system file and trained our subsequent analysis team: Elizabeth Kaye Kasdan, Chris Clark Means, and Norma Yokota;

the journal readers, whose detailed responses to the journals kept by all Sierra freshmen served to stimulate and support students in their new environment — Pamela Burton, Jeanette Eberhardy, Carole Findlay-Ducoff, Holly Magaña, Dave Marrero, Martha Morgan, Molly Slaten, Karen Vogel, and Edward Weeks;

the sophomore student staff, who gave of themselves so extensively and who assisted us in "bridging the generation gap" —

Class of 1979: Mundo Norte (RA), Jeanette Caldeira, Jocelyn Campos, James Harrison, Kim Kreiling, Chris Leatherwood;

Class of 1980: James Harrison (RA), Kevin Clover (RA), Maueen Burris, J. Steven Jennings, Susan Lindsey, Chuan Ren, Valerie Samuel, Norma Yokota; Class of 1981: Maureen Burris (RA), Gregory Bolles, Robert Burbank, James Fiorino, Jose Leal, Grizel Norte, Mary Ann Skorpanich;

Class of 1982: Bridgette Berry (RA), J. P. Congleton, John Elston, Carlyle Kidd, Teresa Martinez, Pamela McZeal, Lisa Stangl;

Ralph L. Mosher and Norman A. Sprinthall, pioneers and innovators of psychological education at the elementary and secondary school levels, who have stimulated my thinking, critically examined what we have tried to do, and cared enough to devote time to helping us think through methods for improving the Sierra Project and this report;

James R. Rest, who read portions of the manuscript in an earlier form and greatly assisted me in solving methodological problems in the data analysis;

Daniel G. Aldrich, Jr., founding chancellor of the University of of California, Irvine, who has created a climate in which research and curriculum development such as that of the Sierra Project are encouraged and supported;

Scott Whiteley, Barbara Tomlinson, and William Craig, who read this manuscript in an earlier form and provided skilled commentary on how to improve its presentation;

Karen Kao, my perpetual critic and colleague, who has aided me in sharpening and articulating my thoughts from their inception to their presence on the printed page;

Helene Hollingsworth, who masterminded the task of getting this manuscript, in all of its phases, to press;

Barbara McKinney, who transcribed the rough manuscripts and consistently incorporated revisions generated by our numerous proofreaders and editors;

Tracey Minkin, who undertook the indexing, and whose perspective from outside helped clarify portions of the book;

Jane DuKet, who typed handwritten sections and helped assure by detailed proofreading a clean and consistent final manuscript;

Herman Williams of the Character Research Press for publishing this book and the leadership of the American College Personnel Association and the American Personnel and Guidance Association for distributing it;

the residents of Sierra Hall, who so wholeheartedly participated in the psychological intervention and its associated research studies and thereby gave us a better understanding of character development in college students.

John M. Whiteley
Irvine, California

DEDICATION

To my children: Elizabeth M. Whiteley
                        Gregory T. Whiteley
                        Jennifer A. Whiteley
                        John M. Whiteley II
                        William C. Whiteley

with hope for their educations for the 21st century

FOREWORD

Nevitt Sanford

American universities have been expanding and becoming differentiated at a rate far beyond their capacity to achieve the integration which is necessary to any living system. Particularly in the years since World War II we have seen a fantastic proliferation of departments, specialities within departments, institutes, centers, and programs, each of which, in the major universities, has behaved as an independent principality, bent on its own aggrandizement, relating less to other substructures in the same institution than to outside constituents, markets, and sources of funds. This has been going on long enough so that this model of a university is widely regarded as just a phenomon of nature, something that the good Lord intended.

Enormous interest is vested in these present structures. It seems that only a few of us old-timers remember the humane and humanizing universities of the 1920's and 1930's, some of which surely achieved greatness — and this without huge inputs of funds from Washington or elsewhere. Their greatness depended on a clear vision of goals and a willingness to organize effort in their pursuit.

In my more despairing moments it seems to me that the modern university has succeeded in separating almost everything that belongs together. Not only have fields of inquiry been subdivided until they have become almost meaningless, but research has been separated from teaching, teaching and research from action, and, worst of all, thought from humane feeling.

The effects of these changes on students, especially undergraduates, have been devastating. It is fair to say that in most of our universities — and in many of our elite liberal arts colleges — a majority of the students suffer from a lack of a sense of community, confusion about values, a lack of intimate friends, a very tenuous sense of self (including serious doubt about their personal worth) and the absence of a great cause, movement, service, religion, belief system, or anything else that they might see as larger than themselves and in which they could become deeply involved.

I conclude from this that those of us who care about the nation's youth and their education must now work to construct conditions and promote values that we once took for granted.

Much of value was taken for granted at the University of Richmond (a small college with a law school) when I was there in the 1920's. I am sure it never occurred to anyone to suggest that we ought to build community. Indeed, to have talked about community at that time and place would have been like talking to a fish about water. It was not only that students and faculty alike generally shared the same values but we all could upon occasion display our genuine school spirit. I belonged to a fraternity and to several athletic teams; and was best friends with a young man who shared my interest in academic work. I never doubted that these young men cared for me and over the years I have always known that when I went back to Richmond we would take up our friendships just where we left off. My older fraternity brothers and teammates took pains to instruct me how to act in various social situations. At the same time I was sometimes able to help some fellow athletes with their homework; they took pride in the fact that one of them could "understand this stuff." I was usually able to hold my own in the innumerable "bull sessions" we had.

I was never close to my professors, being too shy to take questions or problems to any of them. I can, however, call up vivid images of at least a dozen of these men. This, I think, is not so much because they were unusually individualistic, but because they expressed themselves more freely than do professors today. They were teachers above all else; they felt safe in saying what they pleased and, most important, we could "get them off the subject." We wanted to know what they really felt and thought about issues and people, not just about Shakespeare or Bismarck but about H. L. Mencken, the Scopes trial, and the Soviet Union; in sum, about what interested us. Thus, they exposed themselves as whole persons and bearers of value.

One value that was universally espoused was that of liberal education. In "bull sessions" we debated whether the purpose of education was to learn "how to live" or "how to make a living" and came down overwhelmingly on the side of the former. Even those students who were bound for medicine, law, or the ministry thought the way to get started was to "get a liberal education."

Most of us gave little thought to what we would do after college. All we were clear about was that we would stay as close as possible to the city of Richmond and maintain close ties with family and friends. They would find jobs for us, and if we got into trouble they would take care of us. We were under no pressure to establish our "vocational identities." The selves we felt ourselves to be depended instead on such factors as family, locale, region, religion, ethnicity, school, and group memberships; also on interest, activities, and personal characteristics that were confirmed by others. The confirming—or disconfirming—of notions we had about ourselves was fairly easy in an environment where friends and relations cared enough to "straighten each other out."

I, in company with many of my fellows, I believe, had a hard time finding out what I could and could not do, suffering more than a few painful blows to self-esteem in the process; but I never doubted that in some fundamental way I was, or would be, all right. This was not only because I knew I was loved by family and friends but because our professors somehow conveyed the idea that, despite our obvious shortcomings, great things were expected of us; the reason they berated us so often was because they believed that, some day, affairs of great moment could be left safely in our hands.

In sum, we had *community*, every opportunity for intimacy, values that were clearly defined and exemplified by professors, ways of defining ourselves that did not depend on achievement or vocational aspiration, and plenty of ways to satisfy our need for "homonomy." This last is Andras Angyal's term. He wrote that every individual needs not only autonomy but homonomy, "to become an organic part of something he conceives as greater than himself—to be in harmony with super individual units, the social world, nature, God, ethical world order, or whatever the individual's formulation of it may be" (Angyal, 1941, p. 172). There were plenty of things around that people could throw themselves into: the Christian religion, the Baptist Church, Southern culture, the Democratic party, Sigma Phi Epsilon, football—to mention a few.

Richmond was not unique. In fact, it was very much like other small colleges of the time—not only in the South but nationwide. More than that, much of the culture and spirit I have tried to describe prevailed in the universities. To get along at Harvard, where I became a graduate student in 1930, all one had to do was to have some intellectual interests, to respect those of others, and to be civil in argument. The faculty displayed these values; they showed their concern for students and convinced us that they could be trusted. We students, knowing that we were in a system that really worked, felt no need to compete with each other. Instead, mutual help and cooperation were the order of the day and many enduring friendships were formed.

The University of California at Berkeley, in the early 1940's, was even more a community than Harvard, even though there were 20,000 students around. It *felt* like a community. When Provost Monroe Deutsch spoke on formal occasions everybody felt that he spoke for us all. Professors in one department fraternized easily with professors in various others. Graduate students were happy and secure, for they knew that as long as they were serious and willing to work some professor would see them through to their degree. Assistant professors, such as I, were also secure, for we knew that having been brought into a departmental family we would be looked after and promoted in our turn. The psychology department at Berkeley was already famous in the 1930's; yet it was not until 1947 that any assistant professor ever hired by that department was out instead of up.

When I went to work at Vassar College in 1952 I soon felt very much at home. The place was a lot like Richmond. Of course, the academic standards were higher, everybody was more serious about what they were doing, and there was greater liberalism in politics, but there was much of the sort of community I had grown used to. There was universal belief in liberal education and a generally agreed upon set of values, organized around something vaguely defined as "quality." This embodied some intellectual snobbery, but there was much more to it than that. The faculty cared about students and worked hard at their teaching. Although there was some social stratification in the student body there was much sisterliness and open display of loyalty to the school. It was generally agreed that Vassar was a place where "you made your life-long friends."

But Vassar, like almost all other colleges and universities in the country, was to change. Shortly after World War II the federal government began pouring money into the universities to support research and graduate training. Soon the universities were putting more and more emphasis on research, less and less on teaching undergraduates. For example in the late 1940's my colleagues and I in the psychology department at Berkeley set out to make ours the strongest department in the university and the strongest psychology department in the nation. We competed fiercely with other departments around the country in our effort to get the best young researchers. We did not ask if they could teach; to sweeten our offers, we made the proposed teaching load as light as possible and promised our new recruits that they could teach their specialities. The curriculum proliferated wildly. At one time, unbeknownst to anybody in the department, the same text was being used in five courses, each with a different name. When our most senior professor retired there was no one around to worry about the integration of our curriculum. All that mattered was research and publication, and the training of graduate students in various specialities. In these circumstances nobody had time for undergraduates. They would have been dismissed altogether, I believe, were it not for the fact that the budget for psychology depended on how many undergraduate students we had.

What was happening in psychology, as I later learned, was happening in most other departments of the university, and what was happening at Berkeley was happening at universities all over the country. And after 1957, when Sputnik was launched, things took a turn for the worse. Now there was an increased accent on science and technology as a road to "national strength." The kind of science that soon got the upper hand was that modelled after 19th century physics. Understanding was to be achieved by the analysis of phenomena into finer and finer bits. Knowledge of how things fit together could wait. The required rate of publication could not be sustained if professors addressed themselves to large or complicated issues. The research that was to save us from the Russians became more and more trivial. In psychology, issues of great moment were turned into methodological problems.

In the humanities as well as in the sciences the Western techno-scientific approach to knowledge became increasingly dominant. In the excitement following Sputnik there was general acceptance of the notion that American education was mediocre. Professors now felt that they had permission to do, and to do more rigorously, what they wanted to do anyway, that is, concentrate on their scholarly specialties in their teaching as well as in their research. Professors of literature, for example, instead of focusing on the task of making great works available to undergraduates, insisted on close reading, detailed analysis, and interpretation according to their preferred conceptual schemes. In philosophy, professors who wanted to reduce their discipline to arguments about what philosophy is, or to the analysis of linguistic minutiae, took a new lease on life.

Where in the curriculum, then, were students to find anything to nurture the spirit? How were they to attain broad understanding, to find out what it means to be human, to experience wonder, to acquire a sense of values?

The liberal arts colleges, particularly the elitist ones, followed the example of the universities. The departments evaluated themselves primarily on the basis of how many of their students gained admission to good graduate schools. The safest course was to teach these undergraduates what the professors knew would be taught again in graduate school.

By 1964, as it turned out, the situation had become explosive. The student protests that began at Berkeley in September, 1964 were in the beginning protests against the "irrelevance" of the curriculum and the "impersonality" of campus life. Although the students' insistence on educational reform was soon forced into the background by protests against the Viet Nam War, it persisted and became a national movement. Great energy went into this movement, but it suffered from a lack of educational leadership. Many institutions just gave the students what they said they wanted, with small attention to what they needed. Nevertheless many constructive things were done. Whole new institutions were started within and without existing colleges and universities; for example, the experimental colleges within the University of California, Berkeley, and New College in San Francisco. Unfortunately this was almost always done with soft money and very few of the innovations have persisted.

Today the excitement of the sixties and early seventies seems remote. With the end of the Viet Nam War in sight the student movement ran out of steam, as movements do, and inevitably some reaction set in. Up until quite recently, and still, institutions have been busy putting back into place things that were "dislocated" in response to student activism. Neither students nor university officers are thinking about educational reform. They have other things on their minds. Students, for their part, having decided to work within the system, are very much taken up with getting into professional schools and will do whatever is required. Professors, with only pliable students to deal with, feel free to do what they like most and do best, that is, research and teaching their specialties — preferably to graduate students.

Concern with moral values seems to have disappeared from the scene. If the university has any noble purposes, or any purposes beyond preparing students for vocations, keeping the wheels turning, and maintaining the standard of living, there does not seem to be anyone around to say what these purposes are. Even with the emphasis on ethics that followed Watergate, instruction in this area has been focused almost exclusively on how to analyze ethical issues, critique ethical positions, and avoid "moral indoctrination" (Bennett, 1980). Nobody is telling students that they ought to do better or be better persons, or suggesting what *is* better; nor do students have much opportunity to learn from the example of their elders. On every university campus there are, to be sure, professors who have the self-discipline that it takes to discover and to tell the truth. But there are more who present examples of competitiveness and acquisitiveness, absorption in narrow specialities, virtuosity untempered by humane feeling. For better or worse, however, students rarely get to know their professors well enough to consider them as models. "Getting them off the subject" went out of fashion some time ago.

What is even more to be regretted, professors do not know their undergraduate students. Last year I had a letter from a former Stanford student who was in prison for murder. He is a Viet Nam veteran who had become mentally disturbed and deeply involved with drugs. The prosecutor had tagged him a sociopath, and he needed the testimony of someone who knew him when he was a student. He had taken a lecture course from me and, for one quarter in 1963, a course in guided reading and research. We met six or eight times and he submitted a paper. He told enough in his letter about what he had said and what I had said so that, remarkably enough, I remembered him. I believe I was able to be of some help to him. But (and this is the point of the story) I was the only professional person at Stanford who had known him personally and who, as he thought, might conceivably remember him. And he was there for four years. A university can be a very cold place; I have no doubt that it is as cold today as it was in 1963.

One might think that students who are alienated from their professors — and probably from most other adults — would turn to one another for intimacy and support. But not so. Colleagues and graduate students at the Wright Institute, who have been studying student life at Berkeley, tell me that these young people do not know how to make friends or behave on dates — that there is a distressing amount of loneliness on campus. I had observed the same phenomena at Stanford in the early 1960's. Apparently there is so much competition for grades and status, so much uncertainty about who one is and what one can do, that students cannot expose themselves enough to make intimate relationships possible. Most of them, most of the time, are putting on some kind of act.

Equally distressing is the fact that they cannot talk over such problems among themselves. My Wright Institute informants interviewed, in considerable depth, 15 young men who lived in a nearby fraternity house. The plan was to use the major themes that came up in the interview as a basis for group discussion. As expected, the fraternity men enjoyed the interviews; they were open, sincere, willing to talk about serious problems. But when the three interviewers arrived at the fraternity house to hold the discussion the music was turned on, the beer had been distributed, and young women soon arrived. Of course there was no discussion. It was as if each individual personality had been dissolved in the group.

Many students have told me that they and their acquaintances could not organize discussions of serious questions. Not only were they too wary of one another, but there was the ubiquitous TV and record player. This is in contrast not only with the "good old days" but with the recent past when students were involved in efforts at educational or political change. There was plenty of communication among them then, and some of it was the sort that calls for self-revelation and leads to intimacy. What they had primarily was homonomy. And this raises the question of what is there today that students can lose themselves in. For many, no doubt, preparation for their chosen vocation is enough to capture their imaginations and use up their energies. Beyond that the scene appears bleak. There seems to be very little action on the political left. The women's movement, demonstrations against nuclear weapons or in favor of environmental protection are still out there, but much of the life seems to have been drained from them. Clearly we need some new movements and, this time around, something that adults as well as students can throw themselves into. The fact that they long for homonomy is, I believe, one reason why students join cults or new religious groups.

In thinking of the pre-World War II university as a source of ideas about how we might improve the quality of campus life, and better assist students in their self-development, we must remember that the culture which prevailed then had its dark side. At Richmond there was universal and completely thoughtless racism. There were *no* Black students there, or at any college I knew of. Blacks were so submerged that we never saw them except in menial roles; and this state of affairs was regarded as natural. Certainly it was never discussed. I was more aware of anti-Catholicism, and may have participated in it; but the ethnocentrism that I experienced most vividly and expressed with the most enthusiasm was in connection with a traditional football rivalry. On our campus it was generally believed that William and Mary College imported "ringers," (i.e., professional athletes, with strange ethnic backgrounds) who came from places like Jersey City, New Jersey. When we went into a game with this outfit it was virtually "holy war." Some months after graduating from college I was approached on the New York subway by a smiling young man who happily identified himself as someone who had played against me in the last Richmond-William and Mary game. I was struck dumb. Did he not realize that we were enemies, and that I would not be ready to make peace? He must have thought me a fool.

I might say in my own defense that people matured more slowly in those days than they do now, that it is probably better to display one's enthnocentrism on the playing fields than to do so in the streets. More than that, I was still an adolescent when I graduated from college, and adolescents are entitled to some measure of ethnocentrism. Their big problem is what to do about the emotional impulses they regard as low, destructive, and dangerous. The conventional strategy for adolescents, and for people stuck at that stage of development, is to cling to a group or to groups that are seen as good like themselves and to see the "bad" as existing in other people, who are then put beyond the pale.

Can we, then, have community without ethnocentrism? I believe that we can. We may hope that, as they grow older, adolescents will come to see that their impulses need not be projected onto other people or stamped out completely: that they may, instead, be modified or controlled. This kind of development can be brought about through education at the college level. It is partly a matter of learning to think well, and partly a matter of character development. What we desire for our college graduates is a capacity for group loyalty *and* tolerance of other groups, identity *and* intimacy, homonomy *and* autonomy. This requires that their personalities become sufficiently expanded, differentiated, and integrated so that opposite tendencies can be held in consciousness long enough for synergistic resolutions to be found.

I have argued for more than a few years (Sanford, 1956, 1962a, 1962b, and 1980) that the development of such personalities is the overarching aim of education and that all the resources of our educational institutions should be put in its service. As various theorists have insisted, personality functions as a unit; its diverse features develop an interaction one with the other (Allport, 1937; Murray, 1938; Angyal, 1941). Intelligence, feeling, emotion, and action can be separated conceptually but no one of them functions independently of the others. I wrote in 1962: "Just as nothing is truly learned until it has been integrated with the purposes of the individual, so no facts and principles that have been learned can serve any worthy human purpose unless they are restrained and guided by character. Intellect without humane feeling can be monstrous, while feeling without intelligence is childish; intelligence and feeling are at their highest and in the best relation one to another where there is a taste for art and beauty as well as an appreciation of logic and knowledge" (Sanford, 1962b).

I believe the authors of the present volume will agree with this statement, for their work is in the same spirit. Although they focus on character, it is clear that in creating a new educational environment—which they did as part of their Sierra Project—they have been guided by a conception of, and concern with, the whole person.

That environment, which is fully described here, deserves our best attention and careful study. It embodies in some degree all those things whose lack I have bemoaned in the above paragraphs. (In going on so long about the poor quality of student life generally, and about what we know, on the basis of the past, might be possible, my object has been to provide a background against which the significance of the Sierra Project may be highlighted.)

In this residential learning program we find a concern about values, opportunities to serve the larger community, close relations among faculty, staff and students, intensive small group discussions, special curricular experiences designed on the basis of developmental theory—in general a humanitarian and therefore humanizing environment. And all of this at the University of California, Irvine, an institution that prides itself on how rapidly it is becoming a great research university.

There are other projects and programs around the country that are based in theory and directed to the development of the student as a person. For example, at the University of Nebraska-Lincoln and at Azusa Pacific College students are provided with mentors and keep records of their activities and achievements. I know of no program, however, that is as comprehensive and far-reaching in its implications as the one being considered here.

The question is: What are the effects of the living-learning program on the students' development—with special reference to character? Attempts to answer this question for freshmen who spent one year in the project are fully described in this book. Experimental evaluation with the use of tests and control groups was carried out with the rigor one would expect of U.C. Irvine. More to my liking, there was a great deal of interviewing and some case studies.

Finally, I should say that the Sierra Project is not only a set of actions whose effects are then evaluated; it is also pure research on character development. This volume contains a thorough review of the literature on this subject but reports only part of the research results that are or will be available. Later reports will ·deal with the lasting effects of being in the program for freshmen and with the question of which educational procedures or experiences had what kinds of effects on which students. I can hardly wait.

References

Allport, G. W. *Personality: A psychological interpretation.* New York: Holt, 1937.

Angyal, A. *Foundations for a science of personality.* New York: Commonwealth Fund, 1941.

Bennett, W. J. Getting ethics. *Commentary,* 1980, *70* (6), 62-65.

Murray, H. A. *Explorations in personality.* New York: Oxford, 1938.

Sanford, N. Personality development during the college years. *Personnel and Guidance Journal,* 1956, *35,* 74-80.

Sanford, N. Higher education as a social problem In Sanford, N. (Ed.), *The American college.* New York: Wiley, 1962.(a)

Sanford, N. Ends and means in higher education. In K. Smith (Ed.), *Current issues in higher education.* Washington, DC: National Education Association, 1962.(b)

Sanford, N. *Learning after college.* Orinda, CA: Montaigne, 1980.

TABLE OF CONTENTS

INTRODUCTION

John M. Whiteley

The college years represent one of society's last opportunities to influence the next generation of its citizens — those who will lead its institutions and, as parents, will shape the nature of its future generations. The college years also represent a period of human development when young people are especially open to new influences as they make the transition from late adolescence to early adulthood. In the college years, for the first time in their lives, young people are physically and psychologically autonomous from parents, siblings, and previous friends while coming into contact with a wide variety of new associations and ideas in a particularly stimulating environment — one where improving the quality of thinking is a primary goal. These new associations and ideas become important sources of coping with the challenges of college life: developing friendships, learning new intellectual skills, solidifying personal values, focusing career aspirations, and forming more intense and significant intimate relationships.

Universities, however, have organized their relationship to students around the academic disciplines which reflect their principal responsibilities — conducting basic research for society and transmitting knowledge to its citizens. This focus on academic disciplines is an efficient approach to meeting these principal responsibilities, but its consequence is to leave a dominant role in shaping the human development of college students to random events and to the power of the peer culture. Further, there is a growing body of evidence that college students will be more effective in utilizing what they learn in college if they have developed psychological and personal skills in addition to those provided by the traditional academic disciplines.

A substantial research literature identifies the important components of psychological and personal development which strongly affect how acquired academic achievement is used in later life and whether it is used effectively. After reviewing the literature which supports this view, Sprinthall (1980) concluded that "life skills and success after the completion of formal education are more closely related to psychological maturity than to scholastic aptitude or grade point achievement" (Sprinthall, 1980, p. 342). Society, therefore, has a vested interest in developing effective ways to influence the personal development of students during their college years.

The Sierra Project, the subject of this book, is an exploratory effort at influencing the development of college students on one of the dimensions of importance to society: the character of its future citizens. Since the character development of college students has not been the subject of much previous empirical research, the Sierra Project is also a research study both on character development during the college years and on the effects of new approach to character education, drawing heavily from counseling and developmental psychology.

The Sierra Project occurred within the context of a comprehensive, research-oriented major public university. The students who chose to participate did so within the traditional framework of a program of academic study organized around discipline-based instruction. The great majority of students planned on further study beyond the baccalaureate degree, and were consequently involved in academically challenging freshman programs — usually including introductory courses in math, English, chemistry, a foreign language, and so forth, according to their specific academic major and prior preparation.

It is our conviction that the elective academic courses of the Sierra Project — and the extracurricular residence hall experiences it supplies during the freshman year — are flexible enough for students to advance in their core academic work and still participate fully in a special curricular experience intended to influence their character development. That conviction was developed and sustained by our four-year odyssey; we established a longitudinal research program to study students' development on dimensions of character throughout their undergraduate years; organized an integrated and challenging curriculum to foster character development; and worked with the freshmen in the classroom and residence hall to provide the needed intervention.

This book describes our attempt to bring the character development of college students under the influence of higher education to a greater degree. Much of our work has been, of necessity, exploratory and definitional. Our basic intent, however, has been to affirm the importance of developing in college students a greater capacity for ethical sensitivity and awareness, a greater regard for equity in human relationships, and the ability to translate this enhanced capacity and regard into a higher standard of fairness and concern for the common good in all realms of their lives. Our passionate belief is that universities can make a contribution to developing what John Dewey called a "free and powerful character."

Reference

Sprinthall, N.A. Psychology for secondary school. *American Psychologist*, 1980, 35(4), 336-347.

SECTION I.

CHARACTER DEVELOPMENT IN COLLEGE STUDENTS

Section I introduces the reader to character development in higher education, offering a working definition of the term *character development* as it will be used throughout the remainder of this book. It describes in some detail two central constructs of character — moral reasoning and ego development — and presents the theoretical underpinnings of the Sierra Project from developmental and counseling psychology.

Chapter 1 defines the fostering of character as a clear responsibility of colleges and universities and identifies a series of obstacles which have prevented these institutions from meeting that responsibility. The first chapter also presents the development of the Sierra Project — a psychological intervention and research study focusing on the transition from late adolescence to early adulthood — as an attempt to overcome these obstacles.

Chapter 2 defines the terms *character* and *character development* and explores the problems inherent in the imprecise use of the terms.

Chapter 3 presents the theoretical and empirical bases of the central constructs of character addressed by the Sierra Project (moral reasoning and ego development), referring particularly to Kohlberg's theory of moral development and Loevinger's theory of ego development. This chapter simply reviews basic theories, adhering as closely as possible to the intent of the two theorists. This chapter is intended for persons not familiar with this area of developmental psychology.

Chapter 4 sets forth the theoretical underpinnings of the construction of the Sierra Project, concepts drawn from developmental and counseling psychology which informed our planning and implementation.

Chapter 5 reviews the previous research on measuring and changing the level of students' moral reasoning — research which indicates that moral and psychological education curricula can contribute to character development in college students.

Chapter 1

CHARACTER DEVELOPMENT IN HIGHER EDUCATION

John M. Whiteley

The character development of college students has been historically defined as a responsibility of higher education. College catalogs often identify the promotion of character as a goal of the institution. The standards by which institutions of higher education evaluate themselves reflect their sense that the development of character is partly their responsibility. For example, the most recent edition of the *Standards for Accreditation* of the Western Association of Schools and Colleges (1979) calls for education to prepare students for "humane, ethical, and competent participation in society" along with "effective citizenship" (p. 15). Purpel and Ryan (1975) argue persuasively that "educators and the general public must realize that in our schools moral education is an unavoidable responsibility" (p. 662).

In order to meet this "unavoidable responsibility," higher education must confront and overcome a number of obstacles. Understanding what these obstacles are lends clarity to the scope and purposes of the Sierra Project. There have been six obstacles to higher education's meeting its responsibility for character development: 1) the lack of definition of higher education's role in meeting this responsibility; 2) the lack of attention by institutions of higher education to establishing effective character education programs; 3) the lack of agreement on what constitutes character, character development, and character education; 4) the absence of controlled studies of long-term psychological interventions designed to promote character;

3

5) the lack of knowledge concerning which experiences have the greatest impact on promoting individual growth in moral reasoning; and 6) the relative absence of longitudinal studies of character development in college students.

Each of these obstacles contributes to the general problem of determining *how* to go about developing character through higher education programs. As John Dewey remarked in 1897,

> It is commonplace to say that this development of character is the ultimate end of all school work. The difficulty lies in the execution of this idea (p. 28).

Though these remarks were made nearly a century ago, there has been little progress in outlining what specific programs colleges should offer in order to develop character. In the remainder of this chapter, we will elaborate on each of these obstacles and describe how the Sierra Project addressed them.

The first obstacle is that the nation's colleges and universities have neglected to define their responsibility to teach students the "intellectual foundations of morality" (Hutchins, 1972, p. 45). This is also a time in our society's development when "most of the sources that transmit moral standards have declined in importance" (Bok, 1976, p. 26). During the last century, the home, the church, and the community have continued to teach morality but "some of this teaching has become confusing, contradictory, uncertain" (Bettelheim, 1970, p. 537). Martin (1974) warns that the confusion arising in institutions of higher education themselves leads to ethical crises on a host of dimensions. The failure to resolve ethical crises within colleges, and the uncertain and contradictory methods by which society's institutions approach character development, are simply part of a social context which fails to give "adequate attention to the many forces destructively affecting character formation in our young" (*Character*, 1980, *1*(12), p. 12).

Overcoming this first obstacle essentially involved defining the purpose and priorities of higher education's impact on its students. Throughout the development and implementation of the Sierra Project — and in the preparation of this first volume — it has been our conviction that a key purpose of higher education is the development of character. It is, further, our conviction that it is possible to promote character development within the dual context of formal academia and the out-of-class life of students — sacrificing neither academic progress toward graduation nor the extra-curricular sense of community that is such a revered part of college life.

Historically, our colleges and universities have not devoted much time and effort to actual character development activities. This is the second obstacle, and exists despite the unprecedented opportunity for character development provided by the transition from late adolescence to early adulthood. The press of ethical dilemmas in our society, the failure of most institutions of our society to help young people learn to surmount the moral dilemmas they face, and the growth tasks inherent in the transition from late adolescence to early adulthood all combine to create an opportunity for colleges and universities to offer educational programs which give students their first real opportunity to think through their own moral and ethical beliefs. Yet, Bok (1976) finds that "most colleges and universities are doing very little to meet this challenge" (p. 27).

Because of the lack of substantial previous research concerning the promotion of character development in college students, our approach to this second obstacle required a set of inter-related activities: a survey of relevant psychological literature identifying promising theoretical constructs on which to base an intervention (Chapter 4) and a review of the literature that does exist on character development methodology and practice (Chapter 5).

The lack of agreement on what constitutes character, character development, and character education is the third obstacle. This obstacle was addressed by reviewing the use of these terms historically and currently, defining them conceptually (see Chapter 2), and then defining them empirically by three proximate measures of character: moral maturity, principled thinking, and ego development (see Chapter 3).

The fourth obstacle — the absence of controlled studies involving year-long interventions designed to promote character development — was approached in two ways. The first approach was to design and implement a psychological intervention extending throughout the freshman year (see Chapter 6). Accomplishing this was Goal 1 of the Sierra Project. Specifically phrased, the intervention was intended to:

a) facilitate the transition from high school to college life,

b) stimulate psychological development from late adolescence to early adulthood, particularly on dimensions associated with character,

c) foster a consideration of future lifestyle choices and career decisions, and

d) challenge learners to apply their educational experiences to problems in the broader community through community service.

Our second approach was to evaluate the character development of college freshmen using multiple sources of data with an experimental group (Sierra Hall residents) and two control groups (see Chapter 7). Therefore, Goal 2 involved studying college freshmen in the context of an intensive year-long residential program, focusing on their development of three dimensions of character: principled thinking, moral maturity, and ego development.

The fifth obstacle to higher education's meeting its responsibility for character development is our lack of knowledge concerning those collegiate experiences which best promote individual growth in moral reasoning. Collegiate experiences, particularly those taking place within the context of a college living environment, can accentuate the development of character. The diversity of individuals in the residence hall and the clash of new ideas in the classroom become the crucible in which a belief system is formed, tested, rejected, extended. Close interaction with fellow students and professors makes continual thinking about moral choices an almost inescapable part of the college experience. In a context where other students are struggling with similar developmental issues — and where the quality of one's thinking is a most highly valued activity — the stage is set for explorations of moral alternatives and the justification of moral choices.

To address the obstacle created by our lack of knowledge concerning the specific experiences which lead to growth in moral reasoning, Goal 3 involved studying the effects of a variety of freshman-year experiences on our sample group — to investigate which specific experiences have the greatest impact on promoting individual growth in moral reasoning.

The sixth and final obstacle to promoting character development is the absence of longitudinal studies concerning growth in college students on dimensions of character: moral maturity, principled thinking, and ego development. Therefore, Goal 4 of the Sierra Project was to establish and conduct such a four-year longitudinal study of UC Irvine students.

The report on the third and fourth goals of the Sierra Project (investigating the experiences which have the greatest impact on moral reasoning and studying student character development over four years of undergraduate education) will appear in *Character Development in College Students*, Volume III (Whiteley & Associates, in preparation).

This first volume focuses on Goals 1 and 2 of the Sierra Project. It evaluates the effects on freshmen of the psychological intervention provided by the intensive year-long residential program, and examines students' developmental status on three dimensions of character.

Throughout the planning and direction of the Sierra Project and this three-volume series, it has been our conviction that a key purpose of higher education is the development of character. John Dewey's words of 1895 capture the spirit of our philosophy:

> Briefly, only psychology and ethics can take education out of its purely empirical and rule-of-thumb stage. Just as a knowledge of mathematics and mechanics has wrought marvelous improvements in all the arts of construction . . . so a knowledge of the structure and functions of the human being can alone elevate the school from the position of a mere workshop, a more or less cumbrous, uncertain, and even baneful institution, to that of a vital, certain, and effective instrument in the greatest of all constructions—the building of a free and powerful character (p. 5).

References

Bettelheim, B. Moral education. In J. M. Gustafson et al. (Eds.), *Moral education*. Cambridge, MA: Harvard University Press, 1970.

Bok, D. C. Can ethics be taught? *Change*, 1976, *8*, 26-30.

Character, 1980, *1*(12).

Dewey, J. What psychology can do for the teacher. In J. McLellan & J. Dewey (Eds.), *The psychology of number.* New York: Appleton, 1895.

Dewey, J. *Ethical principles underlying education.* Third Yearbook of the National Herbart Society. Chicago: The Society, 1897.

Hutchins, R. M. Second edition/the ideal of a college. *Centre Magazine*, 1972, *5*(3), 45-49.

Martin, W. B. The ethical crisis in education. *Change*, 1974, *6*, 28-33.

Purpel, D., & Ryan, K. Moral education: Where sages fear to tread. *Phi Delta Kappan*, 1975, *56*, 659-662.

Standards for Accreditation. In *Handbook of Accreditation*. Accreditation Commission for Senior Colleges & Universities, Western Association of Schools and Colleges. Oakland, CA: Mills College, 1979.

Whiteley, J. M., & Associates. *Character development in college students* (Vol. III), in preparation.

Chapter 2

CHARACTER DEVELOPMENT IN
THE SIERRA PROJECT:
A WORKING DEFINITION

John M. Whiteley

The purpose of this chapter is to define the concept of character development as it is used in the Sierra Project. We will outline the considerations in choosing our particular definition of *character* and *character development* by analyzing the historical development and current usage of the terms. This background will serve as an explanation of—and a rationale for—the definition we derived (our definition of *character* and *character development* will appear in the concluding section of this chapter).

DEFINITIONS OF CHARACTER

Since *character* and *character development* are terms which have been used to convey very different meanings by different writers, there has been a lack of clarity about the intended meaning of these terms in much of the literature. This situation has been exacerbated by the lack of empirical referents for these terms, both in the data collected in measuring a person's *character* and in the developmental path or paths followed by an individual's *character development*.

The term *character* developed from two Greek words: one which translates as "a distinguishing mark" and the other as the verb "to make" or "to engrave." As early as the 5th century B.C., these words were used to refer to "the distinguishing mark of an individual with respect to his ideals and conduct as judged in terms of values and strength of will" (Jones, 1979, p.700).

Contemporary usage of the word *character* covers a variety of connotations, but basically they are very similar. The publication *Character*, in its statement of purpose, indicates that *character* is often used to relate America's central values to traits which include "persistence, tact, self-reliance, generosity, and loyalty" (*Character*, 1980, *1*(12), p. 12). Jones (1979) similarly notes a popular tendency to interchange the meanings of *morality* and *character*. In current usage, he finds that *character*

1. concerns itself more essentially with volitional reactions of the individual and with the directions of one's striving;

2. concentrates primarily on ethical behavior, on the choice of values, and on the operation of intellectual and volitional factors involved in the converting of such values into practical goals and conduct;

3. is sometimes thought of as synonymous with the moral aspects of behavior;

4. is the organization of an individual's way of thinking and acting where values and volitional factors predominate.

(Adapted from Jones, 1979, p.700)

Peters, in his book *Psychology and Ethical Development* (1974), distinguishes three other current uses of the word *character*. The first use focuses on the individual employment of a specific selection of rules to regulate conduct in both personal deportment and social interaction. The second use connotes the possession of particular patterns of personality traits or a distinctive style of behavior. The third use involves the more encompassing phrase *having character* as it signifies the development of an actual *lifestyle*. When Peters (1974) speaks of an individual as having character, "it is something like integrity, incorruptibility, or consistency" (p. 250).

Drawing heavily on the methodology of Peck with Havighurst, Cooper, Lilienthal, and More (1960), the National Character Laboratory, Inc. defines character as a composite of seven traits: moral stability, ego strength, super-ego strength, purpose of life, spontaneity, friendliness, and the absence of hostility and guile

(*NCL Newsletter,* 1979). These traits are considered by the National Character Laboratory to be both measurable and inclusive under the broad rubric of *character.*

A related approach is taken by the American Institute for Character Education in their *Character Education Curriculum* (undated). Their approach is "based on a worldwide study of basic character traits [which are] shared by all major world religions and cultures" (p. 3). These fifteen character traits are

courage, conviction, generosity, kindness, helpfulness, honesty, honor, justice, tolerance, use of time and talents, freedom of choice, freedom of speech, citizenship, right to be an individual, and right of equal opportunity-economic security (American Institute for Character Education, undated, p. 3).

Clearly, *character* has taken on such a range of colloquial, psychological, and moral connotations that the term is now without precise meaning if unaccompanied by careful explanation. Similarly, the term *character development*—and the educational practices associated with the promotion of it—is in equal need of clarification and definition.

DEFINITIONS OF CHARACTER DEVELOPMENT AND CHARACTER EDUCATION

The term *character development* in common usage frequently refers to one or more of the following: 1) the educational approaches designed to help individuals acquire character, 2) the internal intra-psychic process by which a maturing individual acquires character, or 3) value statements concerning the desired goals of character education programs. Within both the context of contemporary American society and the current literature dealing with character development, there are as many variations on the idea of character development as there are meanings of the word *character.* Peck et al. (1960) drew attention to the problem of differing conceptions of character development when they noted: "There is perhaps no study of human behavior more fraught with risk of subjective bias and culture-bound prejudice than is the study of moral character"

(Preface, p. *v*). There is a consensus among those who write about character development and character education that ours is a society which is "failing to give adequate attention to the many forces destructively affecting character formation in our young" (*Character*,1980, *1*(12), p. 12).

The existing differences in conceptions of the ideal product of character training are, however, considerable. According to one religious educational system, "Godlikeness is the ultimate objective of character development" (Fowler, 1977). Peck et al. would surely term the assimilation of Godlikeness as a venture "fraught with risk of subjective bias."

A central problem for educators discussing the training of character is in the imprecise delineation of and agreement on the goal of such training. Peters (1974) notes that it is

> quite possible for different educators to stress this [character training] and to have quite different conceptions of an ideal man. They might all be agreed on the desirability of developing traits like consistency, integrity, and persistence; yet they might disagree vehemently about which substantive traits were desirable as well as about the type of character that was to be encouraged (p. 250-251).

There is commonality of concern about enduring values— some traits being desirable over others—and the need for improving the way society affects the character of its young people through its institutions. The problem for all members of society, then, is to determine which approaches to education offer the most promise for developing value systems which enhance the common good. Yet, while there is consensus on the importance of these problems—and some consensus on what is the general domain of character —there remains little agreement on methods of developing character, on what the psychological components are that constitute character, and on what an institution should do if it wants to promote character development.

SIERRA PROJECT DEFINITIONS OF CHARACTER, CHARACTER DEVELOPMENT, AND CHARACTER EDUCATION

Given the confusion stemming from the various connotations of *character*, it is of obvious importance to be clear about the conceptual usages of *character*, *character development*, and *character education* as they are employed in the Sierra Project. Further, it is essential to the evaluation phase of the Sierra Project to choose conceptual usages which, at this point in the history of research on character, have empirical referents. The Sierra Project is both an intervention in character education, and a study of character development in the transition from late adolescence to early adulthood. Both aspects of the Sierra Project assume a definition of character which is operational in the sense of being measurable at different points in a longitudinal study.

It was simply not possible to offer a definition of character which is, at the same time, conceptually satisfactory (although this is a judgment which is admittedly subjective) and empirically satisfactory (another subjective judgment) in the sense of having valid and reliable measures (instruments) which could capture all of the various conceptual components of the Sierra Project definition of character. In addition, the measures which do exist are of two very divergent psychological heritages: trait measures and developmental measures. Perhaps another generation of researchers on character development will have more adequate choices at the conceptual and empirical level.

Given the options of the trait and developmental models, we have chosen to work within the developmental model. We consider this model to be more representative of the definition of character and more sensitive to the progression of changes within individuals over time. This choice reflects our judgment that the developmental model captures with greater complexity and accuracy the true nature of this aspect of the human experience. It is beyond the scope of this book to draw detailed comparisons between alternative psychological models, but we feel it is important to note that this choice was made with cognizance of the constructs from the developmental model presented in the next two chapters.

Character, as we have defined it conceptually, has two parts. The first part refers to an *understanding* of what is the right, fair, or good thing to do in a given circumstance. The second part refers to the *ability to do* those things (the courage to act in accordance with one's understanding of what is right, fair, and good). Thus, *character* constitutes understanding what is right and acting on what is right.

Research is just beginning on components of character, and there are presently no reliable or valid measures for both the *understanding* and the *ability to do* components of our conception of character. Over the past decade, however, those working within the developmental framework have made substantial progress in instrument development related to the measurement of the understanding of what is right. This progress presently focuses on two particular measurements: that of moral reasoning and ego development. Although this is a comparatively narrow empirical definition of character, it does focus on how individuals *think* about moral issues and how they may *act* in different situations (rather than on how they actually behave). The measures of moral reasoning chosen were those developed by Kohlberg and his associates (Kohlberg, 1973; Colby, Gibbs, Kohlberg, Speicher-Dubin, & Candee, 1979) on moral maturity, and Rest and his associates (Rest, 1979) involving principled thinking. The measure of ego development which we used is that of Loevinger and her associates (Loevinger & Wessler, 1970; Loevinger, 1976).

Character development, as we have conceptually defined it, refers to the progression of an individual's capacity for *understanding* what is right or good in increasingly complex forms, and the willingness or courage to *act* on those conceptions. Our emphasis is on understanding the internal (intrapsychic) progression within a maturing individual through his/her interaction with others and the environment.

Character education refers to the planned and unplanned experiences which promote the development of *character* in individuals. Within the Sierra Project, the planned portions of the *character education* intervention are the classroom experiences provided by the curriculum modules as briefly described in Chapter 6 of this book, in Whiteley and Loxley (1980), and in a future volume to be published (Loxley & Whiteley, in preparation). The unplanned portions of this *character education* are student interactions with the rest of the educational institution, other institutions of society, family and—particularly—friends and peers.

Our approach to *character education* was to utilize the freshman year experiences of a group of undergraduates in a major research university, presenting them with a structured group of curricular modules spread sequentially over the course of one academic year. The classroom experience occurred in a college residence hall in which these participants lived. Our evaluation of the *character education* intervention involved assessing the effects of the intervention on moral reasoning and ego development (as well as on other psychological dimensions), and observing the development of the college students who participated in the intervention over the four years of their undergraduate experience. Our approaches to studying the components of character education are presented in Chapter 7.

We have offered what, in our view, are proximate conceptual and empirical definitions of *character, character development,* and *character education.* Whether these will prove to be adequate definitions awaits further theoretical advances and the development of a broader array of empirical measures.

References

Character, 1980, 1(12).

Character education curriculum. American Institute for Character Education. Pasadena, CA: Thomas Jefferson Research Center, undated.

Colby, A., Gibbs, J. C., Kohlberg, L., Speicher-Dubin, B., & Candee, D. *Standard form scoring manual* (Parts 1-4). Cambridge, MA: Harvard University, Center for Moral Education, 1979.

Fowler, J. M. The concept of character development in the writings of Ellen G. White (Doctoral dissertation, Andrews University). *Dissertation Abstracts International,* 1977, 38, 3395-3396C. University Microfilms No. 77-27, 581.

Jones, V. Character. In *Collier's Encyclopedia,* Vol. 5. New York: Macmillan Educational Corp., 1979.

Kohlberg, L. *Collected papers on moral development and moral education.* Cambridge, MA: Harvard University Graduate School of Education, Center for Moral Education, 1973.

Loevinger, J. *Ego development: Conceptions and theories.* San Francisco: Jossey-Bass, 1976.

Loevinger, J., & Wessler, R. *Measuring ego development, Volume I: Construction and use of a sentence completion test.* San Francisco: Jossey-Bass, 1970.

Loxley, J. C., & Whiteley, J. M. *Character development in college students* (Vol. II), in preparation.

National Character Laboratory Newsletter, 1979, 9(1), 1-14.

Peck, R. F., with Havighurst, R. J., Cooper, R., Lilienthal, J., & More, D. *The psychology of character development.* New York: Wiley, 1960.

Peters, R. S. *Psychology and ethical development.* London: George Allen & Unwin, Ltd., 1974.

Rest, J. R. *Development in judging moral issues.* Minneapolis, MN: University of Minnesota Press, 1979.

Whiteley, J. M., & Loxley, J. C. A curriculum for the development of character and community in college students. In V. L. Erickson & J. M. Whiteley, (Eds.), *Developmental counseling and teaching.* Monterey, CA: Brooks/Cole, 1980, 262-297.

Chapter 3

CENTRAL CONSTRUCTS OF CHARACTER:
MORAL REASONING AND EGO DEVELOPMENT

John M. Whiteley

Central constructs of character for the Sierra Project are students' level of moral reasoning (principled thinking and moral maturity) and ego development. Both constructs and the approaches to measuring them rely on the theoretical development and empirical research which has progressed dramatically in the past decade. The purpose of this chapter is to present the psychological theories from which our assessments of moral reasoning and ego development were derived.

The first section of this chapter will present Kohlberg's theory of moral development, including the six stages of development he identified. The second section of the chapter will present Loevinger's theory of ego development, including the stages and transitions which she has identified. The third section will explore the theoretical and empirical relationships between moral reasoning and ego development. This is a relatively unexamined area which has implications for curriculum development and the sequencing of educational experiences, as well as for increased understanding of the constructs themselves.

MORAL REASONING

Piaget's (1932/1948) original investigations of moral thinking in children were extended by Kohlberg's (1958) early work in moral reasoning in adolescents. Further research has extended, amplified, and reformulated the constructs from these initial studies to cover the entire life-span (see Rest, 1979a; Haan, 1978; Gibbs, 1977; Gilligan, 1977). For reviews of the empirical documentation of these constructs, see Rest (1979a), Whiteley, Bertin, and Berry (1980), and Lickona (1976).

A central tenet of the theoretical framework of these studies, and our own, is that an individual's moral development proceeds through stages—each of which is qualitatively different from the others. In Kohlberg's six-stage conceptualization (1964, 1969, 1971), the first two stages are *preconventional*:

Stage 1. Punishment and obedience orientation

Stage 2. Naive instrumental hedonism

These first two stages are considered preconventional, in which rules and expectations are viewed from a highly egocentric perspective. Rest (1979b) characterized Stage 1—punishment and obedience orientation—as the morality of obedience, wherein the central standard for determining moral rights and responsibilities is: "Do what you're told" (p. 1.29). At this stage, the individual's concept of fairness arises out of the natural inequality of the parent-child relationship; as long as the individual is obedient, he or she will not be punished by the authority figure. Unfairness, in this system, occurs when the individual is obedient and still receives punishment. This approach to determining right or wrong provides the individual with a primitive framework for surviving in the world.

Rest (1979b) characterized Stage 2—naive instrumental hedonism—as the "morality of instrumental egoism/simple exchange." Here, the concept of fairness arises out of a bargain between parties in which each party has something to gain. Voluntary responsibilities evolve from the specific bargain; moral rights and responsibilities are based on "making a deal."

As conceptualized by Kohlberg (1964, 1969, 1971), the next two stages are *conventional*:

Stage 3. The interpersonal concordance, or "good boy-nice girl" orientation

Stage 4. The "law-and-order," authority-and-social-order-maintaining orientation

These two stages are labeled *conventional* by Kohlberg (1976) because, in these stages, a person "is identified with or has internalized the rules and expectations of others, especially those of authorities" (p. 33)* and is working on the basis of conventions.

Rest (1979b) characterized Stage 3 — interpersonal concordance — as the "morality of personal concordance." The central standard for determining moral rights and responsibilities is: "Be considerate, nice and kind, and you'll get along with people" (p. 1.29). The concept of fairness is generally limited to an individual's primary group, there being no structure for defining fairness beyond it. Stage 3 provides a more stable social environment than does Stage 2, for morality is defined through a broader set of interpersonal relationships rather than through a limited series of individual personal exchanges.

Rest (1979b) characterized Stage 4 — law-and-order — as the "morality of law and duty to the social order." The central standard for determining moral rights and responsibilities is: "Everyone in society is obligated and protected by the law" (p. 1.29). Fairness at Stage 4 is defined as people doing what is expected of them to accomplish society's goals as manifested in socially derived laws. These same laws are then impersonally and impartially applied to all members of society. The individual comes to view any conflict in terms of how it fits into the existing legal strictures of society. Laws, rather than the opinions of others, become the basis of the definition of *fairness*.

As conceptualized by Kohlberg (1964, 1969, 1971), the last two stages are *post-conventional*:

Stage 5. The social-contract legalistic orientation

Stage 6. The universal ethical principle, or conscience, orientation

The final two stages are labeled *post-conventional* by Kohlberg (1976) because a person at these stages has differentiated him or herself "from the rules and expectations of others and defines his [or her] values in terms of self-chosen principles" (p. 33). According to Rest (1979b):

---

*This and all other quotations from this source are from Kohlberg, L. Moral stages and moralization: The cognitive-developmental approach. In T. Lickona (Ed.), *Moral development and behavior*. New York: Holt, Rinehart & Winston, 1976. Reprinted with permission.

> What is distinctive about Stages 5 and 6 is that they face the problem of devising a plan for cooperation that minimizes arbitrary inequities and maximizes the stake each individual has in supporting the social system. Stages 5 and 6 provide a rationale for choosing among alternative social systems and provide principles for creating new laws and arrangements (p. 1.9).

The emphasis in the post-conventional stages is, therefore, on principles for choosing a more just arrangement for individuals within the society.

Rest (1979b) characterized Stage 5 — the social-contract legalistic orientation — as "the morality of societal consensus." The central standard for determining moral rights and responsibilities is: "What laws the people want to make is what ought to be" (p. 1.29). The procedures by which each individual is given an equal voice to determine the framework of society are the central component of fairness at Stage 5. In effect, these procedures are considered to accurately reflect the will of the majority. The principle of consent and the idea that laws should serve the welfare of the greatest number of individuals are also central facets of thinking at this stage. Whereas Stage 4 emphasized the perpetuation of existing social arrangements, Stage 5 emphasizes the choice among conflicting laws and the evolution of new ones.

Rest (1979a) subdivides Stage 5 into three phases. In the first phase, moral obligation evolves via the voluntary cooperation among members of society. In the second phase, attention is given to maximizing human welfare — as demonstrated by the majority will — through procedures for selecting laws (e.g. procedural justice). In the third phase, social obligations are based on basic human rights.

Rest indicates that the major accomplishment of Stage 5 is to provide the constitutional principles (i.e., those principles which advocate consensus government and the acknowledgment of basic human rights). In Stage 5, competing perspectives are coordinated by:

> imagining what rational people would accept. The balancing of interests and the appeal of the arrangement are established by instituting procedures for making laws that are viewed as fair. If a person has been allowed to cast his

vote, to have his day in court (with all due process), to have his basic rights protected, then there are no grounds for complaint (p. 35).

Rest (1979b) characterized Stage 6 — the universal ethical principle, or conscience, orientation — as "the morality of non-arbitrary social cooperation." The key standard is: "How [would] rational and impartial people . . . organize cooperation" (p. 1.29). Stage 6 adopts the Stage 5 approach of anticipating the mind of the rational person, but goes further by attempting to anticipate those principles by which a rational society would choose to govern itself. Thus, at Stage 6, the moral universe is composed of the ethical ideals which would be reasonable for all people from any vantage point.

Kohlberg's (1979) most recent conclusion is that "Stage 6 remains as a theoretical postulate but not an operational empirical entity" (p. 24). There remains clear longitudinal evidence supporting the idea of individuals moving upward from lower stages to higher ones, but as yet there are no Stage 6 subjects in the longitudinal studies of the growth of moral reasoning. Table 3-1 represents Kohlberg's visualization of stage development. It is, to date, one of his most comprehensively developed presentations.

As an elaboration on Kohlberg's basic six-stage sequence, Turiel (1974) has posited the existence of a transitional stage which is relevant to a college-age population located between Kohlberg's Stages 4 and 5 (accordingly labeled Stage 4 1/2). He formulated this transitional stage as a result of studying subjects in the process of moving from Stage 4 to Stage 5. His subjects gave responses which were characterized by a high degree of conflict, internal contradiction, and inconsistency. Their central inconsistency was between relativism and moralism. He found that his subjects typically stated that:

a) all values are relative and arbitrary,

b) one should not judge what another person should do,

c) it is up to every individual to make his [or her] own decisions, and

d) terms like "duty," "good," "should," or "moral" have no meaning.

(Turiel, 1974, p. 19)

TABLE 3-1
THE SIX MORAL STAGES

CONTENT OF STAGE

Level and Stage	What is Right	Reasons for Doing Right	Social Perspective of Stage
LEVEL I—PRECONVENTIONAL Stage 1—Heteronomous Morality	To avoid breaking rules backed by punishment, obedience for its own sake, and avoiding physical damage to persons and property.	Avoidance of punishment, and the superior power of authorities.	*Egocentric point of view.* Doesn't consider the interests of others or recognize that they differ from the actor's; doesn't relate two points of view. Actions are considered physically rather than in terms of psychological interests of others. Confusion of authority's perspective with one's own.
Stage 2—Individualism, Instrumental Purpose, and Exchange	Following rules only when it is to someone's immediate interest; acting to meet one's own interests and needs and letting others do the same. Right is also what's fair, what's an equal exchange, a deal, an agreement.	To serve one's own needs or interests in a world where you have to recognize that other people have their interests, too.	*Concrete individualistic perspective.* Aware that everybody has his own interest to pursue and these conflict, so that right is relative (in the concrete individualistic sense).
LEVEL II—CONVENTIONAL Stage 3—Mutual Interpersonal Expectations, Relationships, and Interpersonal Conformity	Living up to what is expected by people close to you or what people generally expect of people in your role as son, brother, friend, etc. "Being good" is important and means having good motives, showing concern about others. It also means keeping mutual relationships, such as trust, loyalty, respect and gratitude.	The need to be a good person in your own eyes and those of others. Your caring for others. Belief in the Golden Rule. Desire to maintain rules and authority which support stereotypical good behavior.	*Perspective of the individual in relationships with other individuals.* Aware of shared feelings, agreements, and expectations which take primacy over individual interests. Relates points of view through the concrete Golden Rule, putting yourself in the other guy's shoes. Does not yet consider generalized system perspective.
Stage 4—Social System and Conscience	Fulfilling the actual duties to which you have agreed. Laws are to be upheld except in extreme cases where they conflict with other fixed social duties. Right is also contributing to society, the group, or institution.	To keep the institution going as a whole, to avoid the breakdown in the system "if everyone did it," or the imperative of conscience to meet one's defined obligations (Easily confused with Stage 3 belief in rules and authority; see text.)	*Differentiates societal point of view from interpersonal agreement or motives.* Takes the point of view of the system that defines roles and rules. Considers individual relations in terms of place in the system.
LEVEL III—POST-CONVENTIONAL, or PRINCIPLED Stage 5—Social Contract or Utility and Individual Rights	Being aware that people hold a variety of values and opinions, that most values and rules are relative to your group. These relative rules should usually be upheld, however, in the interest of impartiality and because they are the social contract. Some nonrelative values and rights like *life* and *liberty*, however, must be upheld in any society and regardless of majority opinion.	A sense of obligation to law because of one's social contract to make and abide by laws for the welfare of all and for the protection of all people's rights. A feeling of contractual commitment, freely entered upon, to family, friendship, trust, and work obligations. Concern that laws and duties be based on rational calculation of overall utility, "the greatest good for the greatest number."	*Prior-to-society perspective.* Perspective of a rational individual aware of values and rights prior to social attachments and contracts. Integrates perspectives by formal mechanisms of agreement, contract, objective impartiality, and due process. Considers moral and legal points of view; recognizes that they sometimes conflict and finds it difficult to integrate them.
Stage 6—Universal Ethical Principles	Following self-chosen ethical principles. Particular laws or social agreements are usually valid because they rest on such principles. When laws violate these principles, one acts in accordance with the principle. Principles are universal principles of justice: the equality of human rights and respect for the dignity of human beings as individual persons.	The belief as a rational person in the validity of universal moral principles, and a sense of personal commitment to them.	*Perspective of a moral point of view from which social arrangements derive.* Perspective is that of any rational individual recognizing the nature of morality or the fact that persons are ends in themselves and must be treated as such.

From Kohlberg, L. Moral stages and moralization: The cognitive-developmental approach. In T. Lickona (Ed.), *Moral development and behavior.* New York: Holt, Rinehart & Winston, 1976, p. 34-35. Reprinted with permission.

He also found that, while his subjects were committed to positions on particular issues, they viewed moral values in general as arbitrary and, in fact, denied their existence. In Turiel's view, persons at Stage 4 1/2 reject Stage 4 concepts, but have an incomplete understanding of Stage 5 concepts. Their rejection of Stage 4 conceptions has led some researchers to the false impression that the subjects were in fact at Stage 2. Closer examination of the protocols, however, revealed that the subjects thought both moral *and* conventional values were arbitrary and relative. The changes which occur during Stage 4 1/2 include:

a) an increase in awareness of equality and individual rights,

b) a growth in the need for an explanation of collective functioning, and

c) an increase in concern with objective criteria for moral judgments.

(Turiel, 1974, p. 24)

Internal conflict is common during this transitional period. During this stage, conceptions of morality lack a basis in either conventional *or* postconventional thought. Conflict, therefore, is frequent because there is no consistent basis for making moral judgments. The three most common types of conflict are: 1) recognition of the difference between conventional versus principled moral reasoning, 2) a reluctant recognition of one's inconsistency when making moral judgments while concurrently claiming to be relativistic, and 3) a reluctant recognition of the contradictions inherent in viewing the individual and society as competing moral agents. Conflict results from recognizing that, on the one hand, society should not impose judgments on the individual—who has a right to remain free to make his/her own judgments—while on the other hand, recognizing that society rightly promulgates principles of conduct to enhance the common good.

We have seen that a structure for considering moral development in college students is provided in Kohlberg's theory, that there are six stages of moral reasoning, each characterized by an increasing complexity of thought and an increasing adequacy for dealing with the world in terms of principles of justice. There are theorists, however, who believe that moral development must be viewed in a broader context than is provided by cognitive development stage theory. Sanford (1980), for example, observed that "moral development cannot really be separated from the development of the rest of the person" (p. 206). These theorists provide a framework for looking at the relationship between moral reasoning and other forms of personality development. In their view, moral reasoning can be presented as one of the components of a broader construct of personality. For Loevinger, one of those theorists, that broader construct is ego development.

EGO DEVELOPMENT

The approach to ego development underlying the Sierra Project's empirical definition of *character* is that of Loevinger (1966, 1976), and Loevinger and Wessler (1970). As noted above, Loevinger quite clearly subsumes moral development under the concept of ego development:

> ego development includes some topics previously discussed under moral development, socialization, character structure, and even cognitive development. Indeed, the breadth of topics subsumed under *ego development* justifies the term, for nothing less than the ego has so wide a scope (Loevinger, 1976, p. 4).[*]

During the course of ego development, changes occur in the "complexly interwoven fabric of impulse control, character, interpersonal relations, conscious preoccupations, and cognitive complexity, among other things" (p. 26). Loevinger conceptualizes ego development as also occurring in a number of stages, but unlike Kohlberg, does not closely define each stage. Rather, she presents "impressionistic descriptions" from many sources, "corrected by empirical work" (p. 13). (See Loevinger, 1976, Ch. 8 for a discussion of her rationale.) The stages are referred to by a name or a code symbol (rather than by a number) in order to avoid both "cutting off new insights arbitrarily," and reaching a possible "terminological impasse" (p. 14) when and if other stages are later identified.

---

[*]This and all other quotations from this source are from Loevinger, J. *Ego development*. San Francisco, CA: Jossey-Bass, 1976. Reprinted with permission.

Loevinger describes seven discrete stages of ego development, and two additional periods which she terms *transitional*, noting that other researchers might consider these transitional periods to be full fledged stages in themselves. The first stage (coded as "I-1") predates the acquisition of language and is not considered measurable. This stage consists of two phases: a pre-social phase and a symbiotic phase. In the pre-social phase, the self is not differentiated from inanimate objects. The symbiotic phase occurs during the period when the child has a strong attachment to the mother. The child, in this phase, is capable of distinguishing the mother from the rest of the environment, but does not differentiate him/herself from the mother.

Loevinger labels the second stage (coded as "I-2") the Impulsive Stage. At this stage:

> The child's own impulses help him to affirm his separate identity. The emphatic "No!" and the later "Do it by self" are prime examples. The child's impulses are curbed at first by constraint, later also by immediate rewards and punishments (Loevinger 1976, p. 16).

Impulses clearly predominate at this stage, and there is a limited capacity for control. The world is viewed from a perspective which is egocentric and concrete (Hauser, 1976). Loevinger describes the child's orientation as being directed exclusively to the present—with a confounding of motive, cause and logical justification.

The next stage is called the Self-Protective Stage (coded "Delta"). At this stage:

> The first step toward self-control of impulses is taken when the child learns to anticipate immediate, short-term rewards and punishments. Controls are at first fragile, and there is a corresponding vulnerability and guardedness, hence we term the stage Self-Protective (Loevinger, 1976, p. 17).

Hauser (1976) notes that individuals at the Self-Protective Stage recognize that there are rules, but obey them out of self-interest. Obedience is to their own immediate benefit. Interpersonal relations are exploitative and manipulative; morality is defined in terms of expediency. Blame is attributed to "circumstances" or to others. "Don't get caught" is a major operating principle, as is "use rules to your own advantage."

During the next stage, called the Conformist Stage (coded as "I-3"), the individual begins to identify his/her own welfare with that of "the group." This group can be composed of either family members or peers. Rules are then obeyed for the sake of the group, rather than for fear of punishment or hope of immediate reward. Loevinger (1976) states that:

> Disapproval is a potent sanction for the individual at this stage. His moral code defines actions as right or wrong according to compliance with rules rather than according to consequences, which are crucial at higher stages (p. 18).

At this stage, norms involving incidental issues (e.g., norms of conduct or dress) are not differentiated from more serious, obligatory rules. Hauser (1976) draws attention to a tendency of individuals at this stage to value material goods, status, reputation, and appearance. Loevinger indicates that niceness, helpfulness and cooperation with others are also valued. Sex roles are stereotyped at this stage.

The next stage, the Self-Aware Stage (coded "I-3/4"), marks the transition between the Conformist Stage and Stage I-4, the Conscientious Stage. This transitional stage differs from the preceding stage in that individuals' self awareness has so increased that they have come to appreciate multiple possibilities. As Loevinger (1976) notes:

> Where the Conformist lives in a conceptually simple world with the same thing right always and for everyone, the person in the Self-Aware Level sees alternatives. Exceptions and contingencies are allowed for, though still in terms of stereotypic and demographic categories like age, sex, marital status, and race, rather than in terms of individual differences in traits and needs (p. 19).

The modal adult in our society functions at this level. In Hauser's (1976) view, the individual at the Self-Aware stage no longer accepts absolute guidelines provided by external social groups, but instead begins to rely on emerging "introspective capacities [and on] a beginning understanding of psychological causation, self-awareness, and self-criticism" (p. 931).

The next stage is called the Conscientious Stage (coded "I-4"). Loevinger (1976) describes individuals at the Conscientious Stage as possessing the elements of an adult conscience (i.e., goals, capacity for self-criticism, sense of responsibility), a differentiated inner life, and a high degree of conceptual complexity (e.g., thinking in terms of a number of polarities). Rather than perceiving the world in terms of the broad stereotypes characteristic of earlier stages, those in the Conscientious Stage discern individual differences, concerning themselves with their own internal standards for meeting obligations, setting ideals, developing traits, and achieving. They are characterized by a capacity for self-criticism and an ability to rely on their own rather than external opinion (Loevinger, 1976). Thus, at this stage, the norms of external groups are replaced by inner rules. Further:

> At this stage a person is his brother's keeper; he feels responsible for other people, at times to the extent of feeling obligated to shape another's life or to prevent him from making errors. Along with the concepts of responsibility and obligations go the correlative concepts of privileges, rights, and fairness (Hauser, 1976, p. 21).

The next transitional stage is referred to as the Individualistic Level (coded "I-4/5"). A concern for emotional independence and an increased awareness of one's own and others' individuality are marks of this stage. The main growth task is to become more tolerant—both of oneself and of others—as a way to become emotionally independent. When comparing outward appearances to inner realities and making distinctions between process and outcome, discrepancies become apparent. In Loevinger's (1976) view:

> Psychological causality and psychological development, which are notions that do not occur spontaneously below the Conscientious Stage, are natural modes of thought to persons in the Individualistic Level (p. 23).

Loevinger (1976) further observes that as the individual moves from the Conformist to the Conscientious Stage, interpersonal relationships become more intense and are seen, to some degree, in opposition to other characteristics of individuals such as the striving for achievement, moralism, and a sense of responsibility for themselves and others. Conflict is still not accepted as a natural part of the human condition. Hauser (1976) characterizes the transition from the Conscientious Stage to the Autonomous Stage as involving more complex conceptualization. He concurs with Loevinger's identification of the high value placed on interpersonal relations at this transitional individualistic level and its contrast to the high value ideals and achievements at the previous stage.

The capacity to acknowledge and cope with conflicting needs and duties is the "distinctive mark" of the Autonomous Stage (coded "I-5"). Hauser (1976) stresses this capacity, noting that while individuals at previous stages tend to engage in moral condemnation of the choices and solutions of others, those at the Autonomous Stage develop increased tolerance as they develop greater understanding of inner conflict. Characteristic of the person at this stage is the ability "to unite and integrate ideas that appear as incompatible alternatives to those at lower stages; there is a high toleration for ambiguity" (Loevinger, 1976, p. 23). Loevinger characterizes the person at I-5 as striving to be objective about others as well as him/herself. Social ideals (such as justice) are often held at this stage of ego development.

Loevinger (1976) offers Maslow's(1971) model of the self-actualizing person as the best description of the last and highest stage, the Integrated Stage (coded "I-6"). In 1966, she referred to it as: "proceeding beyond coping with conflict to reconciliation of conflicting demands, and, where necessary, renunciation of the unobtainable" (Loevinger, 1966, p. 200). A key distinguishing characteristic of this stage is the ability to transcend the innner conflicts which were encountered, acknowledged, and dealt with at the preceding stage.

According to Loevinger's theory, then, ego development proceeds through a number of stages and transitions. Table 3-2 briefly describes each stage and presents some of the areas in which change occurs as an individual matures and moves through the stages and transitions in ego development.

TABLE 3-2
LOEVINGER'S STAGES OF EGO DEVELOPMENT

Stage	Code	Impulse Control, Character Development	Interpersonal Style	Conscious Preoccupations	Cognitive Style
Presocial			Autistic		
Symbiotic	I-1		Symbiotic	Self vs. non-self	
Impulsive	I-2	Impulsive, fear of retaliation	Receiving, dependent, exploitative	Bodily feelings, especially sexual and aggressive	Stereotyping, conceptual confusion
Self-Protective	Δ	Fear of being caught, externalizing blame, opportunistic	Wary, manipulative, exploitative	Self-protection, trouble, wishes, things, advantage, control	
Conformist	I-3	Conformity to external rules, shame, guilt for breaking rules	Belonging, superficial niceness	Appearance, social acceptability, banal feelings, behavior	Conceptual simplicity, stereotypes, cliches
Conscientious-Conformist	I-3/4	Differentiation of norms, goals	Aware of self in relation to group, helping	Adjustment, problems, reasons, opportunities (vague)	Multiplicity
Conscientious	I-4	Self-evaluated standards, self-criticism, guilt for consequences, long-term goals and ideals	Intensive, responsible, mutual, concern for communication	Differentiated feelings, motives for behavior, self-respect, achievements, traits, expression	Conceptual complexity, idea of patterning
Individualistic	I-4/5	*Add:* Respect for individuality	*Add;* Dependence as an emotional problem	*Add:* Development, social problems, differentiation of inner life from outer	*Add:* Distinction of process and outcome
Autonomous	I-5	*Add:* Coping with conflicting inner needs, toleration	*Add:* Respect for autonomy, interdependence	Vividly conveyed feelings, integration of physiological and psychological, psychological causation of behavior, role conception, self-fulfillment, self in social context	Increased conceptual complexity, complex patterns, toleration for ambiguity, broad scope, objectivity
Integrated	I-6	*Add:* Reconciling inner conflicts, renunciation of unattainable	*Add:* Cherishing of individuality	*Add:* Identity	

NOTE: *"Add"* means in addition to the description applying to the previous level.
From Loevinger, J. *Ego development: Conceptions and theories.* San Francisco, CA: Jossey-Bass, 1976, pp. 24-25. Reprinted with permission.

THE INTERRELATIONSHIPS OF
MORAL REASONING AND EGO DEVELOPMENT

Kohlberg and Loevinger share a common preoccupation with moral development and character. As we have discussed, Loevinger's (1976) broad definition of ego development subsumes such dimensions as moral development, development of cognitive complexity, and development of capacity for interpersonal relations. Loevinger defines ego as a process, with components which are inseparable from the whole. She has established a correspondence between ego development and moral development, outlining the correspondence between her system and Kohlberg's as indicated by Table 3-3.

TABLE 3-3
CORRESPONDENCE BETWEEN
LOEVINGER'S AND KOHLBERG'S SYSTEMS

Approximate ego level	Kohlbergian basis for morality
Presocial	
Impulsive	Punishment and obedience
Self-protective	Naive instrumental hedonism
Conformist	Good relations and approval
Conscientious-Conformist	Law and order
Conscientious	Democratic contract
Individualistic	Individual principles of conscience
Autonomous	
Integrated	

Adapted from Loevinger, J. *Ego development; Conceptions and Theries.* San Francisco, CA: Jossey-Bass, 1976, p. 109. Reprinted with permission.

Loevinger presents a correspondence between: her Impulsive Stage and Kohlberg's Punishment-and-Obedience Stage; her Self-Protective Stage and Kohlberg's Naive-Instrumental-Hedonism Stage; her Conformist Stage and Kohlberg's Interpersonal-Concordance Stage; her Conscientious-Conformist transition and Kohlberg's Law-and-Order Stage; her Conscientious Stage and

Kohlberg's Social-Contract Stage; and her Individualistic Stage and Kohlberg's Universal-Ethical-Principles Stage. Clearly, there are some conceptual similarities between Loevinger's and Kohlberg's systems, particularly in the middle ranges.

Kohlberg, however, disagrees with the view that Loevinger presents in relating ego development and moral development. In order to' elaborate his theoretical differences with Loevinger and other ego developmentalists, Kohlberg presented five of his central beliefs:

1. Cognitive development or structures are more general than, and are embodied in, both self or ego structures and in moral judgment.

2. Generalized ego structures (modes of perceiving self and social relations) are more general than, and are embodied in, moral structures.

3. Cognitive development is a necessary but not sufficient condition for ego development.

4. Certain features of ego development are a necessary but not sufficient condition for development of moral structures.

5. The higher the moral stage, the more distinct it is from the parallel ego stage.

(Kohlberg 1976, p. 53)

While the propositions noted above suggest a high correlation between measures of moral and ego development, Kohlberg (1976) believes that "such a correlation does not imply that moral development can be defined simply as a division or area of ego development" (p. 53).

Kohlberg (1976) suggests that in order to relate experiences to a developing personality or self, individuals' levels of ego and moral development are both helpful. It is important to emphasize — as part of understanding the differences between Kohlberg and Loevinger — that Kohlberg uses ego development theory to understand the relationship of specific experiences to change:

In this sense, ego-development theories represent possible extensions of cognitive-developmental theory as it moves into the study of individual lives and life histories. There is a broad unity to the development of social perception and social values which deserves the name "ego development" (Kohlberg, 1976, p. 52).

Kohlberg's reference to the "broad unity" of ego development is a further key to understanding his viewpoint. He feels that the central unification of ego development is not really parallel to the stages of logical or moral development which involve instead a matter of levels. Therefore, it is a mistake to view moral stages as "simply reflections of broader ego levels" (p.52) because moral stages have a tighter unitary structure. Kohlberg's system of moral structure is defined: "by formalistic philosophy . . . to treat moral development as simply a facet of ego (or of cognitive) development is to miss many of its special problems and features" (Kohlberg, 1976, p. 53).

On the other hand, Loevinger (1976) and Loevinger and Wessler (1970) do treat moral development as a facet of general ego or character development. Kohlberg (1976) describes Loevinger as doing so because she assumes that:

If ego development is seen as the successive restructuring of the relationship between the self and standards, it is natural for ego-developmental theorists to use changes in the moral domain as bench marks (p. 52).

Kohlberg obviously feels that Loevinger and others have failed to provide the necessary specificity in their definitions of moral stages. In Kohlberg's view, Loevinger's inability to differentiate moral from nonmoral items in her ego development measure "simply demonstrates that her criteria of moral development were not more specific than her general criteria of ego development" (Kohlberg, 1976, p. 53). He further contends that if more careful, detailed specifying is not done when moral development is initially defined, then it may be almost inevitable that moral development is found to be simply one facet of ego development. Naturally, Loevinger and associates feel that a broad definition of ego development, one which subsumes moral reasoning, more accurately represents the sequencing of growth.

To clarify her position, Loevinger presented the four character-istics of what she considers to be a "fully-realized contemporary conception" of ego development:

1. stages are potential fixation points;

2. stage conception is structural, with an inner logic to the stages and their progression;

3. specific tests, experiments, or research techniques become the instruments for advancing knowledge in the domain; and

4. the conception is applicable to all ages.

(Adapted from Loevinger, 1976, p. 11)

Loevinger and Kohlberg do agree, however, that there is an interrelationship between moral reasoning and ego develop-ment that occurs predominantly in the intermediary stages though empirical evidence is far from definitive.

Magaña, Whiteley, and Nelson (1980) surveyed the available research literature relating to moral and ego development prior to the beginning of the Sierra Project and found that, as ex-pected, measures of each correlated moderately at specific levels of age and intelligence (see Magaña, Whiteley & Nelson, 1980; Rest, 1979a). They also considered the question of whether at-taining given ego stages was a necessary but not sufficient con-dition for attaining the corresponding moral stage, a question with profound implications for curriculum development. If there is little relationship between growth in each of the sytems, then a moral education curriculum alone should be sufficient to promote moral development. However, if ego development effec-tively sets a ceiling on the potential level of moral develop-ment, then both psychological *and* moral education curricula are necessary.

As a preliminary step in ascertaining the interrelationship of ego and moral development, Magaña, Whiteley, and Nelson (1980) tabulated the number of Sierra subjects whose ego stage was higher than, the same as, or lower than their moral stage ac-cording to the measures described in later chapters. The results of this tabulation are shown in Table 3-4.

TABLE 3-4
A COMPARISON OF KOHLBERG AND LOEVINGER STAGES
FOR THE SIERRA STUDENTS IN THE CLASS OF 1980*

	At Pre-test		At Post-test	
	Males	Females	Males	Females
Loevinger ego development stage higher than Kohlberg moral reasoning stage	15	16	16	15
Loevinger ego development stage the same as Kohlberg moral reasoning stage	5	1	4	3
Loevinger ego development stage lower than Kohlberg moral reasoning stage	2	2	2	1
	22	19	22	19

*From "Sequencing of experiences in psychological interventions: Relationships among locus of control, moral reasoning, and ego development," by H. Magaña, J. M. Whiteley, & K.H. Nelson. In V.L. Erickson & J.M. Whiteley (Eds.), *Developmental counseling and teaching.* Copyright © 1980 by Wadsworth, Inc. Reprinted by permission of the publisher, Brooks/Cole Publishing Co., Monterey, CA.

The tabulations in Table 3-4 indicate that very few subjects attain moral stages that are higher than the corresponding ego stages, though a small number of subjects have comparable levels of moral and ego development. These data suggest that the attainment of a given stage of ego development precedes the attainment of the corresponding moral development stage, these results holding equally true for both sexes.

Sullivan's (1975) data agreed with these findings. He collected scores on the Kohlberg Moral Judgment Interview and the Washington University Sentence Completion Test for Measuring Ego Development from 14 high school students and found that in all but one case, ego stage was higher than moral reasoning stage (see Sullivan, 1975, p. 177).

Magaña, Whiteley, and Nelson (1980) presented two possible explanations for their findings. One explanation is that an individual must first progress to the next ego stage in order to develop the increased logic necessary to attain the corresponding moral stage (so that there is a gap or "lag" in moral development when compared to ego development). Another possible explanation is that the attainment of the next ego stage is a "necessary but not sufficient condition for the development of moral structures" (Kohlberg, 1976, p. 53). This explanation would be appropriate if, in fact, the Loevinger instrument taps those "certain features" of ego development which are "necessary but not sufficient" conditions for the development of a higher level of moral structure. However, neither Kohlberg nor any other theorist has explicated what are the necessary and sufficient conditions for moral development.

In summary, there *is* a correlation both theoretically and empirically between moral reasoning and ego development (for relevant Sierra Project data, please see Chapter 8). Further, level of ego development appears to precede level of moral development. Thus, attempts to raise the level of moral reasoning must take into account the level of ego development of the participants in the intervention.

References

Gibbs, J. C. Kohlberg's stages of moral judgment: A constructive critique. *Harvard Educational Review*, 1977, *47* (1), 43-61.

Gilligan, C. In a different voice: Women's conception of self and of morality. *Harvard Educational Review*, 1977, *47* (4), 481-517.

Haan, N. Two moralities in action contexts: Relationships to thought, ego regulation, and development. *Journal of Personality and Social Psychology*, 1978, *36* (3), 286-305.

Hauser, S. T. Loevinger's model and measure of ego development: A critical review. *Psychological Bulletin*, 1976, *83* (5), 928-955.

Kohlberg, L. *The development of modes of moral thinking and choice in the years ten to sixteen.* Unpublished doctoral dissertation, University of Chicago, 1958.

Kohlberg, L. Development of moral character and moral ideology. In M. L. Hoffman (Ed.), *Review of child development research* (Vol. 1). New York: Russell Sage Foundation, 1964.

Kohlberg, L. Stage and sequence: The cognitive-developmental approach to socialization. In D. A. Goslin (Ed.), *Handbook of socialization theory and research.* Chicago: Rand McNally, 1969, 347-480.

Kohlberg, L. From is to ought: How to commit the naturalistic fallacy and get away with it in the study of moral development. In T. Mischel (Ed.), *Cognitive development and epistemology.* New York: Academic Press, 1971.

Kohlberg, L. Moral stages in moralization: The cognitive-developmental approach. In T. Lickona (Ed.), *Moral development and behavior.* New York: Holt, Rinehart & Winston, 1976, 31-53.

Kohlberg, L. *The meaning and measurement of moral development.* Heinz Werner Memorial Lecture, April 1979.

Lickona, T. (Ed.). *Moral development and behavior.* New York: Holt, Rinehart & Winston, 1976.

Loevinger, J. The meaning and measurement of ego development. *American Psychologist,* 1966, *21,* 195-206.

Loevinger, J. *Ego development: Conceptions and theories.* San Francisco: Jossey-Bass, 1976.

Loevinger, J., & Wessler, R. *Measuring ego development,* Volume I: *Construction and use of a sentence completion test.* San Francisco: Jossey-Bass, 1970.

Magaña, H., Whiteley, J. M., & Nelson, K. H. Sequencing of experiences in psychological interventions: Relationships among locus of control, moral reasoning, and ego development. In V. L. Erickson & J. M. Whiteley (Eds.), *Developmental counseling and teaching.* Monterey, CA: Brooks/Cole, 1980, 298-328.

Maslow, A. H. *The farther reaches of human nature.* New York: Viking Press, 1971.

Piaget, J. *The moral judgment of the child.* (M. Gabain, trans.). Glencoe, IL: The Free Press, 1948. (Originally published 1932).

Rest, J. R. *Development in judging moral issues.* Minneapolis, MN: University of Minnesota Press, 1979. (a)

Rest, J. R. *The impact of higher education on moral judgment development,* Technical Report #5. Minneapolis, MN: Minnesota Moral Research Projects, University of Minnesota, 1979. (b)

Sanford, N. *Learning after college.* Orinda, CA: Montaigne, 1980.

Sullivan, P. J. *A curriculum for stimulating moral reasoning and ego development in adolescents.* Unpublished doctoral dissertation, Boston University School of Education, 1975.

Turiel, E. Conflict and transition in adolescent moral development. *Child Development,* 1974, *45,* 14-29.

Whiteley, J. M., Bertin, B. D., & Berry, B. A. Research on the development of moral reasoning among college students. In M. L. McBee (Ed.), *New directions in higher education*, No. 31: *Higher education's responsibility for moral education*. San Francisco: Jossey-Bass, 1980, 35-44.

Chapter 4

THEORETICAL UNDERPINNINGS FROM DEVELOPMENTAL AND COUNSELING PSYCHOLOGY

John M. Whiteley

The constructs of moral reasoning and ego development—and the relationship between them—have been presented as central to the consideration of character and its development, and form the theoretical backbone of the Sierra Project. One of the goals of the Sierra Project is to stimulate psychological development in the areas of moral reasoning and ego development during the transition from late adolescence to early adulthood.

Unfortunately, there is no blueprint provided in the literature on how to so stimulate development. While the formal curriculum and the informal structuring of experiences in the residence hall provide the vehicle for our approach to fostering character development, there is no well articulated theory of social and personality growth in developmental psychology to specifically guide our intervention. Given the present level of theory, research, and curriculum formulation in developmental education, there is simply not enough known about the optimal match between the developmental level of students and the sequencing of educational experiences to provide direction.

It is not at all clear from previous psychological education programs what kinds of experiences for students at what levels of development lead to specific structural changes in character. As Rest (1977) summarized it, "developmental psychology is in such a state of tentativeness and growth that it cannot furnish detailed, scientifically proven directives for education" (p. 33).

The same constraint applies to the current contribution which counseling psychology can make to developmental education. However, developmental and counseling psychology have made a number of significant contributions to curriculum development, and these contributions have been very influential in the shaping of the Sierra Project.

We will discuss several concepts from developmental and counseling psychology which have particularly influenced the Sierra Project curriculum. Though the day-by-day planning was not based on any specific prescription from either field, the following concepts and skill exercises guided the development of our curriculum in a general way: from developmental psychology, the concepts of structural organization, developmental sequencing, interactionism, and equilibration; from counseling psychology, the concept of a psychological sense of community, the skills of empathy/social perspective-taking, and assertion training.

DEVELOPMENTAL PSYCHOLOGY

Structural Organization of Thinking. Structural organization of thinking refers to the method by which an individual imposes meaning on his or her experience. In Kohlberg's (1969) explanation, "structure" refers to the rules for dealing with information or for relating different events. These internalized rules or conceptual frameworks for problem-solving are basic to how an individual thinks about any particular content or emotional experience.

Piaget (1960, 1964) has indicated that structural organization of thinking may be observed in different stages of development, with each stage different from the others on a number of dimensions. The general characteristics of cognitive stages, as they were identified by Piaget, are:

1. a distinct and qualitative difference between stages of thinking,

2. an invariant sequence in the development of modes of thought,

3. an underlying organization of thought within each sequential stage, and

4. a hierarchy of stages of thinking.

Each stage is increasingly complex; each displaces and reintegrates the cognitive structures found at earlier (and lower) stages. The acquisition of cognitive structures of a more complex nature is an important goal, for these internalized conceptual frameworks endure beyond the recall of specific content. Recognition of the existence of cognitive structures—and of a hierarchy of cognitive stages—is the basis for much of the research in developmental psychology. As Rest (1974a) observed:

> The developmentalist sees cognitive structure as the framework by which affective experiences are interpreted, and by which the strong, emotional experiences of today are translated into the commitments of tomorrow. Structure is emphasized; not the transitory awareness or feeling state (p. 242).*

In the specific area of moral reasoning, the theory that thinking is structurally organized is reflected in the six stages of moral reasoning, each more complex in nature than its predecessor and more adequate in terms of understanding mature and abstract principles of fairness and justice. Improving individuals' abilities to make decisions and solve problems relating to moral issues is the goal of our work in character development, rather than indoctrinating them with a particular set of moral beliefs.

The Sierra Project is a developmental intervention that aims at providing students with experiences which will foster some degree of cognitive reorganization and thereby facilitate the acquisition of higher levels of structural organization. Higher levels of structural organization, reflected in the higher stages of moral reasoning, are characterized by increased intricacy and complexity, allowing the effective solving of problems of scope.

---

*This and all other quotations from this source are from Rest, J. R. Developmental psychology as a guide to value education: A review of "Kohlbergian" programs. *Review of Educational Research*, 1974, *44* (2). Copyright American Educational Research Association. Reprinted with permission.

Developmental Sequencing. Developmental sequencing refers to the belief that there is, in general, a preferred order for presenting educational experiences in order to promote the maximum amount of positive growth. Since the tasks of each stage of development must be mastered before individuals can successfully deal with the experiences addressed by the next stage, educational experiences must be proportionate to an individual's immediate capabilities, as well as his or her potential to grow.

The goal of an educational intervention is to stimulate and accelerate this step-by-step development. As Rest (1974a) noted:

> The adage that the teacher should meet the student at the student's level can be given precise and operational meaning if the course of development is defined and the student's level can be assessed. Knowing the course of development enables one to optimize the match between [students] and curricula and also serves as a guide for sequencing curriculum (p. 244).

Knowing a student's level of development provides a means of identifying those experiences which are likely to be engrossing and therefore lead to further growth. Once these specific experiences are identified, exposure to them can be implemented in a developmentally-based curriculum.

The concept of developmental sequencing provides important information that assists in the planning of a developmental intervention. Rest (1974a) noted two important points in this regard:

1) The characterization of the highest stage of development gives a psychological analysis of some competence — e.g., Piaget's stage of formal operations gives us an analysis of what it means to be logical; Kohlberg's "Stage 6" provides a description of what mature moral judgment consists (p. 243).

2) If the educator has a step by step description of the development of some competence, then he has a means of ordering progress (knowing which changes are progressive), of locating people along this course of development, and therefore, of anticipating which experiences the student will most likely respond to and from which he will profit (p. 244).

For the purposes of the Sierra Project, the concept of developmental sequencing provides both an identification of mature moral judgment and a description of developmental progress in the area of moral reasoning.

Interactionism. The third construct from developmental psychology relevant to the work of the Sierra Project is interactionism. Developmental change results from an individual's active attempts to make sense of experiences which call into question his or her previous assumptions. Learning is not a passive intellectual experience, but rather requires the active involvement of individuals with their environment. In this interactionist framework, experience is necessary both for the full development of a cognitive stage and for the transition to the next stage. Interactionism assumes that changes in experience may affect advancement through cognitive stages, that more or richer experiences will enable individuals to progress at a faster rate through the stages.

The impact of the interactionist position on the curriculum of the Sierra Project is in the devising of conditions to "bring about transformations in the desired direction" (p. 8), in Dewey's (1934/1966) phrase. We attempted to devise experiences which would engage the student in interaction with student peers, with faculty and staff, and with the commmunity at large through field study. The use of journals, in which students were required to reflect critically on the nature of their interactions, was an attempt to promote the development and adoption of new meanings about experiences.

Interactionist assumptions about how to promote structural change form the primary theoretical basis for much of our curriculum. The curriculum is described briefly in Chapter 6 of this volume, in more detail in Whiteley and Loxley (1980), and in Loxley and Whiteley (in preparation).

Equilibration. The fourth concept from developmental psychology which has influenced the work of the Sierra Project is that of equilibration. Equilibration describes the natural and continuous process by which people change their thinking in acquiring more adequate ways of perceiving the world. It is the fundamental theoretical mechanism for change underlying the interactionist approach to fostering the development of higher stages of moral reasoning, and, therefore, is basic to the Sierra

Project approach. Equilibration, or what Piaget (1964) referred to as "self-regulation" (p. 178), has been elaborated upon as a concept by a number of writers including Kohlberg (1969), Langer (1969a, 1969b) and Kegan (1977). Langer's (1969a) characterization of equilibration is helpful in understanding its role in forcing self-development:

> Our own view is that the child is an active operator whose actions are the prime generator of his own psychological development. When he is in a relatively equilibrated state, he will not tend to change; he will only change if he feels, consciously or unconsciously, that something is wrong (p. 36).

Development, therefore, comes from disequilibrium. For Langer (1969a), when affective and organizational disequilibrium are present:

> The energetic or emotional force for change in action is activated, and stabilizing interactions between mental actions and the symbolic media in which they are represented can be constructed in order to generate greater equilibrium. It is this constructive activity that constitutes the force of self-development (p. 36).

Langer also notes that the developmentalist's problem is to identify the individual's internal state of organization to determine when it can contend effectively with disruptions and disequilibrium, and to understand how individuals at different stages of development may accommodate to such disequilibrium.

The task for the educator using an equilibration model for promoting change is to determine ways of increasing the educational impact of an individual's interaction with the environment. This is done with an equilibration analysis employing such notions as "optimal match" and "cognitive conflict." As Kohlberg (1969) stated it:

> such [equilibration] analyses focus upon discrepancies between the child's action system or expectancies and the experienced events, and hypothesize some moderate or optimal degree of discrepancy as constituting the most effective experience for structural change in the organism (p. 356).

As was indicated earlier in this chapter, not enough is known yet about what are the most effective experiences for promoting structural change. The question, of course, is much more refined than the mere identification of those "effective experiences." Enough is now known to direct work toward identifying what experiences, in what order, influence individuals at specific structural levels of development. The equilibration theory is helpful to curriculum development because it provides guidance in assessing stage level, sequencing experiences, and increasing the impact of the environment.

Part of equilibration analysis involves the complementary processes of assimilation and accommodation. These processes suggest how individuals understand new experiences, and how new experiences lead to structural change. Assimilation refers to the process by which the outside world is understood within the framework of an individual's current mode of thinking. The alternate process, accommodation, occurs when existing thought patterns are not adequate to fully understand and integrate new experiences, thereby creating cognitive conflict and disequilibrium. The individual then modifies his or her mode of thinking to incorporate the new experiences.

Kohlberg (1969) states that since "the direction of development of cognitive structure is toward greater equilibrium" (p. 348), accommodation is part of the process by which individuals' modes of reasoning are modified. As Sullivan (1975) puts it,

> When this happens a new, more stable form of thinking is established and the process of equilibration is said to have occurred. . . . Each successive equilibration provides a more complex, more stable way for the individual to interpret and interact with his environment (p. 35).

While assimilation and accommodation are seen as complementary, they are also quite different and, in fact, opposite in function. Distinguishing their differences helps clarify the nature of the growth tasks facing freshmen in Sierra.

Based on our initial normative data, we have concluded that Sierra freshmen have just made the transition from preconventional thinking to the first stage of conventional thinking. As a group, they are experiencing both a new and stressful university environment, and a new — albeit conventional — way of understanding the world. Were it not for assimilation as a thought process, the Sierra freshmen would have no stable, dependable way of relating to those around them. Assimilation, then, results from the desire to transform new experience into the old and familiar, providing some stability and continuity with the past.

During a transition period, the extent to which the college freshman attempts to retain the characteristics of his or her role as a high school student reflects the degree to which he or she is assimilating the new experience and attempting to deal with it in a stable manner—but also thereby preventing growth. Assimilation is vital for fully investigating new issues of living from the new Stage 3 perspective of interpersonal concordance, and vital for exploring peer and university culture to the fullest. This process of promoting growth through Stage 3 thinking competency is an important part of being a freshman within the context of the Sierra Project and the broader university. However, since past ways of approaching the world are not adequate for understanding and managing the new experiences—both those presented by the peer and university culture and those presented by the formal Sierra curriculum—accommodation is an important thought process for promoting new equilibration.

Thus, encouraging the process of reaching toward more adequate ways of viewing the world is an important educational goal. An aim of the Sierra curriculum is to present tasks which are structured in such a way as to foster accommodation and the forming of higher level cognitive structures. We are suggesting that by using the natural change mechanism of equilibration, educators can identify and implement exposure to experiences most appropriate for promoting positive moral development.

A goal of the Sierra Project, then, is to provide experiences which will produce disequilibration, since it is the *process* that each individual undertakes in the face of disequilibrium that promotes growth. At the same time, some balance is necessary. Overly stressing change might well leave a student with a sense of being rootless. A careful monitoring of the amount of dissonance is necessary. As one method of providing sources of stability, we attempted to create a cohesive community. It is to this topic that we now turn.

COUNSELING PSYCHOLOGY

Psychological Sense of Community. A basic educational approach of the Sierra Project was to balance a disequilibrating, growth-producing experience (the transition to college) with experiences promoting some security and feelings of personal belonging. A psychological sense of community encourages feelings of personal belonging. In attempting to foster a sense of community as a source of stability, we encountered a problem of definition.

Community is used to mean many different things, and the literature does not prove particularly helpful in clarifying meaning—or in understanding the interrelationship of a sense of community and character development. It is necessary to define *community* carefully and to articulate its relationship to other concepts. After reviewing the literature, we define a *psychological sense of community* as the following: *the presence of high levels of trust, cooperation, and mutual feelings of security and support among members of a community—with very low levels of alienation and hostility.* The approach to measurement of community which we chose to adopt was the Environmental Assessment Inventory principally developed by an environmental psychologist (Stokols, 1975) whose major interests at the time were the study of alienation, density, stress, and crowding. While our measurement of community was developed by an environmental psychologist (and our curriculum development and delivery were largely from the perspective of counseling psychology), a number of other perspectives shaped our thinking on the characteristics and definition of a psychological sense of community.

Scherer (1972), a sociologist, provides a number of observations about communities which we found to be quite valid. She states that communities will always exist because of human nature, even though sense of community seems under attack by the circumstances of modern social systems. She suggests that community is a complex concept that "may be thought of as the other side of the coin presented in the dominant twentieth century concern with 'alienated' man" (Scherer, 1972, p. 1).* For our purposes, we conceptualize the urge toward community, while complex, as being basic to human nature. By tapping into it as an educational resource, we are reaching a very powerful medium for involving people in changing themselves and for sustaining that involvement.

Sarason has written extensively on community (Sarason, Zitnay, & Grossman, 1971; Sarason, 1972, 1974). He believes that:

> the dilution or absence of the psychological sense of community is the most destructive dynamic in the lives of people in our society. That I hold this belief is less persuasive than the fact that it has been for several hundred years a theme noted and discussed with ever-increasing frequency and urgency in Western Society (Sarason, 1974, Preface, p. *viii*).

A similar view is held by two other psychologists who have influenced our thinking, Carl R. Rogers (1970) and William Coulson (1973), both of whom are humanistically-oriented.

The converging body of literature from sociologists and developmental, clinical, community, and counseling psychologists has drawn attention to the importance of a psychological sense of community. Scholars disagree, however, about specific structures in which it can be developed and about how the development of community is related to fostering other goals, such as character development.

In fact, Sarason (1974) suggests that it is naive to assume that developing a psychological sense of community is a simple vehicle for improving the human condition:

> Agreement on values is easier to reach than agreement about the appropriateness of value-derived actions. This alone should caution one against the tendency, tempting and understandable, to assume that because the psychological sense of community is a value which should inform

---

*This and all other quotations from this source are from Scherer, J. Contemporary community: Sociological illusion or reality? London: Tavistock, 1972. Copyright Jacqueline Scherer. Reprinted with permission.

action, it is a value that ensures certain desired outcomes. The failure to resist this tempting oversimplification leads only to disillusionment (p. 268-269).

Another viewpoint that influenced our thinking about psychological sense of community is that of Kanter (1972) who wrote a sociological perspective on communes and utopias. In the process of exploring their characteristics, she made a number of observations about the nature of community which have proven helpful to us. One observation is that many approaches to community have been based historically on a psychosocial critique of society:

> This critique revolves around alienation and loneliness, both social isolation and inner fragmentation. It holds that modern society has put people out of touch with others and with their own fundamental nature. It rejects established society's emphasis on achievement and instead adopts as its credo "self-actualization" or "personal growth" (p. 7).

This critique is very similar to that held by members of the Sierra Project staff. Our belief is that the nature of the traditional educational experience forecloses certain types of growth, and, importantly for our purposes, character development is one of these. Our aim is to create a climate of community which can foster character development while at the same time provide skills to facilitate academic achievement within the broader university community.

Some aspects of utopias described by Kanter (1972) are similar to the environment we endeavored to foster in the residence hall. The resemblance between the two is in the desired nature of the interpersonal climate, one in which

> people work and live together closely and cooperatively, in a social order that is self-created and self-chosen rather than externally imposed . . . harmony, cooperation, and mutuality of interests are natural to human existence, rather than conflict, competition, and exploitation, which arise only in imperfect societies (p. 1).

Our belief is that we can use that element of human interaction so basic to the utopian dream—community—and utilize it as a force for the development of skills to live more adequately in society. Further, and importantly, the development of a community can be the basis for raising the level of reasoning about moral issues.

It may be that psychological sense of community functions as one of the most powerful forces for influencing moral reasoning. Scherer (1972) notes the power of communities in affecting moral behavior:

> At present, perhaps the most tenacious pull of the community concept is in its moral implications. To share interests and live together requires agreement on rules, concern for others, and a commitment to the group. The idea of belonging, and being a part of a larger association, is most attractive to the insecure and frightened. It can also be a ferocious web of affiliations that strangles individuality and restricts freedom to the confines of the circle. Churches are the most obvious centres of moral communities, but one finds them wherever group goals are symbolic and behaviour is prescribed by ethical regulations (pp. 5-6).

The power of communities to affect moral behavior has been tapped by Kohlberg (1975) and his associates (Kohlberg, Kauffman, Scharf, & Hickey, 1975; Scharf & Hickey, 1976; Kohlberg, Wasserman, & Richardson, 1975; Wasserman, 1976), who have applied the concept of community specifically to the educational task of raising the level of moral reasoning. The term he and his associates used to describe their approach was that of developing a *just community*.

Their initial implementation of the "just community" approach was in a prison (Kohlberg, Kauffman, Scharf, & Hickey, 1975; Scharf & Hickey, 1976) where the social atmosphere and justice structure were modified to stimulate moral growth. Subsequent to the prison work, Kohlberg and his colleagues attempted an intervention designed to develop a just community in a high school (Kohlberg, Wasserman, & Richardson, 1975; Wasserman, 1976).

Kohlberg (1975) clarified the role of the "just community" in stimulating upward movement through the moral stages, saying:

> A just community approach promotes moral character development and responsibility: (a) through living in an atmosphere of fairness and developing relations of loyalty

and trust; (b) by taking responsibility for making and en-
forcing rules on oneself and other members of the group;
and (c) through a better understanding of the society in
which we live (p. 6).

The first of these three points—an atmosphere of fairness, loyalty, and trust—is very similar to what we are attempting to
foster and measure under the rubric of a psychological sense of
community. The second of these points—the taking of responsibility for the group's rules of conduct—was much more difficult for us to implement for several reasons.

First, there are very few rules of conduct for the residence
halls of which Sierra is a part. There are no intervisitation rules:
men and women students are allowed in each other's rooms at
any time. Public consumption of alcohol and smoking of marijuana are not permitted, but students' rooms are not subject to
arbitrary search. The possession of a firearm on a campus of the
University of California is a felony under state law, and this law
is strictly enforced. Students are expected to act as responsible
adults without the university assuming the role of a parent. The
voluntarily chosen obligations of freshmen in Sierra Hall, which
went beyond the obligations of UCI freshmen living in other
dorms, were to participate in the testing program, attend the
Sierra dorm class on a regular basis, and turn in their journals
at specified times. These rules had been accepted by the freshmen prior to their moving in, and there were not many other
outside rules or authority issues with which to contend.

The second reason why it has been difficult for us to get
students involved in setting their own rules is because these
entering freshmen were very conventionally oriented and very
accepting of what they were told. Our initial efforts were aimed
at encouraging them, as much as we could, to develop a critical
and analytic view of staff pronouncements. However, the Sierra
students were more interested in exploring their new freedoms
from parental sanction, and in learning how to survive academically; they simply had little interest in exploring rules. Perhaps
working with students at a higher stage of development would
lead to a different instructional experience. And certainly an
atmosphere of greater campus restriction would provide more
impetus for students to take initiative in setting rules.

The third of Kohlberg's points—establishing a better understanding of society—is something the Sierra curriculum focused
on directly. Field studies were designed to interest Sierra freshmen in accepting greater responsibility for what they were
learning, and for helping them learn more about themselves
and society.

Kohlberg (1975) holds that "moral development arises from
social interaction in situations of social conflict" (p. 6). An important implication of this statement for the "just community" is
the need to establish a system wherein rules and decisions are
made by staff and students in a framework considered fair by
all. Students will, therefore, experience social conflict in democratic interactions in which they can work with each other and
staff to carry out the rules by which they will live. A key premise
is that students should be involved in making the decisions
which greatly affect them. Kohlberg (1975) stated this point when
he noted that the program of a just community school:

> emphasizes the creation of a "constitution" or social con-
> tract that is shared by everyone in the community. This
> process involves the students in taking responsibility for
> developing and enforcing the rules, understanding others'
> points of view, and developing reciprocity in human rela-
> tions (p. 7).

We have commented on the special circumstances surrounding
rules. The formal Sierra curriculum—through the teaching of
empathy and listening skills—aims at increasing student understanding of others' points of view. Reciprocity in human relations is a key part of the informal curriculum of living in the
residence hall situation. It is also part of the formal curriculum,
particularly in the assertion training and community building
modules. Since a key premise in the development of community
is the involvement of the participants, the Sierra Project was
organized in such a manner as to encourage full student and
staff participation.

Empathy, Social Perspective-Taking, and Moral Reasoning. Both
empathy and social perspective-taking are active skills which
are very important in the development of higher levels of moral
reasoning. Empathy allows a person to more accurately perceive and understand the thoughts and feelings of another on
an intimately personal level. Social perspective-taking extends

that perception and understanding to encompass a broader spectrum of concerns: socio-economic, political, racial, etc.

Three separate groups of researchers, working quite independently and with different methodological approaches, have identified the theoretical and empirical relationships between empathy and moral reasoning. We will review their work and indicate the approach we have found most relevant to the psychological education and longitudinal research aspects of the Sierra Project.

The first group of researchers is Mosher and Sprinthall and their associates (Mosher & Sprinthall, 1970, 1971). Their pioneering work in psychological education promoted personal development during adolescence, making it "a central focus of education, rather than pious rhetoric at commencement, a second-order concern of the English curriculum or the private guilt of committed teachers and counselors" (Mosher & Sprinthall, 1971, p. 3). Their discovery of the relationship between empathy and moral reasoning was made while teaching high school students an experimental course in counseling skills.

From their background in counselor education, both researchers realized the effects which counselor training can have on a participant,

> that the seminar and practicum experiences in counseling were powerful tools for raising questions of personal identity, the meaning of a helping relationship, understanding one's self and others in comprehensive ways, the complexity of hearing and responding to another person's ideas and feelings, the importance of emotions, etc.; in short, the whole array of questions counselors have traditionally confronted as a result of supervised counseling experience (p. 15-16).

The counseling skills taught by Mosher and Sprinthall were assessed using three scales developed by Carkhuff (1969): empathy, genuineness, and immediacy. While their control group (a psychology class with no counseling skill training) showed no change in moral reasoning and ego development, the experimental group changed significantly—both empathy and immediacy increased as a result of the counseling training. This work has been replicated by subsequent researchers, including Sullivan (1975) and Dowell (1971).

The second group of researchers exploring the relationship between empathy and moral reasoning is Hogan and his associates (Hogan, 1969, 1973; Hogan & Dickstein, 1972; Greif & Hogan, 1973). In the Greif and Hogan (1973) paper, empathy is defined as "sensitivity to the needs and values of others" and is conceptualized as a "major element in role-theoretical accounts of interpersonal behavior" (p. 280). The role-theoretical literature providing background for the conceptualization included Cottrell (1971), Goffman (1959), Kelly (1955), McDougall (1960), Mead (1934), and Sarbin and Allen (1968).

Greif and Hogan's (1973) work relates empathy to moral development and moral conduct. Instead of references to Kohlberg and his developmental stage approach to measurement, Greif and Hogan drew on the work of Hogan (1973), Baier (1966), and Wright (1971). For Hogan (1973), moral conduct can be explained and the development of moral character described in terms of five concepts: moral knowledge, socialization, empathy, autonomy, and a dimension of moral judgment.

The work of Hogan and his associates is essentially a trait model in contrast to Mosher and Sprinthall's developmental model. The measurements of empathy used by Mosher and Sprinthall (1971) in their research were derived from the client-centered approach to psychotherapy. Hogan (1969), however, derived a scale to measure empathy from the California Personality Inventory and the Minnesota Multiphasic Personality Inventory.

The relationship between social perspective-taking and moral reasoning was explored by Selman and associates (Selman, 1971, 1976a, 1976b; Selman & Byrne, 1974; Selman & Damon, 1975). Selman's research has centered on the development of role-taking ability and social perspective-taking, particularly as it affects the development of moral reasoning in children. Selman (1976b) makes a crucial distinction between moral judgment and social role-taking. In his view, moral judgment considers "how people *should* think and act with regard to each other." In contrast, social role-taking considers "how and why people do *in fact* think about and act toward each other" (p. 307).

Selman's methodology has been similar to that of Piaget (1929) and Kohlberg (1969): dilemmas are used to elicit the structure of moral reasoning which the child draws upon in resolving the issues of competing claims. Although Selman presents a fixed series of dilemmas, the probe questions that follow are more variable and open-ended in order to identify the underlying logic that the person is using to resolve the problem. Once Selman has completed the clinical interview, the child's thinking is scored for its structural aspects from three perspectives (Selman, 1976b):

(1) the subject's own point of view,

(2) the different viewpoints of each character in the dilemma, and

(3) the relationships among these various perspectives (p. 302).

Selman's approach also provides a scale for measuring the child's conception of the motives and feelings of others as these relate to moral judgments. Selman (1976b) describes role-taking as a social cognition intermediate between logical and moral thought:

> According to this outlook the child's cognitive stage indicates his level of understanding of physical and logical problems, while his role-taking stage indicates his level of understanding of the nature of social relationship, and his moral judgment stage indicates the manner in which he decides how to resolve social conflicts between people with different points of view (p. 307).

This outline of the parallel structured relationship between social role-taking and moral judgment stages is an important contribution. Since Selman's work has been primarily with children, it is not directly applicable to the work of the Sierra Project; however, extrapolating from his work with children and considering it in concert with the work of Hogan and his associates and Mosher and Sprinthall and their associates, there is a clear indication in the literature that empathy and moral reasoning are integrally related.

Because of its greater applicability to late adolescence and early adulthood, because of its conceptual foundation on a developmental model which is particularly relevant theoretically to our attempt to promote growth in moral reasoning and ego development, and because of the fact there are well-developed and researched instructional techniques associated with it, the Sierra Project uses the methodology and assumptions of the Mosher-Sprinthall approach.

As part of using this approach, we assumed that empathy training could have a very significant impact on the growth of moral reasoning—that the teaching of counseling skills in general and, in particular, those of empathic understanding could stimulate moral growth past the initial egocentric, self-consciousness of Stage 3. This empathy training helps students set aside the "self" and learn to listen to another person.

Learning to listen to others and understanding their feelings, however, is only part of the growth problem; another part is to learn to stand up for oneself. At Stage 3, the challenge is to maintain one's psychological rights against the demands of significant others and of the group. We use assertion training as the vehicle for teaching this ability.

In our model, assertion training builds upon the individual's capacity to see others' perspectives and listen to what they have to say. As a part of their transition from Stage 3, it is important for students to learn to be able to respond with empathy and with respect for the rights of all parties involved including themselves. In utilizing an intervention which encourages students to learn self-direction and independence, we also assume that we are assisting students to seek more field independence, a factor in the ultimate transition from conventional to post-conventional thinking.

Assertion Training. Assertion training is the final concept from counseling psychology which underlies the Sierra Project. It is designed to assist individuals in learning to identify their own personal rights and the rights of others, and then to resolve differences fairly. Assertion training is viewed as providing the students with skills to help them live more effectively. As applied in the Sierra Project, assertion training specifically helps students rethink their beliefs about issues of fairness and justice, provides them with the skills to put their beliefs into action, and helps them reconsider their sex role choices.

Like the concept of a psychological sense of community, assertion training is not the sole province of counseling psychology. In its early formulation by Salter (1949), in a book entitled *Conditioned Reflex Therapy* and in the pioneering work by Wolpe and

Lazarus in the 1950's and 1960's (Wolpe, 1958, 1969, 1970; Wolpe & Lazarus, 1966; Lazarus, 1968; Wolpe, Salter, & Reyna, 1964), assertion training was largely the province of behavior therapists, its applications largely oriented to therapy patients.

The widespread application of assertion training techniques to the general public as a means of helping them live more effectively is largely a phenomenon of the 1970's. The specific approaches to assertion training focused on particular needs — sexuality assertiveness training, assertion training for job interviews, and assertion training for women — have been provided largely by counseling psychologists concerned with helping normal people eliminate counterproductive interpersonal behavior.

The trend toward the increased use of assertion training is based on a realization that individual change does not always require extensive psychotherapy, and on an attempt by the counseling profession to provide the opportunity for such change to a much broader section of the population. Assertion training reflects a movement toward providing counseling for all who think that they can work on their psychological concerns and benefit from counseling. The increasing number of techniques and procedures which are based upon a "health" rather than "illness" model of psychotherapeutic intervention reflect this trend; assertion training falls into the "health" model category.

Assertiveness has been variously characterized. R. M. Whiteley (1976) described it as:

> the direct, honest, and appropriate expression of one's thoughts, opinions, feelings, or needs. Assertive behavior involves a high regard for one's own personal rights *and* the rights of others. It is ethical and responsible, yet firm. Unassertive behavior is characterized by communicating less than one wishes in an avoidant, passive, or wishy-washy manner. Assertiveness is differentiated from aggressive behavior, where one expresses oneself in a direct and even honest manner but where one is also attempting to hurt, put down, embarrass, or upset another person (p. 233-234).

In working with students, a first task is to help them learn to discriminate among assertive, nonassertive, and aggressive behaviors. College freshmen are established in an environment where they are more free to fully express themselves than at any previous time in their lives. Learning to identify their own personal rights is often a new, challenging, and liberating experience in and of itself. Becoming cognizant of the rights of others in different situations is also often a new experience.

Assertion training, according to Lange and Jakubowski (1976), incorporates four basic procedures:

1. teaching people the differences between assertion and aggression and between nonassertion and politeness;

2. helping people identify and accept both their own personal rights and the rights of others;

3. reducing existing cognitive and affective obstacles to acting assertively, e.g., irrational thinking, excessive anxiety, guilt, and anger; and

4. developing assertive skills through active practice methods (p. 2).

Assertion training may include behavioral rehearsal, modeling, successive approximation as a method of response shaping, positive reinforcement, and cognitive restructuring of the belief systems which direct behavior. It is a psychological intervention which treats intrapsychic or mediating variables of behavior. Specific, overt behaviors as well as feelings, thoughts, and fantasies are the subject matter of behavior change in most models of assertion training.

Within the Sierra Project, the personal growth component of assertion training is viewed as providing the students with skills to help them live more effectively in their adult lives. In addition to its providing skills for living more effectively, we also see assertion training as offering specific contributions toward promoting character development. This is the fundamental reason that assertion training has been accorded a place in our curriculum.

Assertion training assists with character development by offering a means of helping students rethink their beliefs about issues of fairness and justice, and their own and others' rights and mutual obligations. By providing students with the skills to implement their newly acquired conceptions, assertion training can provide a life-long contribution to these individuals' daily conduct.

The contribution of assertion training differs depending on the stage level of the subject. In the Sierra population, almost everyone clustered around Stage 3. The transitions we were trying to effect, then, were either from Stage 2 to Stage 3, or from Stage 3 to Stage 4. The remainder of this section will focus on the theoretical issues in each transition that influence how assertion training is employed in character development.

Assertion training as an intervention was expected to affect individuals at Stage 2 differently than those at Stage 3. For Stage 2 individuals, assertion training is aimed at those specific beliefs frequently associated with that stage and their consequences:

1. the "What's in it for me" orientation which leads to aggressive behavior and a lack of regard for the rights of others; and

2. the "It's not fair if I don't get what I want" and "It's not how you play the game but whether you *win*" orientation that leads to exploitative and unfair actions, usually of an aggressive nature.

With a Stage 2 individual, assertion training attempts to accomplish the following:

1. promote perspective-taking by helping people identify the rights of others in interpersonal transactions;

2. help individuals develop a belief system in which the rights of others are respected and acknowledged;

3. help people move from aggressive behavior to more appropriate assertive behavior;

4. promote a belief system which devalues the cognitive antecedents of some aggressive behaviors characteristic of Stage 2 such as "it is good to win over others," or "it is my basic right in life," or "as a prerequisite to feeling OK about myself, I must get my way at the expense of others"; and

5. give people practice in stating their goals for an interpersonal transaction in terms of their own behavior rather than what they want from others.

Changing from aggressive behavior to appropriate assertive behavior (point #3) will result in different consequences; those individuals who behave assertively are much more likely to receive approval from others than those who behave aggressively. With Stage 2 persons, assertion training will increase the availability and potential of approval as a consequence of their behavior. This increase should thereby make it a more potent reinforcer which, in turn, should lead to valuing approval as a positive consequence of one's behavior.

For Stage 3 individuals, assertion training attempts to deal with the following characteristics frequently associated with this stage:

1. approval seeking;

2. avoidance of conflict;

3. avoidance of risk-taking which might jeopardize relationships;

4. lack of discrimination regarding what and whose approval is valued;

5. immediacy of approval in relationship transactions which determines the rightness and wrongness of actions; and

6. lack of tolerance for differences in others.

With a Stage 3 individual, assertion training attempts to accomplish the following:

1. develop a concern for and awareness of personal rights in relationships, both those belonging to oneself and to others;

2. promote a belief system which helps people give themselves permission to have personal rights and to act on those rights;

3. encourage people to choose goals for themselves independently of the demands or pressures from others;

4. promote using oneself as the evaluator of behavior rather than relying on others to determine the evaluation; and

5. break down sex role stereotypes through developing a concept of personal rights which is broader than sex-type role behavior.

The object of the fifth goal is to establish a basis for new behavior choices by helping people identify contradictions between personal rights and socially prescribed sex role imperatives. Stage

3, the preponderant level of Sierra students, has a central theme of social relationships organized around conformity to the personal expectations of others.

Selman (1971) distinguished between Stage 3 individuals and those at a lower level on the dimension of reciprocal role-taking. Stage 3 individuals can be mutually aware of each other's point of view, whereas lower stage individuals cannot. Rest (1974b) drew attention to an additional feature of Stage 3 thinking: the capacity to view social interaction over time. As he phrased it, "Each party knows what the other expects, wishes, and acts to support those expectations" (p. 11). The core characteristic of Stage 3 in Rest's (1974b) presentation is the "establishment and maintenance of positive, stable, reciprocal relationships whereby each party in the relationship is kind, thoughtful, and helpful" (p. 11). Within one's circle of family and friends, an action is characterized as good if it is "well motivated" and shows a concern for the approval of the "significant other." Even without a consideration of its stage change implications, assertion training is a mode of intervention which leads to more satisfying living within Stage 3. Respecting others' rights will result in their approval; obtaining your rights without interfering with another will maintain approval. Such an approach helps preserve relationships over time.

Assertion training also contributes to the transition to Stage 4. Once an individual moves beyond his or her intimate circle, Stage 3 no longer provides guidelines for living. Roles are no longer specified personally. Rights and responsibilities are not defined so that persons outside a close association know what to expect. In Stage 4, roles and responsibilities are defined impersonally. Rest's (1974b) characterization of Stage 4 is that:

> The stabilization and coordination of human interaction depends on people knowing what to expect from each other. Stage 4 establishes this by law: norms for behavior that are publicly set, knowable by all members of society, categorically and impartially applied, and enforced impersonally as a society-wide concern (p. 16).

When used for promoting transition to Stage 4, assertion training forces the participants to consider the rights of people beyond their immediate circle, and with a conflict resolution model, it presents skills to help maintain the established order. Stage 4 individuals attempt to maintain social order for its own sake. Conflict resolution is a necessary skill for maintaining order.

The core of the application of assertion training in the transition from Stage 3 to Stage 4 is analyzing individuals' belief systems, and assisting them to rethink their beliefs toward different conclusions about the role of conflict and approval-seeking in their lives. This is the cognitive restructuring approach to assertion training, not the strictly behavioral approach.

The basic assertion training procedure of identifying one's own rights in a situation is a challenge for a Stage 3 person, whose actions are directed toward *avoiding conflict* and *seeking approval*. The notion that an individual has rights beyond the approval of others is a new concept for a Stage 3 person. This is a Stage 4 concept in itself, as there is an explicit treatment of rights as vested in law and society. Rights are presented in assertion training as based beyond the approval system of one's immediate circle.

For young people making the transition from adolescence to young adulthood, from high school to college, we have found that introducing a belief system which tells them they may choose goals that other people would not want them to have is captivating emotionally and intellectually. Assertion training oriented this way capitalizes on a very powerful issue of emotional development and a key source of conflict with parents and other significant adults. The subject of rights is presented as having a context larger than one's immediate personal transactions.

This Stage 3/4 transition presents a new kind of risk-taking. The Sierra context, with an emphasis on a psychological sense of community, provides a level of security which allows the participants to take risks. Our experience with a very conventional population is that there is a lot of risk and psychological stress associated with the Stage 3/4 transition.

In view of the degree of risk and psychological stress associated with the Stage 3/4 transition, it is not surprising that the conflict-resolution component of assertion training may help make it such an impetus for structural change. Stage 4 differs from Stage 3 in the conflict resolution model: at Stage 4, assertion training provides individuals with the skills to act assertively and achieve their legitimate ends without interfering with the rights of others in the process. This new skill facilitates learning to act successfully in relation to society. It requires a higher level of empathy and social role-taking because individuals must be aware of themselves, be aware of the point of view of others in the conflict, and have the capacity to see how each relates to the other in the conflict. The principles of fairness and justice provide the basis for resolving the conflict.

How these principles are employed, of course, determines the stage level at which the resolution will occur. A successful resolution, taking all the parties' perceptions as well as their interaction into account, reflects at least a Stage 4 accomplishment. Individuals fixed at Stage 3 are too emotionally torn between potentially losing their status as "nice persons" and fully engaging themselves in an open process of conflict resolution. Assertion training provides the structure in which Stage 3 issues can be shifted into Stage 4 conceptualizations, a process which can and does (in the Piagetian framework) render assimilation ineffective, place an emphasis on accommodation, and lead to a higher level of equilibration.

Assertion training is also a vehicle for helping students rethink their sex role choices. Traditional sex role stereotyping in our society tends to support a belief system that many assertive actions are not appropriate for women. R.M. Whiteley (1977) identified the following assertive behaviors as being excluded from or minimized in the traditional female sex role:

1. initiating behaviors;
2. problem solving, particularly analysis, evaluation;
3. verbally defending and supporting one's point of view;
4. directness;
5. positive self-presentation;
6. expressing negative feelings or giving negative feedback;
7. setting limits on the behavior of others in relation to self;
8. striving for personal power and achievement (p. 3).

Assertion training challenges the socialization messages and stereotyped thinking which maintain the nonassertive behaviors in women and restrict the actions of both sexes. R.M. Whiteley (1977) and her colleagues use cognitive restructuring procedures as a model for encouraging behavior change in women, basing their interventions on the work of Ellis (1962, 1973), Meichenbaum (1977), and Beck (1976). Cognitions which maintain nonassertive or aggressive behaviors are conceptualized by R. M. Whiteley (1977) as "irrational thinking styles, irrational belief systems, and instances of deficiencies in problem-solving abilities and coping skills" (p. 4). Following cognitive restructuring, behavioral rehearsal is employed to enable students to try out their newly conceived behaviors.

Assertion in the sense of recognizing one's own and others' rights is a task which can be accomplished by a person at Stage 3. Erickson (1973) locates the typical American woman in our society at Stage 3. This suggests that their developmental stage may account for the large numbers of women who have been able to benefit from assertion training. They can conceptualize the issues surrounding personal rights and opt for new values. R. M. Whiteley (1976) presented this part of the desired outcome of the assertion training process:

> In many areas there is a double standard of behavior for men and women. When these areas involve the violation of one's personal human rights, assertion training can help a person sort out the rights involved; determine whether the behavior is, in fact, unassertive, assertive, or aggressive; and choose responses to communicate one's thoughts, feelings, or needs in a direct, honest, and appropriate manner. Thus, the cultural stereotypes that restrict personal expression are rejected in favor of *human* values. Men and women are not encouraged to give up the masculine or feminine qualities they value, but rather to have greater access to the full range of healthy thoughts, feelings and behaviors available to all human beings (p. 234).

Learning to recognize new human values and acquiring the skills to implement them is a valued part of the Sierra curriculum for the freshmen. Their enthusiasm for assertion training reflects the positive personal growth and competencies which they achieve. Further, the aspects of assertion training identified above are highly compatible with the basically Stage 3 conventional orientation which predominates with our group of students.

Thus far, we have outlined and described the basic concepts that have influenced us from the inception through the implementation of the Sierra Project. Our work in the Sierra Project, however, is basically experimental. The final chapter of this section, "Research on Measuring and Changing the Level of Moral Reasoning in College Students," will close our look at the remaining body of literature and research that has shaped the Sierra Project.

References

Baier, K. *The moral point of view: A rational basis of ethics.* New York: Random House, 1966.

Beck, A. *Cognitive therapy and the emotional disorders.* New York: International Universities Press, 1976.

Carkhuff, R. R. *Helping and human relations.* (Vol. I and Vol. II). New York: Holt, Rinehart, & Winston, 1969.

Cottrell, L. S. Covert behavior in interpersonal interaction. *Proceedings of the American Philosophical Society,* 1971, *115,* 462-469.

Coulson, W. R. *A sense of community.* Columbus, OH: Merrill, 1973.

Dewey, J. The need for a philosophy of education. In R. D. Archambault (Ed.), *John Dewey on education: Appraisals.* New York: Random House, 1966. (Originally published 1934).

Dowell, R. C. *Adolescents as peer counselors: A program for psychological growth.* Unpublished doctoral dissertation, Harvard University, 1971.

Ellis, A. *Reason and emotion in psychotherapy.* New York: Lyle Stuart, 1962.

Ellis, A. Rational-emotive therapy. In R. J. Corsini (Ed.), *Current psychotherapies.* Itasca, IL: Peacock, 1973.

Erickson, V. L. *Psychological growth for women: A cognitive-developmental curriculum intervention.* Unpublished doctoral dissertation, University of Minnesota, 1973.

Goffman, E. *The presentation of self in everyday life.* New York: Doubleday Anchor, 1959.

Greif, E. B., & Hogan, R. The theory and measurement of empathy. *Journal of Counseling Psychology,* 1973, *20*(3),280-284.

Hogan, R. Development of an empathy scale. *Journal of Consulting and Clinical Psychology*, 1969, *33*(3), 307-316.

Hogan, R. Moral conduct and moral character: A psychological perspective. *Psychological Bulletin*, 1973, *79*(4), 217-232.

Hogan, R., & Dickstein, E. A measure of moral values. *Journal of Consulting and Clinical Psychology*, 1972, *39*(2), 210-214.

Kanter, R. M. *Commitment and community: Communes and utopias in sociological perspective.* Cambridge, MA: Harvard University Press, 1972.

Kegan, R. G. *Ego and truth: Personality and Piaget paradigm.* Unpublished doctoral dissertation, Harvard University, 1977.

Kelly, G. A. *The psychology of personal constructs.* (Vol. I). *A theory of personality.* New York: Norton, 1955.

Kohlberg, L. Stage and sequence: The cognitive-developmental approach to socialization. In D. A. Goslin (Ed.), *Handbook of socialization theory and research.* New York: Rand-McNally, 1969, 347-476.

Kohlberg, L. *Latest version of the theory of the just community school.* Unpublished manuscript, Harvard University, 1975.

Kohlberg, L., Kauffman, K., Scharf, P., & Hickey, J. The just community approach to corrections: A theory. *Journal of Moral Education*, 1975, *4*(3), 243-260.

Kohlberg, L., Wasserman, E., & Richardson, N. The just community school: The theory and the Cambridge cluster school experiment. In L. Kohlberg (Ed.), *Collected papers on moral development and moral education* (Vol. II). Cambridge, MA: Harvard University Center for Moral Education, 1975.

Lange, A. J., & Jakubowsky, P. *Responsible assertive behavior: Cognitive-behavioral procedures for trainers.* Champaign, IL: Research Press, 1976.

Langer, J. Disequilibrium as a source of development. In P. H. Mussen, J. Langer, & M. Covington (Eds.), *Trends and issues in developmental psychology.* New York: Holt, Rinehart, & Winston, 1969. (a)

Langer, J. *Theories of development.* New York: Holt, Rinehart, & Winston, 1969. (b)

Lazarus, A. A. Behavior therapy in groups. In G. M. Gazda (Ed.), *Basic approaches to group psychotherapy and group counseling.* Springfield, IL: Thomas, 1968.

Loxley, J. C., & Whiteley, J. M. *Character development in college students* (Vol. II), in preparation.

McDougall, W. *An introduction to social psychology.* London: Methuen, 1960.

Mead, G. H. *Mind, self, and society from the standpoint of a social behaviorist.* Chicago: University of Chicago Press, 1934.

Meichenbaum, D. *Cognitive-behavior modification: An integrative approach.* New York: Plenum, 1977.

Mosher, R. L., & Sprinthall, N. A. Psychological education in secondary schools: A program to promote individual and human development. *American Psychologist,* 1970, *25,* 911-924.

Mosher, R. L., & Sprinthall, N. A., et al. Psychological education: A means to promote personal development during adolescence. *The Counseling Psychologist,* 1971, *2*(4), 3-82.

Piaget, J. *The child's conception of the world.* New York: Harcourt, Brace, 1929.

Piaget, J. The general problems of the psychobiological development of the child. In J. M. Tanner & B. Inhelder (Eds.), *Discussions on child development: Proceedings of the fourth meeting of the World Health Organization study group on the psychobiological development of the child,* Geneva, 1956 (Vol. IV). New York: International Universities Press, 1960.

Piaget, J. Cognitive development in children. In R. E. Ripple & V. N. Rockcastle (Eds.), *Piaget rediscovered: A report of the Conference on Cognitive Studies and Curriculum Development.* Ithaca, NY: Cornell University School of Education, 1964.

Rest, J. R. Developmental psychology as a guide to value education: A review of "Kohlbergian" programs. *Review of Eduational Research,* 1974, *44*(2), 241-259. (a)

Rest, J. R. *Major concepts in moral judgment development.* Unpublished manuscript, University of Minnesota, 1974. (b)

Rest, J. R. Comments on the deliberate psychological education programs and the Toronto moral education program in secondary education. *The Counseling Psychologist,* 1977, *6*(4), 32-34.

Rogers, C. R. *Carl Rogers on encounter groups.* New York: Harper & Row, 1970.

Salter, A. *Conditional reflex therapy: The direct approach to the reconstruction of personality.* New York: Creative Press, 1949.

Sarason, S. B. *The creation of settings and the future societies.* San Francisco: Jossey-Bass, 1972.

Sarason, S. B. *The psychological sense of community: Prospects for a community psychology.* San Francisco: Jossey-Bass, 1974.

Sarason, S. B., Zitnay, G., & Grossman, F. K. *The creation of a community setting* (Vol. I). Syracuse, NY: Syracuse University Press, 1971.

Sarbin, T. R., & Allen, V. L. Role theory. In G. Lindzey & E. Aronson (Eds.), *The handbook of social psychology.* Reading, MA: Addison-Wesley Press, 1968.

Scharf, P., & Hickey, J. The prison and the inmate's conception of legal justice. *Criminal Justice and Behavior,* 1976, *3*(2), 107-122.

Scherer, J. *Contemporary community: Sociological illusion or reality?* London: Tavistock Publications, 1972.

Selman, R. L. The relation of role-taking ability to the development of moral judgment in children. *Child Development,* 1971, *42*(2), 79-91.

Selman, R. L. A developmental approach to interpersonal and moral awareness in young children: Some theoretical and educational implications of levels of social perspective taking. In T. C. Hennessy (Ed.), *Value and moral development.* New York: Paulist Press, 1976. (a)

Selman, R. L. Social-cognitive understanding: A guide to educational and clinical practice. In T. Lickona (Ed.), *Moral development and behavior.* New York: Holt, Rinehart, & Winston, 1976, 299-316. (b)

Selman, R. L., & Byrne, D. F. A structural-developmental analysis of levels of role-taking in middle childhood. *Child Development,* 1974, *45*, 803-806.

Selman, R. L., & Damon, W. The necessity (but (insufficiency) of social perspective-taking for conceptions of justice at three entry levels. In D. J. DePalma & J. M. Foley (Eds.), *Moral development: Current theory and research.* New York: Wiley, 1975, 57-73.

Stokols, D. Toward a psychological theory of alienation. *Psychological Review,* 1975, *82*(1), 26-44.

Sullivan, P. J. *A curriculum for stimulating moral reasoning and ego development in adolescents.* Unpublished doctoral dissertation, Boston University School of Education, 1975.

Wasserman, E. R. Implementing Kohlberg's "just community concept" in an alternative high school. *Social Education,* 1976, *40*, 203-207.

Whiteley, J. M., & Loxley, J. C. A curriculum for the development of character and community in college students. In V. L. Erickson & J. M. Whiteley, (Eds.), *Developmental counseling and teaching.* Monterey, CA: Brooks/Cole, 1980, 262-297.

Whiteley, R. M. Assertion training for women. In M. Harway, H. S. Astin, J. M. Suhr, & J. M. Whiteley, *Sex discrimination in guidance and counseling*. Report prepared by Higher Education Research Institute under Contract 300-75-0207 with the Education Division, National Center for Education Statistics, U.S. Department of Health, Education and Welfare, February 1976.

Whiteley, R. M. *Cognitive restructuring of assertive behavior for women*. Paper presented at the American Psychological Association Convention, 1977, San Francisco.

Wolpe, J. *Psychotherapy by reciprocal inhibition*. Stanford, CA: Stanford University Press, 1958.

Wolpe, J. *The practice of behavior therapy*. New York: Pergamon Press, 1969.

Wolpe, J. The investigation of assertive behavior: Transcripts from two cases. *Journal of Behavior Therapy and Experimental Psychiatry*, 1970, *1*, 145-151.

Wolpe, J., & Lazarus, A. A. *Behavior therapy techniques: A guide to the treatment of neuroses*. New York: Pergamon Press, 1966.

Wolpe, J., Salter, A., & Reyna, L. J. *The conditioning therapies: The challenge in psychotherapy*. New York: Holt, Rinehart, & Winston, 1964.

Wright, D. S. *The psychology of moral behaviour*. Harmondsworth, England: Penguin, 1971.

Chapter 5

RESEARCH ON MEASURING AND CHANGING THE LEVEL OF MORAL REASONING IN COLLEGE STUDENTS

John M. Whiteley and Barbara D. Bertin

Previous research on moral reasoning has established that: 1) individuals differ markedly in their moral conceptions; 2) the underlying developmental order and logic of these individuals' moral judgments can be identified and studied empirically; and 3) certain types of educational experiences encourage individuals to attain more adequate and complex conceptions of justice and fairness in their relationships. Much in the research literature can aid our understanding of the transition in moral development which occurs between late adolescence and early adulthood; accumulated intervention studies suggest alternative choices for educational or experimental programs which can have an impact on raising the level of moral reasoning.

This chapter will briefly survey some of the previous research on moral reasoning during the transition from late adolescence to early adulthood.[1] The first section will discuss various research reports on the developmental status of moral reasoning in college students. It is necessary to establish the level of moral reasoning in a group of students before developing a curriculum which will be effective in promoting increased levels of that reasoning. For example, curriculum intended to promote

---

[1]See Rest (1979b), Lockwood (1978), and Erickson and Whiteley (1980) for more extensive reviews.

transition from conventional to post-conventional thinking may be beyond the comprehension of, and therefore ineffective with, individuals making a transition from preconventional to conventional thinking.

The second section of this chapter will review a number of interventions previously employed with college students. These interventions have utilized two general types of programs: those focused on moral education and those focused on psychological education. Research on both types of curricula has provided valuable suggestions for promoting character development through in-class interventions.

THE DEVELOPMENTAL STATUS
OF COLLEGE STUDENTS
IN REGARD TO MORAL REASONING

Empirical assessment of the developmental status of moral reasoning in college students has been primarily done by means of two instruments: the Moral Judgment Interview (MJI) and the Defining Issues Test (DIT). These instruments are, to date, the most valid measures of moral reasoning.

The Moral Judgment Interview is a structured individual interaction between tester and subject in which subjects are asked to respond to the issues raised by a series of moral problems. Testers encourage the subjects to clarify the reasons for their particular responses. Scorers can then identify the structure of the subject's moral reasoning as reflected in the answers given in the interview. Results of the Moral Judgment Interview are usually reported by the Moral Maturity Score (MMS), a weighted average of a subject's stage usage.

In considering research using the MJI, it is necessary to keep certain factors in mind. Because the MJI scoring system has changed during the 1970's, scores as reported in the research literature are not necessarily comparable. Further, scores are highly dependent upon the form of the test used (written or oral), the edition of the scoring system applied to the test results, and the training and ability of the scorers. Finally, Gilligan (1977) and Holstein (1976) have argued that there is a sex bias in the MJI which artificially lowers the stage scores assigned to women.

Most studies of college students using the MJI place college students between Stages 3 and 4 1/2. For the college educator, these findings are very important since curricula must be aimed at a student's current level of development to produce maximum growth in moral reasoning. Because of their developmental stage, most college students would most likely profit from curricula attempting to facilitate a transition from stage 3 to Stage 4 reasoning or to promote a shift within Stage 3.

The Defining Issues Test (DIT), a paper-and-pencil test exploring level of moral reasoning, is a recognition task requiring subjects to convey how they would make decisions about the moral issues raised by a series of dilemmas. An advantage of the DIT is that it can be easily administered and objectively scored.

Results of the Defining Issues Test are usually reported as a P Index representing the degree to which a subject uses principled moral considerations in making moral decisions. DIT scores appear to increase with the level of education, with Rest (1979a, p. 110) reporting an average P score of 21.9% for junior high school students, 31.8% for senior high school students, and 42.3% for college students. Rest's review of the accumulated research (Rest, 1979b) suggests that moral judgment is more closely related to education than to age. His research data indicates that P scores increase for as long as individuals remain in school but reach a plateau upon their leaving school. Although adults continue to encounter moral dilemmas throughout life, they do not appear to increase in level of moral reasoning. Because level of moral reasoning appears static for individuals who are no longer involved in formal education, we must consider what characteristics of formal education may be stimulating moral reasoning. While empirical evidence documents the leveling off of growth in moral reasoning which occurs when individuals leave school (Rest, 1979b), we know very little about how different types of educational experiences and programs may alter levels of moral reasoning.

INTERVENTION STUDIES IN
EDUCATIONAL SETTINGS DESIGNED TO
RAISE THE LEVEL OF MORAL REASONING

There has been relatively little research on educational programs designed to promote an increase in college students' level of moral reasoning. During the past decade, most attempts to raise the level of moral reasoning within an educational setting were focused on junior high and high school students. Still, these studies provide college educators with background on methodology and curriculum development. Rest (1979b) reviewed 16 intervention studies utilizing the DIT with junior high, high school, and college-age subjects, grouping the studies into four types: 1) short-term interventions; 2) interventions predominantly involving social studies or civics curricula; 3) interventions encouraging general personality and social development (including Deliberate Psychological Education programs); and 4) interventions primarily addressing problems of moral philosophy. These studies suggest that changes in DIT scores, if they occur at all, are slight. There are two possible interpretations of these data: either the curricula used in the interventions were unsuccessful in influencing moral reasoning, or the DIT measure did not accurately reflect changes in moral reasoning which did occur.

We identified less than a dozen interventions at the college level using either the MJI or the DIT as a measure. We have chosen to classify these interventions into two broad categories — Moral Education programs and Psychological Education programs — and have selected four representative approaches for review.

Moral Education Programs. Moral education programs involve direct classroom discussions of moral dilemmas and ethical issues which encourage students to clarify and justify their moral reasoning. Representative intervention programs in this category are those of Justice (1977) and Boyd (1976). The curriculum components of each contain many useful and innovative instructional approaches and are therefore described in detail below.

Justice's (1977) basic instructional assumption was that human learning occurs "as a cognitive-development/interactional phenomenon" (p. 32-33). The central objective of his curriculum was the equilibration of moral reasoning, particularly of principled moral reasoning. As part of this central objective, Justice anticipated that his curriculum would:

(1) broaden [students'] concepts of morality;

(2) increase their awareness of [themselves] as moral beings;

(3) increase their awareness of others as moral beings;

(4) become more prone to reason through a moral issue before taking a public stand on it;

(5) become more attentive to the reasoning behind the moral positions of others;

(6) become more tolerant for diversity of moral positions among others;

(7) be motivated to develop more clearly principled moral judgment;

(8) have an increased sense of competence in moral decision making;

(9) be helped in building conceptual skills in assessing the developmental stage of moral reasoning in self and others;

(10) have increased insight into the influence of various disciplinary interventions on their own moral developmental history; and

(11) be prepared to make more effective disciplinary intervention into the moral development of others.

(Justice, 1977, pp. 35-36)

The instructor's role was to facilitate students' non-judgmental confrontations of themselves and each other. The students were graded on their knowledge of moral development theory, the quality of their case studies, and their skill in analyzing the quality of moral reasoning.

In the first week of the four-week course, students were taught how to analyze moral reasoning through readings, lectures, and discussions.[2] During the second and third week of the course, students applied this analysis to situations presented in moral

[2] See Justice (1977), pp. 37-38 for details.

dilemma exercises. Through these exercises, Justice attempted to approximate the "personal experience" and "moral stimulation" components that Kohlberg (1973) thought necessary in order for students to move from conventional to post-conventional moral reasoning. Initially, invited guests (a criminal court judge, a philosopher, a historian, a student leader) presented the moral dilemma exercises; subsequently, class participants presented personal moral dilemmas which were discussed in small groups. This method accommodated Leming's (1974) observation that an individual's level of moral reasoning changes as issues become more personally relevant. Membership in small groups was rotated to maximize students' exposure to a wide variety of viewpoints.

During the final week of the course, students produced moral development case studies for a child, a youth, an adult, and themselves. (A case study of a literary character could be substituted for one of the four.) The goal of this exercise was to

> help participants integrate their learning, allow further opportunity for practical life situation application and generate moral reflection beyond that which might issue from moral dilemma exercises (Justice, 1977, p. 41).

Justice found that the experimental group showed a statistically significant increase in principled moral reasoning (an increase in mean P score from 45.2 to 49.8). However, the size of the sample was small (22 in the experimental group), and there was wide variation in score patterns (ten subjects increased, four did not change, and eight decreased). Obviously, more research is necessary before the full impact of this type of intervention can be understood.

In contrast, Boyd's (1976) approach involves a more direct teaching of moral development theory. He designed his curriculum "to help students work through concerns about egoism and relativism that often impede the transition from conventional to principled moral judgment" (Boyd, 1976, p. vi).* In the

---

*This and all other quotations from this source are from Boyd, D. R. *Education toward principled moral judgment: An analysis of an experimental course in undergraduate moral education applying Lawrence Kohlberg's theory of moral development.* Unpublished doctoral dissertation, Harvard University, 1976. Reprinted with permission.

reasoning of people at this level of transition Boyd expected to find:

> (1) an assimilation of most of the major differentiations and integrations that characterize stages 1-4, (2) a curious synthesis of stage 5 social contract/ utilitarian justifications and quasi-stage 2 egoism, (3) a rather unstable usage of an overall mixture of stages 2-5, and (4) a strong tendency to be uncritically relativistic (and, on the other hand, occasionally absolutely certain) about their moral judgments (Boyd, 1976, p. 69).

Boyd felt that relativism could "lead a person away from conventional moral reasoning, but not in any satisfactory positive direction" (p. 69), while egoism, a characteristic of Stage 2 thinking, could contribute to the search for stability. Thus, the adolescent, at the same time, presents questions, doubts answers, and attempts to discern whether either is reasonable.

Boyd's curriculum was first offered as a semester-long class to 60 students at Harvard University. It followed a lecture-discussion session format, with one lecture and one discussion session per week. There was a radical difference between the lectures and the discussion meetings, the lectures being provided "from within an explicitly paternalistic framework" (p. 72); for example, Kohlberg, in his guest lecture, described college students as floundering in a "moral no-man's land," then told these students that he could rescue them and "set them on the path to 'the right way' of solving moral problems" (Boyd, 1976, pp. 72-73).

The discussion sessions, in contrast, were structured to facilitate interaction among students around questions of morality. Students discussed their perceptions of the lectures and readings and considered concrete dilemmas suggested by other students or the instructor. Students were first asked how they would resolve dilemmas, and then why they would choose that solution to draw out the reasoning. Boyd often modified these dilemmas to make them personally relevant for particular students or used the position taken by someone else to demonstrate points. He explored the reasoning underlying students' responses or indicated possible consequences of particular lines of reasoning; he restructured an original dilemma (or introduced a second superficially similar dilemma) in order to confront contradictions or inconsistencies in students' thinking. Finally, he suggested alternate ways to consider dilemmas and solutions which involved a developmentally higher level of moral reasoning. Boyd hypothesized that these exercises would enhance students' growth by making them "more aware of the boundaries of the structure of [their] own reasoning, and . . . produce some disequilibrium that could be channeled into restructuring" (p. 89).

Boyd focused required readings on "students' own moral reasoning . . . as subject matter" (p. 75), including a number of topics which Boyd himself viewed as useful toward this end:

Week 1   Kohlberg's stage theory of moral development.

Week 2   Judgment-behavior issues and coding instructions.

Week 3   Cultural relativism and ethical relativism.

Week 4   The relationship between metaethical and normative thinking; the relationship between religious and moral beliefs; the relationship between moral and political thinking.

Week 5   Psychological and ethical egoism, hedonism.

Week 6   Bag of Virtues; the logic of praise and blame.

Week 7   The claims of social order.

Week 8   The social contract and utilitarianism.

Week 9   Ideologies of natural law and/or personal conscience.

Week 10   Universalizable principles of justice.

Week 11   Beyond morality: the relation of the moral good to truth and beauty.

(Adapted from Appendix A,
Boyd, 1976, pp. 268-274)

Boyd offered a second version of his curriculum as a ten-week discussion seminar at the University of Washington. Sixteen students met four hours weekly: two hours in a large group and two hours in smaller groups. The content of the curriculum was similar to the first version, with the primary goal being "to promote the development of rational autonomy in principled moral judgment" (Boyd, 1976, p. 92; see pp. 91-117 for further details.) However, this second version was more broadly conceived and utilized the discussion format of the first curriculum version to a greater extent. The use of more "natural" dilemmas in open class discussions allowed a greater integration of the "second-order" concerns of relativism and psychological egoism which formed the core of both versions of Boyd's curricula.

Both versions of Boyd's moral curriculum used forms of the MJI to assess changes in students' moral reasoning. A written form of the MJI was administered at both the beginning and the end of the first course, and scores indicated that students had advanced approximately one-fifth of a stage. An oral form of the MJI was used for interviewing students at the beginning and end of the second course as well as nine months later. These interviews were broader in scope than the standard MJI interview, yielding a more phenomenological description of the students' thinking. Boyd found that the students in the second course advanced approximately one-third of a stage. Boyd further distinguished three qualitatively different starting points for students and examined the occurrence of differing patterns of change according to initial categorization of students. (See Boyd, 1976, pp. 118-237 for details.)

In discussing the delivery of his curriculum, Boyd mentioned two points which we found germane to the Sierra Project: the need to modify the instructional format to accommodate students' varying levels of moral reasoning, and the signficant impact of students' initial levels of moral reasoning on curriculum delivery. Our handling of these issues will be discussed at length in later chapters.

The Boyd and Justice curricula both focus directly on raising the level of moral reasoning in college students, building upon the general direction of earlier approaches for high school students first initiated by Blatt (1970). They use an approach principally involving dialogue and intellectual confrontation with peers and professor, accompanied by readings and study of the theory of moral development itself. However, they do not explicitly consider the context of broader personality growth within which moral reasoning develops.

In the work of the Sierra Project, such a direct approach to raising the level of moral reasoning was not taken for two reasons. First, our review of research, buttressed by our own findings (Magaña, Whiteley, & Nelson, 1980), showed that the level of ego development sets the ceiling for the level of moral reasoning. We therefore assumed that successfully raising the level of moral reasoning in college students required a more broadly based curriculum. Second, at the time we undertook planning for the Sierra Project in the fall of 1974, the scoring system for the MJI was in a state of flux, and research on moral reasoning in college students using that measurement system was less than a decade old. We were concerned that teaching the theory might artificially affect the research results: that we might inadvertently "teach the test."

Psychological Education Programs. While both moral education and psychological education programs share a concern with moral reasoning, psychological education programs generally tend to consider a broader range of human experiences. Moral reasoning is only one part of a psychological education curriculum which also includes training in such areas as establishing relationships, developing communication skills, and recognizing and analyzing moral and ethical dilemmas. Representative programs which fall into this category are those of Brock (1974), Mosher and Sprinthall (1971), and the Sierra Project.

Brock (1974) focused on cognitive development in young adults, designing a 22-hour seminar-clinical curriculum to "effect structural psychological development" (p. 62). The curriculum for the experimental group had three components. The first component involved training in communication skills, facilitating student ability to relate to each other "in more personally risk taking ways" (p. 61). The primary goal of this component was to help students establish relationships and note communication patterns.

The second component—training in active listening skills—was intended to help students make the distinction between

> content and feeling, [as this] would be instrumental in creating a broader awareness of the multiple aspects of self and others. It [training in active listening skills] would also allow students to maximize the cognitive disequilibrium they could create for each other (Brock, 1974, p. 66).

Brock's use of curricular experiences to create disequilibrium derives from the cognitive-developmental model which characterizes change as a response to the disequilibrium that is created by new information. Brock considers such disequilibrium important because it emphasizes "the multiple possible causes of behavior and the range of choices for action" (p. 67). Experiences which required students to take responsibility, practice roles, and actively involve themselves in discussions were used to further amplify the disequilibrium.

The third component of Brock's curriculum involved exercises in recognizing and analyzing moral dilemmas. Students discussed various ethical situations they encountered, including those presented in the Milgram (1963) film and those they had observed as part of their clinical experiences. Disequilibrium was again considered the agent of change, with instructors modeling higher stage reasoning. On measures of moral reasoning and ego development, Brock found no difference between the control and experimental groups.

At the time they conducted their intervention and its evaluation, Mosher and Sprinthall's (1971) work challenged the traditional roles of high school teachers and guidance counselors. Their intent was to produce systematic educational experiences which would "affect directly the personal development of adolescents." In so doing, Mosher and Sprinthall hoped to elevate personal development to a central role in education. Though this work was done in a different setting and without a residential component, Mosher and Sprinthall's (1971) intervention was a seminal psychological education intervention which conceptually has much to offer educators at the college level.

Mosher and Sprinthall's work was produced by a group of counseling psychologists and teachers "frustrated by the gap between what they taught and offered adolescents and what they knew their students' lives and concerns to be" (pp. 3-4). They began with a critique of secondary education and its failures — failure to provide sufficiently for the personal and ethical development of students and failure to create a climate which significantly influences their intellectual development.

To remedy these problems, Mosher and Sprinthall developed a curriculum in personal and human development which provided "a comprehensive set of educational experiences designed to affect personal, ethical, aesthetic and philosophical development in adolescents and young adults" (Mosher & Sprinthall,

1971, p. 9). They conceived their curriculum as a series of courses "dealing with the principal tasks and tensions" (p. 13) experienced by individuals as they progress through the life cycle. They envisaged courses on child development and child care, middle childhood, adolescence, the psychology of interpersonal relations and marriage, the psychology of work, and the psychology of aging.

Mosher and Sprinthall's (1971) intervention was a seminar and practicum in counseling with a dual focus: 1) studying the themes which adolescents bring to counseling and 2) learning the process of listening and responding to others' feelings and ideas. Students in the course participated in role play, simulated counseling, and actually counseled other students. They studied the developmental themes of other adolescents as well as experiences from their own lives. To evaluate the impact of the course, Mosher and Sprinthall used measures of empathy, ego development, and moral reasoning. Students changed significantly on all three measures as compared to a control group enrolled in a "traditional" psychology class.

The Sierra Project, in its efforts to raise the level of students' moral reasoning, is more similar to psychological education approaches than to moral education approaches. Rather than teaching developmental theory or introducing systematic exercises presenting artificial moral dilemmas, we used those moral dilemmas which arise from the natural living experiences of the residence hall. We based much of our theoretical approach on relevant constructs from counseling and developmental psychology, designing the Sierra Project curriculum in accordance with accumulated research findings which suggest the need for fostering a broader range of psychological growth than strictly moral development.

References

Blatt, M. M. *The effects of classroom discussion program upon children's level of moral judgment.* Unpublished doctoral dissertation, University of Chicago, 1970.

Boyd, D. R. *Education toward principled moral judgment: An analysis of an experimental course in undergraduate moral education apply-*

ing Lawrence Kohlberg's theory of moral development. Unpublished doctoral dissertation, Harvard University, 1976.

Brock, S.A. *Facilitating psychological growth in post-adolescents: A cognitive-developmental curriculum intervention and analysis.* Unpublished doctoral dissertation, University of Minnesota, 1974.

Erickson, V. L., & Whiteley, J. M. (Eds.). *Developmental counseling and teaching.* Monterey, CA: Brooks/Cole, 1980.

Gilligan, C. In a different voice: Women's conception of self and of morality. *Harvard Educational Review,* 1977, 47(4), 481-517.

Holstein, C. B. Irreversible, stepwise sequence in the development of moral judgment: A longitudinal study of males and females. *Child Development,* 1976, 47, 51-61.

Justice, G. E. *Facilitating principled moral reasoning in college students: A cognitive-developmental approach.* Unpublished doctoral dissertation, Saint Louis University, 1977.

Kohlberg, L. *Collected papers on moral development and moral education.* Cambridge, MA: Harvard University, Center for Moral Education, 1973.

Leming, J. S. Moral reasoning, sense of control, and social-political activism among adolescents. *Adolescence,* 1974, IX (36), 507-528.

Lockwood, A. L. The effects of values clarification and moral development curricula on school-age subjects: A critical review of recent research. *Review of Educational Research,* 1978, 48(3), 325-364.

Magaña, H., Whiteley, J. M., & Nelson, K. H. Sequencing of experiences in psychological interventions: Relationships among locus of control, moral reasoning, and ego development. In V. L. Erickson & J. M. Whiteley (Eds.), *Developmental counseling and teaching.* Monterey, CA: Brooks/Cole, 1980 298-328.

Milgram, S. Behavioral study of obedience. *Journal of Abnormal and Social Psychology,* 1963, 67, 371-378.

Mosher, R. L., & Sprinthall, N. A., et al. Psychological education: A means to promote personal development during adolescence. *The Counseling Psychologist,* 1971, 2(4), 3-82.

Rest, J. R. *Development in judging moral issues.* Minneapolis, MN: University of Minnesota Press, 1979. (a)

Rest, J. R. *The impact of higher education on moral judgment development,* Technical Report #5. Minneapolis, MN: Minnesota Moral Research Projects, University of Minnesota, 1979. (b)

SECTION II.

PROMOTING CHARACTER DEVELOPMENT
IN COLLEGE FRESHMEN:
A DESCRIPTION OF THE SIERRA PROJECT

This section describes the Sierra Project itself—where it was located, what occurred within it, who participated in it, and how we evaluated it. In order that future researchers can have a full understanding of the context in which we worked and the approaches we used to evaluate that work, we have divided Section II into two chapters. Chapter 6 describes the nature of the Irvine campus of the University of California, the residence hall complex in which the Sierra Project occurred, the participants, the staff, and the curriculum. Chapter 7 describes the rationale behind our multifaceted evaluation plan and introduces our four methods of evaluation.

Chapter 6

THE CONTEXT, PARTICIPANTS, STAFF, AND CURRICULUM OF THE SIERRA PROJECT

John M. Whiteley

This chapter will present the physical context of the Sierra Project, describe the demographic and psychological characteristics of the participants, and provide a brief description of the curriculum and its sequencing. Extended discussions of the curriculum are presented in Whiteley and Loxley (1980), Loxley & Whiteley (in preparation).

PHYSICAL CONTEXT

The Sierra Project curriculum intervention and the research associated with it are being conducted at the Irvine campus of the University of California. UCI is one of the youngest campuses in the nine-campus University of California system, and one of the most comprehensive in the scope of its academic and research programs. In its first 16 years, UCI has grown from 1,500 to over 11,000 students, offering academic degrees from the B.A. through the Ph.D. and M.D.

UCI places high priority on the quality of its scholarship and research, primarily emphasizing academic standards. In the tradition of land-grant colleges, it also relates to the community — particularly through its extension division, applied research programs, and health science programs such as a regional medical center. In a commencement address at UCI in June of 1980, UC President Emeritus Clark Kerr stated that:

> By the time this Class of 1980 celebrates its 20th reunion in 2000, Irvine will rank even higher in the world of scholar-

ship than it does now, and its degrees will be of even higher value in the United States and around the world. It most likely will stand as the most successful totally new American university founded in the second half of the 20th Century (*SEED*, 1980, p.2).

While UCI does have an attractive climate, new facilities, and an emphasis on research and scholarly accomplishment, it does not naturally foster a sense of on-campus community. During the period of time covered by the freshman portion of the Sierra Project (1975-1979), approximately only 25 percent of undergraduates were housed on campus. A student union, the University Center, was not completed until January 1981. The average commuter student drove 11 miles or more each way to school, and was part of on-campus life mainly between 9:00 a.m. and 5:00 p.m.

The Sierra Project occurred in Sierra Hall, one of 23 individual residence halls located in the Mesa Court undergraduate housing complex. This housing complex is considered by students to be a particularly attractive place to live as reflected by an occupancy rate of over 99 percent, a waiting list at the start of each academic year of over 1,000 students, and a "return rate" request of over 70 percent from one year to the next. Each individual residence hall houses 40-60 students; Sierra Hall houses 50 students in a comfortable wood, stucco, and glass two-story structure with two large common rooms shared by all Sierra residents. Students live in suites housing eight to ten students, each suite having its own living room.

Academically, the Sierra Project consists of a four-unit, lower division course offered each quarter — Social Ecology 74: Moral Development and Just Communities. Students who elect to live in Sierra Hall do so with the understanding that they will concurrently enroll in this class. In addition, Sierra residents can elect a two-unit laboratory course (offered in both the winter and spring quarters) which involves working at least five hours per week in a paraprofessional counseling or service role in the surrounding community. Modeled after the work of Mosher and Sprinthall (1970, 1971) on deliberate psychological education, the laboratory course was designed to encourage students to apply the skills learned in class to problems in the community.

Approximately 40 percent of the Sierra students did elect the community service course but anecdotal reports suggest that closer to 70 percent would have participated were it not for the time restrictions imposed by the structured academic curriculum of the freshman year; the science curriculum is particularly intense, and science majors make up 40 percent of the Sierra population.

In the initial year of the Sierra Project (1975-76) 138 of the 800 freshmen choosing to live on campus requested placement in Sierra Hall. We attribute their interest to the promise of close involvement with other students, staff, and faculty and to a highly supportive personal environment compared to other opportunities on campus. Each year of the project, as the Classes of 1980, 1981, and 1982 entered UCI, there was sufficient demand to fill Sierra Hall only with students who had volunteered to participate in the academic class and the other components of the intervention.

A year of preliminary preparation was necessary before commencing work with the first group of students. We needed to propose new academic courses, and to obtain the cooperation and sanction of the Program in Social Ecology that provided the instruction and offered the course credit. The proposal for the new courses then had to be approved by the campus faculty through the Academic Senate. We obtained the cooperation of the professional staff responsible for managing the Housing program—both to insure the proper assignment of students and student staff to the selected residence halls, and to develop a procedure for fully informing potential student participants about the project. Since there was an experimental evaluation component to the project, we also needed the approval of the Human Subjects Review Committee.

We began the project with freshmen who entered UCI in the fall of 1975, and have studied the four classes of Sierra freshmen and freshman control groups. Each class is hereafter referred to by its year of projected graduation and by group (e.g., Sierra students who entered in the fall of 1975 are referred to as the Sierra Class of 1979).

PARTICIPANTS

The participants in the Sierra Project evaluation consisted of three groups of students from each of the Classes of 1979, 1980, 1981, and 1982. Those three groups of students are the residents of Sierra Hall, the residents of Lago Hall (Control Group I), and the members of several other control groups (Control Group II) which are described in detail in Chapter 7.

Students in Sierra Hall (all freshmen) participated in the intervention and constituted our "experimental" group. Lago residents were also all freshmen living in an identical physical facility, with equal proportions of men and women. The major difference between these groups was that Sierra freshmen had requested to participate in the intervention (including the academic class) whereas the Lago residents had not.

However, with the Class of 1979, the 138 students who had indicated an interest in the intervention were randomly assigned to either Sierra or Lago. We did this in order to attempt "partialing out" the effects of motivation by having a control group that was as equally motivated as the experimental group. This goal was not achieved for two reasons. The first reason was that in subsequent years (the Classes of 1980, 1981, and 1982), there were not enough students interested in Sierra Hall and its academic class to allow random assignment between Sierra and Lago. The second reason was that we made many changes in the research procedures and curriculum modules after our initial experience with the Class of 1979. Our research procedures and curriculum intervention with the Classes of 1980, 1981, and 1982, however, are sufficiently similar to be comparably evaluated.

Demographic Characteristics of the Participants

Evidence of cohort differences in previous life span developmental research (see Chapter 7) influenced our decision to collect fairly detailed background and attitudinal data on our research population. Appendix A presents the following background data for members of Sierra, Lago (Control Group I), and Control Group II for the Classes of 1979-82:

Political orientation

Estimated parental income

Father's occupation

Father's education

Mother's occupation

Mother's education

Vocational choice

Choice of major

Because of the importance of cohort differences, we have distinguished each class in reporting this descriptive information. In addition to the information cited above, we have collected other information including intellective data from our test battery, information about students' expectations of the university and of the residence hall community, and data on these students' psychological development on dimensions associated with character.

Intellective Characteristics of the Participants

Our intellective data is based on results from the Scholastic Aptitude Verbal and Mathematical Tests of the College Entrance Examination Board. The data for our sample is presented in Table 6-1.

The diversity of these students' socio-economic backgrounds and the presence of students for whom English is a second language are reflected in the wide range of SAT scores within Sierra. The range of SAT verbal scores (from 200 to 700) indicates that the verbal facility of our participants functions as both a source of diversity and an instructional problem. Similarly, the range of scores on SAT mathematics was nearly as extreme, the spread being from 240 to 770.

Most of the tests administered as part of the Sierra Project have an extensive verbal dimension; these results may therefore have been influenced by students' verbal facility. There is also debate among researchers as to whether there are cultural and

Character Development in College Students

sex biases on some of the tests; it is also possible that students' socio-economic backgrounds may have influenced our test results.

TABLE 6-1
SCHOLASTIC APTITUDE TEST
VERBAL AND MATHEMATICAL SCORES FOR PARTICIPANTS IN
SIERRA, UCI*, UC AS A WHOLE*, AND NATIONAL NORMS*

	SAT-Verbal			SAT-Math		
	$\overline{X}$	s.d.	Range	$\overline{X}$	s.d.	Range
Class of 1979						
(Enter in 1975)						
Sierra	462.12	111.63	230-640	505.76	114.10	280-770
Lago	469.03	97.62	320-680	524.19	113.87	280-690
Control	540.91	73.41	430-690	595.46	79.67	470-700
All UCI	501					
All UC	510					
National Norms	434					
Class of 1980						
(Enter in 1976)						
Sierra	451.33	109.61	200-700	492.00	111.50	240-650
Lago	462.94	103.24	280-650	536.47	125.94	280-750
Control	493.16	96.84	270-690	568.68	100.06	320-730
All UCI	493					
All UC	507					
National Norms	431					
Class of 1981						
(Enter in 1977)						
Sierra	474.12	99.19	260-670	531.18	98.04	290-640
Lago	490.91	67.68	390-660	575.22	90.50	350-750
Control	496.84	109.70	330-710	556.89	96.32	410-720
All UCI	479					
All UC	504					
National Norms	429					
Class of 1982						
(Enter in 1978)						
Sierra	420.93	106.39	220-620	480.93	114.24	280-720
Lago	510.97	96.21	300-760	581.94	104.77	340-760
Control	518.28	102.23	290-720	570.69	96.25	330-760
All UCI	485					
All UC	505					
National Norms	429					

*Sources: UC Systemwide Administration Admissions Office; CEEB College Bound Seniors Report

Participants' Expectations for Community

The measure of community is helpful in understanding the expectations that Sierra freshmen hold for their college experience. Our measure of community consisted of selected items from the Environmental Assessment Inventory (Stokols, 1975), which has scales relating to physical conditions of the dormitory, quality of social relationships, expectations about dormitory life and its degree of importance, and the amount of control one expects to have over the environment.

The items most germane to a psychological sense of community were the following (answered on a 7-point scale from "strongly disagree" to "strongly agree"):

There will be a lot of trust between us.

There will not be much competition between us.

We will try to make each other feel secure.

We won't feel alienated from each other.

There will be no hostility between us.

We will be considerate of each other's feelings.

We will confide in each other about most personal problems.

The other item which is germane is answered on a 7-point scale ranging from anonymous (1) to personal (7):

Consider the interactions you will have with others in your dorm. To what extent do you expect to relate to others on either a personal or anonymous basis?

We used these eight items to measure the expectations which Sierra Project freshmen have for levels of community upon entering UCI. The EAI was administered three times during the freshman year — allowing us to assess students' entering expectations, and then to contrast those expectations with their perceptions of actual experiences. Table 6-2 describes the students' expectations of their environment in terms of the eight scales of expected psychological sense of community.

TABLE 6-2
EXPECTATIONS OF A PSYCHOLOGICAL SENSE OF COMMUNITY:
SELECTED ITEMS FROM THE ENVIRONMENTAL ASSESSMENT INVENTORY[1]

CLASS OF 1979

ITEM NO.	ITEM[2]	SIERRA male/female		LAGO male/female	
		n=28	n=24	n=20	n=22
1	There will be a lot of trust among us.	5.61	5.83	5.35	5.55
2	There will not be much competition among us.[3]	4.61	4.79	4.95	4.14
3	We will try to make each other feel secure.	5.54	5.83	5.55	5.46
4	We won't feel alienated from each other.	5.54	5.54	5.35	5.64
5	There will be no hostility among us.	4.43	5.08	4.40	4.32
6	We will all be considerate of each other's feelings.	5.18	5.50	5.35	5.59
7	We will confide in each other about most personal problems.[4]	4.18	4.42	4.90	4.36
8	Consider the interactions you will have with others in your dorm. To what extent do you expect to relate to others on either a personal or anonymous basis?	5.57	5.50	5.55	5.86
	TOTAL COMMUNITY SCALE (ALL THE ABOVE ITEMS COMBINED)	5.08	5.31	5.18	5.12

TABLE 6-2 (CONTINUED)

CLASS OF 1980

ITEM NO.	ITEM[2]	SIERRA male/female n=15	n=14	LAGO male/female n=16	n=13	CONTROL male/female n=20	n=12
1	There will be a lot of trust among us.	5.20	5.57	5.94	5.77	5.50	5.50
2	There will not be much competition among us.[3]	5.67	6.00	6.13	6.39	5.75	6.00
3	We will try to make each other feel secure.	5.13	5.42	5.44	6.00	5.40	5.50
4	We won't feel alienated from each other.	5.13	5.50	5.63	5.15	5.45	5.67
5	There will be no hostility among us.	4.13	4.57	5.88	5.69	5.90	5.92
6	We will all be considerate of each other's feelings.	5.07	5.86	5.50	6.23	5.75	6.08
7	We will confide in each other about most personal problems.[4]	4.07	4.36	4.69	5.39	4.70	5.42
8	Consider the interactions you will have with others in your dorm. To what extent do you expect to relate to others on either a personal or anonymous basis?	4.73	4.93	5.31	6.00	5.67[5]	4.67[5]
	TOTAL COMMUNITY SCALE (ALL THE ABOVE ITEMS COMBINED)	4.89	5.28	5.57	5.83	5.52	5.60

TABLE 6-2 (CONTINUED)

CLASS OF 1981

ITEM NO.	ITEM[2]	SIERRA		LAGO		CONTROL	
		male n=14	female n=21	male n=16	female n=19	male n=10	female n=13
1	There will be a lot of trust among us.	4.29	5.72	5.13	5.58	5.20	5.69
2	There will not be much competition among us.[3]	5.00	5.95	5.25	5.47	5.50	5.77
3	We will try to make each other feel secure.	4.43	5.72	4.81	5.47	5.20	5.85
4	We won't feel alienated from each other.	4.14	5.38	5.31	5.21	5.40	5.31
5	There will be no hostility among us.	4.64	4.95	4.38	4.53	4.10	4.62
6	We will all be considerate of each other's feelings.	4.86	5.76	4.81	5.58	4.80	5.62
7	We will confide in each other about most personal problems.[4]	3.15	4.90	4.38	4.37	4.20	4.54
8	Consider the interactions you will have with others in your dorm. To what extent do you expect to relate to others on either a personal or anonymous basis?	4.64	5.62	5.25	4.95	4.00	4.92
	TOTAL COMMUNITY SCALE (ALL THE ABOVE ITEMS COMBINED)	4.37	5.50	4.92	5.15	4.80	5.29

TABLE 6-2 (CONTINUED)

CLASS OF 1982

ITEM NO.	ITEM[2]	SIERRA male/female		LAGO male/female		CONTROL male/female	
		n=21	n=25	n=16	n=18	n=6	n=8
1	There will be a lot of trust among us.	5.14	5.40	5.56	5.72	5.50	6.00
2	There will not be much competition among us.[3]	5.52	5.84	5.88	6.00	5.67	6.13
3	We will try to make each other feel secure.	5.29	5.72	5.44	5.89	4.83	5.50
4	We won't feel alienated from each other.	5.05	5.63	5.69	6.00	5.67	5.75
5	There will be no hostility among us.	4.86	5.36	4.88	5.33	6.33	4.88
6	We will all be considerate of each other's feelings.	5.24	5.88	5.31	5.78	6.00	5.63
7	We will confide in each other about most personal problems.[4]	4.38	4.88	4.27	4.83	4.50	4.88
8	Consider the interactions you will have with others in your dorm. To what extent do you expect to relate to others on either a personal or anonymous basis?	4.86	5.56	5.69	6.11	5.50	5.50
	TOTAL COMMUNITY SCALE (ALL THE ABOVE ITEMS COMBINED)	5.04	5.53	5.36	5.71	5.50	5.53

[1] Figures shown are means. Key: Items 1 through 7: 1 = strongly disagree, 7 = strongly agree. Item 8: 1 = anonymous, 7 = personal.

[2] For the Class of 1982, all items were written in present tense.

[3] For the Classes of 1980, 1981, and 1982, was written as "We will generally cooperate with each other."

[4] For the Classes of 1980, 1981, and 1982, was written as "We will be able to confide in each other about most personal problems.

[5] n = for this item, this group, this year.

As an inspection of Table 6-2 reveals, entering Sierra students (and our other groups as well) had a relatively high level of expectation for a psychological sense of community. For example, on a scale of 1 to 7 (1 being a low expectation for community and 7 being a high expectation), Sierra men entering in the Class of 1979 had an average score of 5.61 on trust, 5.54 on alienation, and 5.18 on consideration of feelings. Sierra women in the same class had average scores of 5.83 on trust, 5.54 on alienation, and 5.50 on consideration of feelings.

Status of Participants on Dimensions of Character

To provide a full picture of participants in the Sierra Project, we will briefly describe here the results of our assessments of central measures of character. Chapters 5 and 7 present detailed information about the instruments used to assess the developmental status of our students.

We had three measures of character. The first, the Defining Issues Test, measures moral reasoning in terms of six stages and a P score (the percentage of principled thinking involved in making responses on the test). Table 6-3 presents the scores of UCI entering freshmen for the Classes of 1980, 1981, and 1982 in terms of P score, as well as the national norms developed by Rest (1979, p. 110) for junior high school, senior high school, college, and graduate students.

Our students fall in the expected range between senior high school students and college students. On the basis of this test, Sierra participants may be characterized as predominately conventional in their moral reasoning.

The second measure of character was the Moral Judgment Interview for assessing moral reasoning. Table 6-4 presents the Moral Maturity Scores (MMS) of freshmen entering Sierra for the Classes of 1980, 1981, and 1982.

We interpret the level of moral reasoning illustrated by these test scores to indicate that Sierra students are very conventional thinkers. As a group, they are very closely clustered around Stage 3, Interpersonal Conformity. Students at the Interpersonal Conformity stage have an orientation toward making judgments in terms of the approval of those around them, particularly what "good boys" and "good girls" would do in a given situation.

TABLE 6-3
PERCENTAGE OF PRINCIPLED MORAL REASONING
(P-SCORES) OF ENTERING UCI FRESHMEN AND NATIONAL
NORM COMPARISONS ON THE DEFINING ISSUES TEST

	n	mean P-score	s.d.
Class of 1980			
Sierra	33	32.52	12.63
Lago	23	37.29	11.13
Control	18	35.53	14.38
Class of 1981			
Sierra	20	42.75	15.62
Lago	25	38.92	13.74
Control	26	43.88	15.11
Class of 1982			
Sierra	33	36.61	14.84
Lago	25	36.47	11.60
Control	26	44.71	14.96
National Norms[1]			
Junior high students	1322	21.90	8.50
Senior high students	581	31.80	13.50
College students	2479	42.30	13.20
Graduate students	183	53.30	10.90

[1]From Rest, J.R. *Development in judging moral issues*, p. 110. University of Minnesota Press. Copyright ©1979, University of Minnesota. Reprinted with permission.

TABLE 6-4
MORAL MATURITY SCORES (MMS) OF ENTERING UCI
FRESHMEN FROM SIERRA HALL BASED ON THE MORAL
JUDGMENT INTERVIEW

	n	mean[1]	s.d.
Class of 1980			
Sierra	41	311.37	39.34
Class of 1981			
Sierra	40	315.83	19.58
Class of 1982			
Sierra	40	313.89	25.03

[1]See Colby, Gibbs, Kohlberg, Speicher-Dubin & Candee, 1979, part 2, for details concerning the computation and interpretation of the MMS.

Our final measure of character was ego development as assessed by the Washington University Sentence Completion Test (WUSCT). The scores of our entering freshmen on ego development are presented in Table 6-5.

TABLE 6-5
**LEVEL OF EGO DEVELOPMENT OF ENTERING UCI FRESHMEN
FROM SIERRA HALL BASED ON THE WASHINGTON
UNIVERSITY SENTENCE COMPLETION TEST FOR MEASURING
EGO DEVELOPMENT**

	n	mean[1]	s.d.
Class of 1980			
Sierra	44	4.66	1.24
Class of 1981			
Sierra	38	4.79	1.14
Class of 1982			
Sierra	46	4.33	0.99

[1]Key:
1 = I-2	6 = I-4
2 = Δ	7 = I-4/5
3 = Δ/3	8 = I-5
4 = I-3	9 = I-5/6
5 = I-3/4	10 = I-6

Our students were clustered between Stages I-3 and I-3/4 on the WUSCT. Stage I-3 represents thinking with a "simplistic conventionality" that fails to question the world. Stage I-3/4 represents the transition from conformity to conscientiousness, where the individual can see multiple possibilities and alternatives. Loevinger and Wessler (1970) captured the distinctiveness of the I-3 to I-3/4 transition characterizing entering Sierra Project freshmen when they observed:

> In place of the I-3 tendency to classify actions in mutually exclusive categories of right and wrong, the I-3/4 subject tends to think about appropriateness, what is right for the time and place and the situation. There are contingencies, exceptions, and comparisons, though they are global and often banal (p. 71).

To summarize, Sierra Project students — in terms of intellective, community, and psychological factors — are quite homogeneous and rather conventional on such dimensions of character as principled thinking, moral maturity, and ego development; on the other hand, they are also quite diverse in ethnic background, socio-economic background, and verbal preparation, as well as in the range of their educational and occupational aspirations.

STUDENT AND PROFESSIONAL STAFF: DESCRIPTION AND ROLES

The student staff (normally sophomores) are our front line teachers. They live in the residence halls, interacting as more than peers and different from formal instructors. These students have been either enrolled in the Sierra Project program as freshmen or deeply immersed in the conceptual framework of the project through course work in developmental or counseling psychology. Our sophomore staff serves as leaders of the small groups (see below for a description of these groups) which function in the winter and spring quarters. In this role, the student staff helps freshmen plan several spring quarter classes. Terms in conventional use which characterize parts of the roles of this student staff include: peer advisor, teaching assistant, peer counselor, teaching aide, participant-observer, role model, and friend. The student staff as it actually functions in Sierra Hall reflects the personalities of the particular incumbents and the demands of the particular situation.

The professional staff also functions as teachers. Particularly in the fall quarter, and to a lesser extent in the winter quarter, one or more of the professional staff serves in the traditional professorial role — specifying the content of weekly classes, defining assignments and requirements. By spring quarter, a goal of the professional and student staff is to involve freshman students in taking more responsibility for their own learning.

An important part of the teacher role, as we implement it, involves the psychologist as educator. Assertion training and empathy skills, for example, are presented in much the same way as most other psychologists would present the material. A developmental intervention such as this, however, need not be directed by psychologists. Teaching character development skills and establishing a sense of community are not the sole province of psychology any more than that of any other discipline. However, the Sierra Project is deeply rooted in the idea of psychologist as educator; the Project would simply be quite different if planned and implemented from another disciplinary perspective.

The teacher's role varies considerably from fall quarter to spring quarter. In the fall quarter, the teachers are quite explicit about defining students' tasks since entering freshmen have a high need for structure. Student tasks in the winter quarter are predominantly psychological in nature (assertion training, socialization, sex roles, life and career planning). Teachers-as-psychologists offer instructional experience to students designed to teach them new skills or understandings.

In the spring quarter, the role of the teacher is to directly encourage students to assume responsibility for thinking about what they are learning. Associated with the modules for winter and spring quarters are small group discussions (Triple I-D groups), named by the students to stand for "Intensive Interpersonal Interaction and Discussion" groups. These small groups, consisting of one sophomore student staff member and approximately eight freshmen, are favorably evaluated by both freshmen and student staff. By the spring quarter, aided by the work done in these Triple I-D groups, students' thinking is sufficiently stimulated to aid them in becoming active learners.

The basic intervention is influenced profoundly by the fact that it occurs within the context of a residence hall. Community as it develops is enhanced by the 24-hour day living arrangement; the hours per week devoted to the formal class are few by comparison. If the Sierra Project had been administered to commuter rather than residential students, the psychological intervention would have been relegated to a much smaller portion of a freshman's time and attention. We doubt that the Sierra curriculum would have as great an impact as it does were it not for the level of community generated in the residence hall.

SIERRA CURRICULUM

The intent of the original group that planned the Sierra Curriculum was to develop a series of discrete modules which could either be implemented singly or be presented in a sequential order. Interested educators could then use the entire program or select only those modules which served their particular instructional purposes. The modules as they were originally conceived are as follows:[1]

Unit 1.   *Survival Skills*: teaching freshmen the learning skills which will help them succeed academically in the university: organizing their time, studying effectively, and preparing for examinations.

Unit 2.   *Empathy/Social Perspective-taking*: developing students' empathy—their ability to understand the point of view of another and to communicate that understanding—which involves basic listening and communication skills.

Unit 3.   *Community Building*: working together with students to create an atmosphere of openness, trust, and group support in an environment which encourages the resolution of conflict through democratic decision-making.

Unit 4.   *Conceptions of Lifestyle*: helping students consider themselves and their lifestyle choices in relationship to how other people have chosen to live, with particular reference to different value choices and perspectives on the world.

Unit 5.   *Sex-role Choices*: helping students consider various sex-role expectations within society and the implications of these expectations for two-person relationships and for partnerships between men and women.

---

[1]In Whiteley and Loxley (1980), there is a presentation of the sequencing of the modules on a week-by-week basis (see pp. 263-265) and a more extensive report of the content of each of the modules and classes on pages 266-296.

Unit 6.   *Assertion Training*: teaching students methods for identifying the personal rights involved in a conflict situation, and for resolving that situation in a way which assures one's own legitimate rights without violating those of others.

Unit 7.   *Career Decision-making*: encouraging students to apply what they already know or can learn about themselves to formulate their educational and long-term career plans—with an emphasis on helping them identify career fields consistent with their values and abilities.

Unit 8.   *Community Service*: providing students with the opportunity to apply the skills they have been learning in Sierra to a social-action setting in the community, allowing them to have positive contact with agencies outside the university community while still receiving support from the campus.

Unit 9.   *Life Planning*: challenging students to plan their lives on paper, determining what kind of persons they would like to be and how they would like to live. One format for this was to ask students to write their own "obituaries," emphasizing the value choices, goals, and key decisions which they will have made in the course of full productive lives.

Unit 10.   *Conflict Resolution in Society*: encouraging student participation in SIMSOC (Gamson, 1972a; 1972b), a commercially available simulation game in which students are given only a vaguely structured role and allowed to form their own society. As implemented in Sierra Hall, SIMSOC emphasizes survival issues, personal goals, problems of power and authority, and consideration of the type of society which will provide the most good for the most people—using principles of fairness and justice as well as conflict resolution skills.

Unit 11.   *Race-role Choices*: helping students consider differing race-role stereotypes in our society—and their impact on interpersonal relationships — as well as the bases of racial prejudice and lack of mutual understanding.

As is apparent from their descriptions, these modules vary greatly in terms of their scope and content. Unit 1, Survival Skills, would not be included if the population were other than entering freshmen. With our group, however, the initial psychological stress and anxiety levels are so high that there is no real point in trying to move to other subject matter without first focusing on learning skills, time management, and methods for coping with the expectations and demands of a major university curriculum.

Unit 2, Empathy/Social Perspective-taking, is one of the key components of character development. It is based theoretically on three independent but converging bodies of research (Greif & Hogan, 1973; Selman, 1976a, 1976b; Mosher & Sprinthall, 1971) which indicate a relationship between increased ability to empathize and increased level of moral reasoning. (See Chapters 4 and 5 for details.)

Unit 3, Community Building, grew out of three other bodies of research and literature. The first is the work of Lawrence Kohlberg and his associates (Kohlberg, 1975; Kohlberg, Wasserman, & Richardson, 1975; Wasserman, 1976) on the creation of just communities and the relationship of participation in the just community to increased levels of moral reasoning. The second is the work of Carl Rogers and his associates (Rogers, 1970; Coulson, 1973) on the importance of community, particularly on the signficant roles of empathy and trust. The third is the work of Seymour Sarason (Sarason, Zitnay, & Grossman, 1971; Sarason, 1972; Sarason, 1974) which emphasizes the value of a psychological sense of community and people's striving to be a part of a network of intimate relationships. (See Chapter 4 for details.)

Unit 4, Conceptions of Life Style, and Unit 9, Life Planning, ultimately did not prove of interest to the freshmen of Sierra Hall. Upon reflection, we decided that since the freshmen were just entering a new collegiate life, they were not psychologically ready to begin to prepare for life after college. These units, therefore, did not appear to be important components of a freshman year curriculum. However, we have found them to be relevant to the needs of juniors and seniors participating in a program for upperclass students modeled after the Sierra Project.[2]

Unit 5, Sex-role Choices, particularly the portions that relate to two-person relationships, was of deep interest to freshmen. As the year started, most of our sample were still involved with high school friends. By the start of winter quarter, these high school friendships lessened in importance as the students became intensely involved in exploring two-person relationships on the campus. Also, the largely egalitarian student culture challenged many students' previously-held beliefs about the roles of men and women in society. This unit was, therefore, a significant vehicle for encouraging them to rethink the basis of relationships. Questions about what is fair for both partners in a relationship, how another human being perceives one's actions, and whether stereotypic sex-role behaviors are a sound basis for enriching partnerships were very relevant and challenging topics for the group.

Unit 6, Assertion Training, helped individuals to identify both their own and others' rights in a situation, and to work out methods for achieving their desired goals without interfering with the rights of others. Elaborating on the traditional assertion training format, the staff emphasized the use of principles of fairness and justice as a basis for conflict resolution.

Unit 7, Career Decision-making, was a unit which appealed to some of our freshman group. In the first year, 1975-76, all students were invited to participate in SIGI (System of Interactive Guidance and Information), a computer-based career decision-making and counseling system developed by the Educational Testing Service which was available on the Irvine campus. However, of the 44 Sierra and Lago control subjects, only 21 chose to participate. We concluded that Unit 7, like the units on lifestyle choices and life planning, is more relevant to upperclassmen than to freshmen.

Unit 8, Community Service, was based on the research of Mosher and Sprinthall and their associates (1971) on deliberate psychological education. These researchers found significant gains in level of moral reasoning and ego development in stu-

---

[2]This program, "Stepping Stones," will be described in a forthcoming volume (Whiteley & Associates, in preparation).

dents participating in community service which involved the application of cross-age counseling and teaching skills. Approximately 40 percent of Sierra students chose to participate in our community service component.

Unit 10, Conflict Resolution in Society, is an important component of community building since it helps students get to know each other. Originally scheduled late in the year, the unit has been moved up to the start of the fall quarter. This alteration of the schedule of units has been used with the Classes of 1980, 1981, and 1982 with positive results.

Unit 11, Race Roles, was not an original component in the planning of the Sierra Project. It developed naturally out of the experiences within Sierra Hall during our exploratory year with the Class of 1979. The relatively proportional representation of Asians, Blacks, Hispanics and Anglos in Sierra Hall made this module a valuable one for challenging stereotypes, encouraging the rethinking of beliefs, and facilitating more complex ways of thinking.

Students in the Sierra Hall were required to participate fully in every module we offered except Unit 8, Community Service. Units 4, 7, and 9 were not considered to have a direct theoretical relationship to character development, but were included because of their relevance to college students and their contribution to future planning. We have incorporated all three units into our subsequent project with juniors and seniors. We considered the other seven units (excluding Unit 1, Survival Skills) to be the core curriculum for promoting higher levels of moral reasoning.

The core curriculum for character development consisted, therefore, of modules on empathy/social perspective-taking, community building, sex-role choices, assertion training, community service, conflict resolution, and race roles.

Each of the educational modules described above required careful planning for its development, implementation, and evaluation. The process involved in developing the modules, their actual presentation in the class, and the students' evaluations of them are presented in the next volume in this series (Loxley & Whiteley, in preparation).

References

Coulson, W. R. *A sense of community.* Columbus, OH: Merrill, 1973.

Gamson, W. A. *SIMSOC simulated society* (2nd ed.): *Instructor's manual.* New York: Free Press, 1972. (a)

Gamson, W. A. *SIMSOC simulated society* (2nd ed.): *Participants' manual.* New York: Free Press, 1972. (b)

Greif, E. B., & Hogan, R. The theory and measurement of empathy. *Journal of Counseling Psychology,* 1973, 20(3), 280-284.

Kohlberg, L. *Latest version of the theory of the just community school.* Unpublished manuscript, Harvard University, 1975.

Kohlberg, L., Wasserman, E., & Richardson, N. The just community school: The theory and the Cambridge cluster school experiment. In L. Kohlberg (Ed.), *Collected papers on moral development and moral education* (Volume II). Cambridge, MA: Center for Moral Education, Harvard University, 1975.

Loevinger, J., & Wessler, R. *Measuring ego development* (Volume I). San Francisco: Jossey-Bass, 1970.

Loxley, J. C., & Whiteley, J. M. *Character development in college students* (Volume II), in preparation.

Mosher, R. L., & Sprinthall, N. A. Psychological education in the secondary schools: A program to promote individual and human development. *American Psychologist,* 1970, 25(10), 911-924.

Mosher, R. L., & Sprinthall, N. A. Psychological education: A means to promote personal development during adolescence. *The Counseling Psychologist,* 1971, 2(4), 3-82.

Rest, J. R. *Development in judging moral issues.* Minneapolis, MN: University of Minnesota, 1979.

Rogers, C. R. *Carl Rogers on encounter groups.* New York: Harper & Row, 1970.

Sarason, S. B. *The creation of settings and the future societies.* San Francisco: Jossey-Bass, 1972.

Sarason, S. B. *The psychological sense of community: Prospects for a community psychology.* San Francisco: Jossey-Bass, 1974.

Sarason, S. B., Zitnay, G., & Grossman, F. K. *The creation of a community setting* (Vol. I). Syracuse, NY: Syracuse University Division of Special Education and Rehabilitation and the Center on Human Policy, 1971.

SEED Alumni Journal, University of California, Irvine. 1980, *10*(1), 2.

Selman, R. L. A developmental approach to interpersonal and moral awareness in young children: Some theoretical and educational implications of levels of social perspective taking. In T. C. Hennessy (Ed.), *Values and moral development.* New York: Paulist Press, 1976, 127-139. (a)

Selman, R. L. Social-cognitive understanding: A guide to educational and clinical practice. In T. Lickona (Ed.), *Moral development and behavior.* New York: Holt, Rinehart & Winston, 1976, 299-316. (b)

Stokols D. Toward a psychological theory of alienation. *Psychological Review,* 1975, *82*(1), 26-44.

Wasserman, E. R. Implementing Kohlberg's "just community concept" in an alternative high school. *Social Education,* 1976, *40,* 203-207.

Whiteley, J. M., & Associates. *Character development in college students* (Vol. III), in preparation.

Whiteley, J. M., & Loxley, J. C. A curriculum for the development of character and community in college students. In V. L. Erickson & J. M. Whiteley (Eds.), *Developmental counseling and teaching.* Monterey, CA: Brooks/Cole, 1980, 262-297.

Chapter 7

APPROACHES TO THE EVALUATION OF CHARACTER DEVELOPMENT

John M. Whiteley

The Sierra Project approach to the evaluation of character development in college students was multifaceted, reflecting the complex nature of the project and the lack of developmentally oriented instruments expressly measuring the broad concept of character development. This chapter articulates our basic research questions and explains the evaluation procedures we followed to address them. The basic questions are as follows:

Did the Sierra Project intervention produce changes? If so, did those changes endure?

Did certain parts of the intervention, under particular conditions, produce specific identifiable developmental changes? If so, what were they?

Who benefited most from the intervention in our particular population of students?

What experiences had the most impact on students, particularly on their thinking about moral decisions?

Each of these basic questions was approached by a quite different evaluation method. The next sections of this chapter will present each of these different methods (and the questions they addressed).

EVALUATION AND DURATION OF CHANGES: THE SURVEY DESIGN

The question of whether the intervention produced changes, and whether those changes, endured was approached through a longitudinal survey design. Students were tested at the beginning and end of their freshman year, then at the end of their sophomore, junior, and senior years. The Survey Design consisted of the following measurements:

Moral Reasoning

Moral Judgment Interview (Kohlberg, 1973; Colby, Gibbs, Kohlberg, Speicher-Dubin, & Candee, 1979): a one-hour individually administered structured interview proposing moral dilemmas for the subject to resolve. The interviewer uses open-ended questions to draw out the logic underlying the interviewee's solutions. When the measure is scored, the subject can be placed at one of six stages of moral reasoning.

Defining Issues Test (Rest, 1979): a paper-and-pencil measure, developed from Kohlberg's Moral Judgment Interview, which asks individuals to rate the importance of various factors in resolving moral dilemmas. Individuals' scores reflect the percentage of moral principles used in reasoning and making decisions, and allow them to be located at one of the six stages of moral reasoning.

Ego Development

Washington University Sentence Completion Test for Measuring Ego Development (Loevinger & Wessler, 1970; Loevinger, 1976): a paper-and-pencil instrument designed to assess an individual's level of ego development expressed in terms of stages.

Locus of Control

Rotter I-E Scale (Rotter, 1966): a paper-and-pencil measure assessing individuals' perceptions of internal and external factors which govern behavior and events, e.g., perceptions and expectations of the social environment, themselves, and others.

Psychological Sense of Community

Environmental Assessment Inventory (Stokols, 1975): a paper-and-pencil instrument focusing on individuals in a social context. The instrument measures the individual's investment in the social environment and his/her perception of the degree of trust, security, competition, etc., in the environment. For this research, we constructed an eight-item "psychological sense of community" scale from the larger pool of EAI items.

Keniston Alienation Scale (Keniston, 1965): a paper-and-pencil measure which asks individuals to determine the extent to which they feel themselves to be an active part of the community or group. Other questions probe the degree of faith and trust individuals have in other members of the group.

Self-Esteem

Janis and Field Personality Questionnaire (Hovland & Janis, 1959): a paper-and-pencil instrument which measures various aspects of personality, centering on self-esteem. We used the 23-item portion measuring feelings of adequacy and inadequacy. Individuals rate themselves on a 5-point scale, responding to such questions as: "How much do you worry about how other people regard you?"

Attitude Toward People

"People in General" portion of the Environmental Assessment Inventory (Stokols, 1975): a paper-and-pencil instrument which focuses on attitudes toward people in general. We used the 11-item portion of the Environmental Assessment Inventory which asks subjects to rate "people in general" on a series of continua such as "aggravating versus soothing," and "harmful versus beneficial."

Sex Role Choices

Bem Sex Role Inventory (Bem, 1974, 1975): a paper-and-pencil measure which asks individuals to rate themselves with respect to 60 masculine, feminine, and neutral personality characteristics. Individuals receive three separate scores: masculinity and femininity scores (each of which independently reflects the extent to which subjects endorse masculine and feminine items), and an androgeny score which reflects the individual's relative endorsement of masculinity and femininity.

Participant Information

Background Questionnaire (adapted from Whitla, 1977): a paper-and-pencil measure requesting information concerning subjects' family backgrounds, expectations about college in general (and UCI in particular), choices of academic major, and possible career directions. Other items ask individuals to rate factors influencing their career decisions, their preferences for leisure activities, their perceptions of their own abilities in relation to those of others, and the values they hold about the potential outcomes of their college experiences.

Student Experience at College

College Experience Questionnaire (adapted from Whitla, 1977): a paper-and-pencil measure which elicits information about important experiences occurring during the college years, and individuals' opinions about those experiences. Additional items specific to UCI were constructed by K. H. Nelson, J. Eberhardy, and K. Kerr.

The Survey Design, through the use of the various instruments described above, serves to evaluate the impact of the Sierra experience on college freshmen. It measures their developmental status as it pertains to character. The results from this approach to evaluation are reported in Chapter 8. When repeated over the four years of undergraduate study, the Survey Design also allows us to assess whether changes occurring in the freshman year persist over time. The results from the four-year longitudinal study will appear in a further volume of this series (Whiteley & Associates, in preparation).

There are several important decisions to be made when employing a longitudinal study: establishing a method for dealing with (class) differences from year to year, choosing statistical techniques for analyzing the data, and selecting a control population or populations.

The approach we took in studying cohort differences has been discussed in Chapter 6, with Appendix A providing additional descriptive data. Our considerations when choosing statistical techniques for analyzing the data from the Survey Design will be discussed in Chapter 8 (along with the presentation of the results). Our rationale for selecting the control populations will be presented in a later section of this chapter.

EXAMINING EFFECTS OF COMPONENTS OF THE INTERVENTION: THE TOPICAL DESIGN

To investigate whether certain portions of the intervention — under particular conditions — produced specific changes in freshmen, we used both a Topical Design and an Intensive Design. Data from a variety of measures were collected before and after specific modules of the curriculum were presented. The Topical Design centered on an evaluation of the effects of each curriculum module. The assertion training module, for example, was evaluated by means of student reports and the College Self-Expression Scale (Galassi, Delo, Galassi, & Bastien, 1974; Galassi & Galassi, 1974). The GAIT Empathy Scale (Goodman, 1972), the Carkhuff Empathy Scale (Carkhuff, 1969), and the Carkhuff Gross Rating of Facilitative Functioning (Carkhuff, 1969) were used to evaluate the empathy training. The results from the Topical Design evaluation will appear in the second volume of this series (Loxley & Whiteley, in preparation).

EVALUATING INDIVIDUAL VARIATION IN RESPONSE TO THE INTERVENTION: THE INTENSIVE DESIGN

Like the Topical Design, the Intensive Design is an evaluation approach which applies only to the experimental population. In the Intensive Design, the focus is on the in-depth case study of the individual. For the Classes of 1980 and 1981, there were several preliminary case studies undertaken from sources such as freshmen journals, sophomore staff journals, and staff reports. A rigorous application of the Intensive Design was not fully implemented until the Class of 1982 since a properly trained staff was unavailable until then.

With the Class of 1982, however, staff was available to implement the Intensive Design to a fuller extent. A detailed report of this study by Resnikoff and Jennings is provided in Chapter 10. These researchers attempted to discover how different kinds of students were influenced by specific conditions in their college experiences. They used a methodology structured to gain a phenomenological view of students' thoughts, feelings, and behavior over the course of the year in order to investigate the impact of various aspects of the University environment.

Seventeen students volunteering for the Intensive Design study were stratified according to sex; seven students were then chosen randomly for the study. The seven students were interviewed weekly for the first month of school, then bi-monthly for the remainder of the academic year. Interviews were semi-structured, designed to allow students to report recent events and experiences and their reactions to them. We assumed that those incidents which remained in students' minds were of particular importance to them. The two researchers (Resnikoff and Jennings) alternated in interviewing each student in order to provide a check on the reliability of researcher perceptions. In addition, data from other sources were gathered: the curriculum coordinator kept detailed notes of class events; sophomore staff members provided observations on events occurring during the year; the Intensive Design students kept detailed journals of their activities, often reflecting on and interpreting their experiences.

The data collected from the nine months of case-study fell into two major categories: the first category included those events and reactions which were common to a number of Sierra students; the second category included those events and reactions which were unique to a particular student. The latter category involved changes in individuals which could be traced to the specific beliefs, values, and personal styles of these individuals rather than to the common experiences of college freshmen.

The Intensive Design allows us to develop tentative explanations for individual variation in outcomes, and to generate new theoretical hypotheses for further exploration and systematic testing. By providing an in-depth view of the changes occurring in students — and by relating those changes to events — the Resnikoff and Jennings approach helped identify important sources of change in students' thinking and behavior.

IDENTIFYING CHARACTERISTICS
OF THOSE WHO CHANGE THE MOST:
A STATISTICAL ANALYSIS OF THE SURVEY DESIGN

The evaluation approach taken by Magaña (1979) and reported in Chapter 9 attempts to detect which students in our population benefited the most from the Sierra Project intervention. Multidimensional scaling and hierarchical cluster analysis were used to differentiate among individuals in the Sierra sample she studied. The measures from the survey design, including those appraising the level of moral reasoning, ego development, locus of control, self-esteem, alienation, sex role identification, and attitudes toward people, served as data sources.

Magaña's approach was to group students according to similarities on dimensions of character measured in the initial testing. The clusters of students so identified were then examined at subsequent testings to see if the extent and type of change occurring between testings varied with their membership in a particular cluster. Magaña attempted, therefore, to determine whether meaningful patterns of individual differences existed in the sample. If those patterns were found to exist, Magaña's next task was to discover whether there were significant differences in the rate and nature of change for students whose initial types of profiles were different.

IDENTIFYING IMPACTFUL EXPERIENCES:
PERCEPTIONS OF THE PARTICIPANTS

A final approach utilized in evaluating the Sierra Project was to focus directly on students' perceptions of what had most affected their thinking on moral decisions. The Topical and Intensive Designs had provided some sources of data on experiences occurring during the freshman year which participants in the intervention felt were particularly influential.

To investigate what students thought had most influenced their thinking about moral decisions, we asked a student participant from the Class of 1979 to assess the intervention from a retrospective viewpoint. Lee's approach, reported in Chapter 11, was to ask students from the Class of 1979 to recall experiences and influences contributing to their thinking about moral issues. We assumed that those impressions and reactions salient enough for students to remember five years later would reflect their special perceptions of Sierra and of their own growth in moral reasoning. This retrospective evaluation was administered to 14 members of the Class of 1979 during the year following their graduation.

Our final evaluation approach, also focusing on students', retrospective perceptions of their experiences during the Sierra Project, used a modification of The Moral Reasoning Experience Check List, a structured interview developed by Volker (1979).

The modified check list was administered to a small sample of students from the Class of 1979 at the end of their senior year, and later to samples of freshmen from the Classes of 1983 and 1984. At the end of their freshman year, these students were asked to reflect upon experiences which they recalled as affecting their moral reasoning. They were also given the Defining Issues Test (Rest, 1979) and the Sociomoral Reflection Measure (Gibbs, Widaman, & Colby, 1981; Gibbs & Widaman, in press). This study was therefore designed to identify important experiences contributing to students' growth in moral reasoning as reported immediately following the students' freshman year; results of this study will be presented by Burris (in preparation) and by Whiteley and Associates (in preparation).

SELECTION OF THE CONTROL POPULATIONS

Perhaps the most perplexing design problem we have encountered is in regard to the nature of our control populations. Control populations are central to the generation of accurate information about the developmental status of college freshmen, the effect of the freshman year, and the longitudinal study of the development of moral reasoning in college students. Yet, since our research is conducted in a "natural laboratory" setting, we have no "control" over the participation of subjects. Attrition in the sample, expected when we began the study, has occurred (see Table 7-2 later in this chapter). We expected that our control populations would suffer the greatest attrition, since they have very little, if any, vested interest in the study while the Sierra

Hall population of volunteers had a certain spirit of involvement, an expressed interest in participating in the Sierra Project. We therefore decided to have two control groups: Control Group I (Lago Hall residents) and Control Group II (random or collateral control students). Control Group I consists of freshmen who had elected to live in all-freshmen residence halls. For the Class of 1979, residents of both Sierra and Lago Halls had volunteered for participation in the Sierra Project. In the Classes of 1980, 1981, and 1982, Lago residents, while also freshmen in living situations identical to those of students in the Sierra experimental group, did not request the Sierra curriculum.

Control Group II consists of subjects selected from the entire freshman populations of UC Irvine. Our original intent for Control Group II was to select freshmen from the Classes of 1979, 1980, 1981, and 1982 who were not residents of Sierra or Lago Halls, and to follow these individuals throughout the four years of their undergraduate study. Through examining the data received from the Class of 1979 when they were freshmen, we learned that our Control Group II attrition was so extensive that it was unrealistic to expect to retain a representative sample of that control group over all four years of undergraduate study (see Table 7-1). We therefore elected the collateral control approach for the Classes of 1980, 1981, and 1982.[1] Schaie (1973) notes that collateral control groups are those selected "in absence of total control over one's subjects" (p. 255). They allow the scrutiny of experimental attrition and can be used to determine whether the residual sample of a longitudinal study has remained representative of its parent population.

Schaie (1973) goes on to say, "Most longitudinal studies will simply be limited by the nature of their sample of survivors, and the findings reported therefrom should be carefully identified

[1]In the fall of 1976, we had not yet elected the collateral control approach. For that testing, Control Group II was composed of the residents of Mirkwood Hall, another all-freshman residence hall. However, beginning in the spring of 1977, Control Group II members were only those students selected through the collateral control approach. For purposes of clarity, Control Group II will refer to all control groups other than the residents of Lago Hall.

as being restricted to similar populations" (p. 256).* Our "sample of survivors," as far as the initial Control Group II (random control) sample for the Class of 1979 was concerned, turned out to be small and unrepresentative.

TABLE 7-1
ATTRITION FOR THE CLASS OF 1979
FROM PARTICIPATION IN THE TESTING

Population	Fall Testing 1975	Spring Testing 1976	Spring Testing 1977
Sierra	46	42	34
Control Group I (Lago)	42	36	12
Control Group II (Random Control)	23	14	5

PROBLEMS OF SAMPLING

There are three problems of sampling related to the Survey Design of the Sierra Project. The first problem concerns the high attrition rate of subjects in any longitudinal research project, a circumstance which is exacerbated for the Sierra Project by the high student attrition rate of major research universities. The second problem concerns the validity of results stemming from repeated measurements. A final problem focuses on the interpretation of these results in discerning distinctions between developmental change and initial developmental differences.

By way of addressing the attrition problem, as previously noted we chose the collateral control group approach. This approach allowed us to randomly select as members of Control

---

*This and all other quotations from this source are from Schaie, K. W. Methodological problems in descriptive developmental research on adulthood and aging. In J. R. Nesselroade & H. W. Reese (Eds.), *Life-span developmental psychology: Methodological issues.* Copyright 1973, Academic Press. Reprinted with permission.

Group II students who had not been residents of Sierra or Lago Halls and who had not been previously selected as subjects. This approach could then be reapplied at each subsequent testing, thus keeping sample cell sizes stable. However, the high level of attrition which occurs in any major research-oriented university substantially affects our sample. As Table 7-2 reveals, less than half (44%) of entering freshmen at UC Irvine remain to graduate from this institution in four years.

TABLE 7-2
ENROLLMENT AND ATTRITION VS. TIME (CUMULATIVE)
Total = 340

	Dropout		Graduated		Remaining	
	#	%	#	%	#	%
1st Year (1970-71)	66	19	-	-	274	81
2nd Year (1971-72)	130	38	3	1	207	61
3rd Year (1972-73)	153	45	12	4	175	51
4th Year (1973-74)	167	49	151	44	22	7
5th Year (1974-75)	172	51	163	48	5	1

Source: Adapted from Table 4, page 19. **Graduation and Attrition at the University of California, Irvine: A Longitudinal Study of Freshmen Entering in Fall 1970.** Report-0AA-76-R2, February 1976 by Susan Weeks.

One of our basic assumptions (and hopes) is that the sample sizes for Sierra, Control Group I, and Control Group II will remain large enough over four years of follow-up to make meaningful generalizations from the longitudinal study. Longitudinal research on college-age populations in naturalistic settings must confront the problem of whether final samples are representative of the population as a whole, and proceed in such a manner as to allow for the high attrition rates of both longitudinal studies and college enrollment.

The second sampling problem concerns the validity of results obtained from studies using repeated measurements. Schaie (1973) describes the problem as:

> In any repeated measurement study, moreover, a sample ceases to be representative of its parent population as soon as it has been tested once, in the sense that its response characteristics have, of necessity, been modified by the initial assessment in a manner which is not characteristic of the parent population. That is, at subsequent measurement points, it will differ from any other random population sample in that the assessment tools or situations have previously been applied to the longitudinal sample, but to no other (p. 255).

Our sample is particularly susceptible to the effects of repeated measurements since alternative forms do not exist for several of our key instruments for assessing character and its development. Because the measurements of moral reasoning (the DIT and the MJI) and ego development (WUSCT) assess the structure of students' thinking as opposed to its content, the effect of repeated test administrations is minimized. In assessing the growth of subjects' moral reasoning, for example, we look at the principles on which they base their solutions rather than at the specific solutions. Because of this one can "fake low" but cannot "fake high" on instruments like the Defining Issues Test (Rest, 1979) and the Washington University Sentence Completion Test for Measuring Ego Development (Loevinger & Wessler, 1970; Loevinger, 1976).

Another aspect of the Sierra Project which reduces the effect of repeated test administrations is the relatively long period of time between testings — nine months to one year — which probably diminishes students' "test-wiseness" to repeated measurements. We intend to make our data available to persons interested in investigating how samples such as ours differ from the parent populations as a consequence of these test effects.[2]

A final problem of sampling for the Sierra Project lies in the distinction we must make between developmental change and initial developmental differences. Initial differences between classes (for example, between the Class of 1979 and the Class of

[2]Our data will be made available at the Henry Murray Research Center, Radcliffe College, 10 Garden Street, Cambridge, MA 02138.

1980) may simply reflect a pattern that is "characteristic of the particular sociocultural conditions existing at the time of testing" (Huston-Stein & Baltes, 1976, p. 180). Huston-Stein and Baltes (1976) also point out that similarities among different age groups can mask ontogenetic patterns, influencing longitudinal assessments of cohort groups. As they state it:

> Longitudinal assessments of one cohort may reflect cultural-social changes or invariances as well as ontogenetic patterns, not to mention problems of retest effects and selective dropouts. They may also be affected by the interaction of ontogenetic development with historical events particular to that cohort (Huston-Stein & Baltes, 1976, p.180).

The last decade has seen both student turmoil and quietude on campuses; the experiences of one class of students have been quite different from those of other classes. In addition, the differing educational approaches of schools and the diversity of students' family life further increase the disparity of previous experiences of the four experimental classes in Sierra Hall. The intent of the research design of the Sierra Project is to make it possible, over the course of the longitudinal study, to separate these varying effects of age, cohort, and time of measurement.

REFLECTIONS ON THE SIERRA APPROACH TO EVALUATING CHARACTER DEVELOPMENT

Our working definition of character development, the state of development of current methods of measurement, our research and curriculum goals, the voluntary status of Sierra Project participants, the skills of our staff, and the naturalistic setting all contributed to the form which our evaluation has ultimately taken.

Had we limited ourselves to only a few approaches to evaluation, we would have missed important data necessary for us to address central questions, to understand what students were experiencing, and to understand how they were changing. A basic strength of this multidimensional approach to evaluation is that important aspects of the complexity of the Sierra Project can be captured and analyzed. Each of our different sources of data collection and analysis served to provide quite valuable perspectives on the process of character development and its influences during the four years of undergraduate study.

References

Bem, S. L. The measurement of psychological androgyny. *Journal of Counseling and Clinical Psychology*, 1974, *42*(2), 155-162.

Bem, S. L. Sex role adaptability: One consequence of psychological androgyny. *Journal of Personality and Social Psychology*, 1975, *31*(4), 634-643.

Burris, M. P. *The influences of college experiences on moral reasoning.* Master's thesis, University of California, Irvine, in preparation.

Carkhuff, R. R. *Helping and human relations* (Vols. I and II). New York: Holt, Rinehart & Winston, 1969.

Colby, A., Gibbs, J. C., Kohlberg, L., Speicher-Dubin, B., & Candee, D. *Standard form scoring manual* (Parts 1-4). Cambridge, MA: Harvard University, Center for Moral Education, 1979.

Galassi, J. P., Delo, J. S., Galassi, M. D., Bastien, S. The college self-expression scale: A measure of assertiveness. *Behavior Therapy*, 1974, *5*, 165-171.

Galassi, J. P., & Galassi, M. D. Validity of a measure of assertiveness. *Journal of Counseling Psychology*, 1974, *21*(3), 248-250.

Gibbs, J. C., & Widaman, K. F. *Social intelligence: Measuring the development of sociomoral reflection.* Englewood Cliffs, NJ: Prentice-Hall, in press.

Gibbs, J. C., Widaman, K. F., & Colby, A. *Construction and validation of a simplified, group-administerable equivalent to the Moral Judgment Interview.* Unpublished paper, Ohio State University, 1981. (Originally presented at the meeting of the American Psychological Association in Montreal, September 1980.)

Goodman, G. *Companionship therapy.* San Francisco: Jossey-Bass, 1972.

Hovland, C. I., & Janis, I. L. (Eds.). *Personality and persuasibility.* New Haven, CN: Yale University Press, 1959, 300-305.

Huston-Stein, A., & Baltes, P. B. Theory and method in life-span developmental psychology: Implications for child development. In H. W. Reese (Ed.), *Advances in child development and behavior* (Vol. II). New York: Academic Press, 1976, 169-188.

Keniston, K. *The uncommitted: Alienated youth in American society* (1st ed.). New York: Harcourt, Brace, 1965.

Kohlberg, L. *Standard scoring manual.* Unpublished manuscript, Harvard University, Center for Moral Education, 1973.

Loevinger, J. *Ego development: Conceptions and theories.* San Francisco: Jossey-Bass, 1976.

Loevinger, J., & Wessler, R. *Measuring ego development, Vol. I: Construction and use of a sentence completion test.* San Francisco: Jossey-Bass, 1970.

Loxley, J. C., & Whiteley, J. M. *Character development in college students* (Vol. II), in preparation.

Magaña, H. A. *Individual differences on multiple assessments and their relationship to rate of development: Implications for developmental research and intervention.* Unpublished doctoral dissertation, University of California, Irvine, 1979.

Rest, J. R. *Development in judging moral issues.* Minneapolis, MN: University of Minnesota Press, 1979.

Rotter, J. B. Generalized expectancies for internal versus external control of reinforcement. *Psychological Monographs: General and Applied,* 1966, *80* (1, Whole No. 609).

Schaie, K. W. Methodological problems in descriptive developmental research on adulthood and aging. In J. R. Nesselroade & H. W. Reese (Eds.), *Life-span developmental psychology: Methodological issues.* New York: Academic Press, 1973, 153-180.

Stokols, D. Toward a psychological theory of alienation. *Psychological Review,* 1975, *82*(1), 26-44.

Volker, J. M. *Moral reasoning and college experience.* Project Report #4, Higher Education and Cognitive-Social Development Project. University of Minnesota: Department of Social, Psychological, and Philosophical Foundations of Education, 1979. National Institute of Education, #NIE-G-79-0021.

Whitla, D. K. *Value added: Measuring the outcomes of undergraduate education.* Cambridge, MA: Harvard University, Office of Instructional Research and Evaluation, 1977.

Whiteley, J. M., & Associates. *Character development in college students* (Vol. III), in preparation.

SECTION III.

EVALUATING THE CHARACTER DEVELOPMENT OF COLLEGE FRESHMEN

Section III presents the results from each of our four approaches to evaluation. Chapter 8 reports the results from the psychological testing of Sierra and control group students at the beginning and end of their freshman year. Chapter 9 reports the statistical analysis of student clusters, identifying the characteristics of those individuals who appear to benefit most from the Sierra intervention. Chapter 10 reports the results of a concurrent case study based on frequent interviews with seven Sierra freshmen. Chapter 11 reports the results of a series of interviews with former Sierra freshmen by one of their classmates—conducted five years after they had participated in the program.

Chapter 8

EFFECTS OF THE FRESHMAN YEAR

John M. Whiteley

This chapter presents the results of analyses of the data collected as part of the Survey Design. These results will be presented in terms of two different sets of questions. First,

1. Are there changes during the freshman year which appear common to all of the groups sampled?

2. Are there changes during the freshman year which are different for students in Sierra Hall (the experimental group) than for students in the two control groups?

In the second set of questions, we will focus on the presentation of results concerned with a more specific area; namely, the three different measures of character development and their interrelationship:

3. What is the empirical interrelationship of the three different measures of character development in college students?

4. Within the Sierra Hall group, what changes occurred during the freshman year on the measures of character development?

5. Are there patterns of developmental change during the freshman year which are related to the level of moral reasoning or ego development?

1. ARE THERE CHANGES DURING THE FRESHMAN YEAR WHICH APPEAR COMMON TO ALL OF THE GROUPS SAMPLED?

Analysis of variance is utilized to distinguish differences among groups of scores when there is more than one factor involved (i.e. sex, class, group); it estimates the amount of variance attributable to each of these factors and their interaction, including a built-in error variance factor. The Repeated Measures Analysis of Variance (RMAV), as described by Jenrich and Sampson (1979), was performed in order to determine the effects of time (pre- versus post-testing), sex, cohort group, and treatment condition—as well as to identify any interactions among these factors. A RMAV further examines the differences in scores from multiple testings (e.g. pre-test and post-test). Statistical tests[1] indicated that our data met the requirements of the RMAV to appropriately apply and interpret its methods.

Our use of the RMAV essentially allows us to determine the amount of variance that can be accounted for by the various treatment conditions (participation in the Sierra psychological intervention program or participation in Control Group I or II) and testing occasions (pre- or post-test). It also permits us to make inferences about what changes occur during the freshman year.

We will report the results from the RMAV by psychological construct—as assessed by the appropriate instrument in the Survey Design. In the case of each construct, the relevant table (8-1 through 8-6) will provide descriptive data (number of subjects, mean pre-test scores and post-test scores according to groups, grand pre- and post-test scores, and the summary of the results of the RMAV). We chose the following basic categories to use in analysis:

Class: differences among the Classes of 1980, 1981, and 1982, i.e. cohort differences.

Sex: differences between scores for male and female subjects.

[1]The statistical tests performed on these analyses and our assumptions in choosing them are described in a paper by Elizabeth Kaye Kasdan deposited at the Henry Murray Research Center, Radcliffe College, 10 Garden Street, Cambridge, MA 02138.

Change over time: changes occurring during the freshman year as assessed by the interval between pre-test and post-test.

Group: differences among the three populations of our project: Sierra (Experimental Group), Control Group I (Lago), and Control Group II (Random Control).

Notations such as Class × Sex or Change over time × Sex refer to the interaction between those categories.

Moral Reasoning (Defining Issues Test)

Table 8-1 presents the results of the analysis of scores on the measure of moral reasoning which reflected students' use of principled thinking. Inspection of Table 8-1 reveals that freshman students as a group made a large and statistically significant gain (p<.0001) in moral reasoning over the course of their first year of college study when the measure focused on their percentage of principled thinking. This gain was characteristic of all three classes studied. Sex of students did not influence the degree of change over the freshman year, even in the case of women in the Class of 1981, who entered the university scoring at a very high level. There were significant differences among the cohort groups in the percentage of their responses which were based on principled moral reasoning, men and women in the Class of 1981 both entering and leaving at a level higher than that of the other two classes (p<.0003).

Locus of Control (Rotter I-E Scale)

Results pertaining to any changes in perceived locus of control occurring in the freshman year are displayed in Table 8-2. On this measure, higher scores reflect a more external orientation; lower scores, a more internal orientation. Inspection of Table 8-2 reveals that freshmen as a group tended to develop a more external locus of control during the course of their freshman year (p<.02). As would be predicted from previous research, women consistently exhibited a more external orientation than men (p<.04).

TABLE 8-1
MEAN TEST SCORES AND REPEATED MEASURES ANALYSIS OF
VARIANCE RESULTS FOR THE DEFINING ISSUES TEST
MEASURE OF MORAL REASONING FOR FRESHMEN IN THE
CLASSES OF 1980, 1981, and 1982

	n[1]	Mean Pre-test Score	Mean Post-test Score
Class of 1980			
all males[2]	34	34.43	41.56
all females	35	30.97	38.82
Class of 1981			
all males	11	46.18	50.73
all females	34	45.29	45.21
Class of 1982			
all males	33	34.95	39.30
all females	40	41.83	43.21
ALL GROUPS $\overline{X}$	187	38.12	42.20

Repeated Measures Analysis of Variance

	Degrees of Freedom	F Value	Significance
Class	2	8.39	.0003
Sex	1	.02	ns[3]
Class x Sex	2	2.66	.0728 (ns)
Change over Time	1	15.88	.0001
Change over Time x Class	2	2.87	.0592 (ns)
Change over Time x Sex	1	1.19	ns
Change over Time x Class x Sex	2	.59	ns

[1]n's are smaller than reported elsewhere because the repeated-measures-analysis-of-variance requires that complete data (all testing times) be available for all subjects used; hence, subjects on whom we have incomplete data are not used in this analysis.
[2]For this analysis, males and females from all groups are combined.
[3]ns = not significant at the .05 level of confidence.

Psychological Sense of Community (Scale constructed from items on the Environmental Assessment Inventory)

The results of the statistical analysis of the eight-item Psychological Sense of Community Scale (PSCS) — constructed from the Environmental Assessment Inventory — are provided in Table

TABLE 8-2
MEAN TEST SCORES AND REPEATED MEASURES ANALYSIS OF VARIANCE RESULTS FOR THE ROTTER I-E SCALE FOR FRESHMEN IN THE CLASSES OF 1980, 1981, and 1982

	n[1]	Mean Pre-test Score	Mean Post-test Score
Class of 1980			
all males[2]	41	10.98	10.98
all females	35	11.86	11.71
Class of 1981			
all males	27	8.78	9.67
all females	47	10.81	10.81
Class of 1982			
all males	47	9.66	10.83
all females	53	10.32	11.60
ALL GROUPS $\bar{X}$	250	10.44	11.01

Repeated Measures Analysis of Variance

	Degrees of Freedom	F Value	Significance
Class	2	2.29	ns[3]
Sex	1	4.31	.0389
Class x Sex	2	.29	ns
Change over Time	1	5.41	.0208
Change over Time x Class	2	3.00	.0518 (ns)
Change over Time x Sex	1	.45	ns
Change over Time x Class x Sex	2	.42	ns

[1]n's are smaller than reported elsewhere because the repeated-measures-analysis-of-variance requires that complete data (all testing times) be available for all subjects used; hence, subjects on whom we have incomplete data are not used in this analysis.
[2]For this analysis, males and females from all groups are combined.
[3]ns = not significant at the .05 level of confidence.

8-3. Only students from Sierra (the experimental group) and Lago (Control Group I) were sampled.

Results from the first assessment reveal what freshmen *expected* to find in terms of a psychological sense of community; those from the second reflect what students perceived as the psychological sense of community they had actually *experienced* during their freshman year.

A most striking finding is the high level of expectation our entering students had for community as a part of college life. Since each of the eight items was rated on a scale of 1 to 7, students total ratings could have ranged from 8 to 56. As inspection of Table 8-3 reveals, both Sierra and Lago students had scores which averaged above 42 on the pre-test. While there were no initial group differences, there were sex differences — women had higher expectation for community than men ($p < .04$).

When students reported the psychological sense of community which they felt during the freshman year, there was a significant difference between their ratings of expected and experienced community ($p < .0001$); students perceived themselves as experiencing less than they had expected. Cohort differences appeared which were highly significant, members of the Class of 1980 perceiving their community to be at a higher level than did the members of the Classes of 1981 and 1982 ($p < .0001$).

Notable findings on this scale include the high level of ex-

TABLE 8-3
MEAN SCALES SCORES AND REPEATED MEASURES ANALYSIS OF VARIANCE RESULTS FOR THE PSYCHOLOGICAL SENSE OF COMMUNITY SCALE (FROM THE ENVIRONMENTAL ASSESSMENT INVENTORY) FOR FRESHMEN IN THE CLASSES OF 1980, 1981, and 1982

	n^1	Mean Pre-test Score	Mean Post-test Score
Class of 1980			
Sierra Males	12	38.58	41.50
Lago Males	10	48.70	39.90
Sierra Females	14	42.57	45.79
Lago Females	9	48.44	40.89
Class of 1981			
Sierra Males	13	34.62	36.08
Lago Males	9	40.11	30.78
Sierra Females	21	44.00	33.62
Lago Females	15	39.93	31.00
Class of 1982			
Sierra Males	21	40.33	35.86
Lago Males	15	42.87	35.20
Sierra Females	24	44.25	37.38
Lago Females	18	45.67	33.78
ALL GROUPS $\overline{X}$	181	42.49	36.51

TABLE 8-3 (CONTINUED)

Repeated Measures Analysis of Variance

	Degrees of Freedom	F Value	Significance
Group	1	.06	ns[1]
Sex	1	4.37	.0381
Class	2	17.51	.000
Group x Sex	1	2.87	.09 (ns)
Group x Class	2	1.42	ns
Sex x Class	2	.03	ns
Group x Sex x Class	2	.10	ns
Change over Time	1	52.19	.000
Change over Time x Group	1	17.92	.000
Change over Time x Sex	1	3.05	.08 (ns)
Change over Time x Class	2	3.81	.024
Change over Time x Group x Sex	1	1.44	ns
Change over Time x Group x Class	2	1.93	ns
Change over Time x Sex x Class	2	1.26	ns
Change over Time x Group x Sex x Class	2	1.99	ns

[1]ns refers to not significant at the .05 level of confidence.

pected psychological sense of community, the consistent perception of less community experienced than was expected for all groups, and the presence of differences between classes.

Alienation (Keniston Alienation Scale)

Table 8-4 presents the results of the RMAV of scores on the Keniston Alienation Scale. On this measure, the higher the score, the greater the degree of alienation.

As Table 8-4 indicates, there were significant sex differences on this measure; men were more alienated than women (p < .0002). While neither cohort (class) nor change over time showed significant effects, their interaction was highly significant (p < .00001). Both men and women in the Class of 1980 became less alienated

TABLE 8-4
MEAN TEST SCORES AND REPEATED MEASURES ANALYSIS OF VARIANCE RESULTS FOR THE KENISTON ALIENATION SCALE FOR FRESHMEN IN THE CLASSES OF 1980, 1981, and 1982

	n[1]	Mean Pre-test Score	Mean Post-test Score
Class of 1980			
all males[2]	41	35.02	31.20
all females	32	35.44	28.59
Class of 1981			
all males	28	34.79	34.71
all females	51	27.80	29.27
Class of 1982			
all males	52	31.12	34.25
all females	58	26.24	29.21
ALL GROUPS X	262	30.92	31.05

Repeated Measures Analysis of Variance

	Degrees of Freedom	F Value	Significance
Class	2	1.74	ns[3]
Sex	1	13.93	.0002
Class x Sex	2	1.79	ns
Change over Time	1	1.04	ns
Change over Time x Class	2	23.69	.0000
Change over Time x Sex	1	.28	ns
Change over Time x Class x Sex	2	1.47	ns

[1] n's are smaller than reported elsewhere because the repeated-measures-analysis-of-variance requires that complete data (all testing times) be available for all subjects used; hence, subjects on whom we have incomplete data are not used in this analysis.
[2] For this analysis, males and females from all groups are combined.
[3] ns = not significant at the .05 level of confidence.

as the year progressed, while women in both 1981 and 1982 and men in 1982 became more alienated; men in the Class of 1981 remained essentially unchanged on this dimension.

The Keniston Alienation Scale has unfortunately not been subjected to detailed psychometric study. It is, therefore, not known how sensitive the scale is (how responsive it is to situational events), nor is it known what its reliability is with a sample such as ours.

Self-Esteem
(Janis and Field Personality Questionnaire)

Data from the Janis and Field Personality Questionnaire measurement of self-esteem were subjected to the repeated measures analysis of variance. Descriptive data and the summary of the RMAV are found in Table 8-5. On this measure, the higher the score, the lower the level of self-esteem.

TABLE 8-5
MEAN TEST SCORES AND REPEATED MEASURES ANALYSIS OF VARIANCE RESULTS FOR THE JANIS & FIELD PERSONALITY QUESTIONNAIRE MEASURE OF SELF-ESTEEM FOR FRESHMEN IN THE CLASSES OF 1980, 1981, and 1982

	n[1]	Mean Pre-test Score	Mean Post-test Score
Class of 1980			
all males[2]	38	36.47	37.13
all females	30	44.37	42.90
Class of 1981			
all males	27	38.78	36.85
all females	48	38.67	36.02
Class of 1982			
all males	48	37.03	37.69
all females	55	39.40	41.69
ALL GROUPS X̄	246	38.89	38.72

Repeated Measures Analysis of Variance

	Degrees of Freedom	F Value	Significance
Class	2	.73	ns[3]
Sex	1	3.58	.0596 (ns)
Class x Sex	2	1.40	ns
Change over Time	1	.32	ns
Change over Time x Class	2	2.45	.0888 (ns)
Change over Time x Sex	1	.07	ns
Change over Time x Class x Sex	2	.65	ns

[1] n's are smaller than reported elsewhere because the repeated-measures-analysis-of-variance requires that complete data (all testing times) be available for all subjects used; hence, subjects on whom we have incomplete data are not used in this analysis.
[2] For this analysis, males and females from all groups are combined.
[3] ns = not significant at the .05 level of confidence.

As inspection of Table 8-5 reveals, the analysis failed to find differences according to cohort, sex, or change over time. The data exhibited two trends approaching significance: women tended to have lower self-esteem than men ($p < .0596$) and some cohort groups tended to show different patterns of change over the course of the year ($p < .0888$).

Attitude Toward People (The "People-in-General" part of the Environmental Assessment Inventory)

Table 8-6 presents the results from the RMAV of the "People-in-General" measure reflecting attitudes toward people from the Environmental Assessment Inventory. On this measure, the lower the score, the less positive the individual's attitude toward people.

Table 8-6 reveals that freshmen became less positive toward people over the course of their first year in college ($p < .0019$), and women were more positive toward people than men ($p < .0259$), though the magnitude of the difference was slight.

Sex Roles (Bem Sex-Role Inventory)

Starting with 1975-76, we measured sex-role characteristics using the Bem Sex-Role Inventory, first introduced by Bem in 1974. This scale remains a promising research instrument, allowing separate study of masculinity and femininity as well as providing a measurement of psychological androgeny. There is, however, continuing debate on the methodology of assessing androgeny (Kaplan, 1979) and on the meaning of validation studies such as Bem's (1974) of androgynous and nonandrogynous individuals. Since research on this aspect of the scale is obviously in an early state of development, we did not analyze androgeny scores. We conducted separate analyses of the Masculinity-Femininity Scales for men and women in the three groups for each of the Classes of 1980, 1981, 1982.

Our analysis revealed no consequential differences; therefore, the tables containing our data and analyses are not reported in this text.[2] Men scored higher than women on the Masculinity

[2]This and all other data obtained from the Sierra Project Survey Design is available at the Henry Murray Research Center, Radcliffe College, 10 Garden Street, Cambridge, MA 02138.

TABLE 8-6
MEAN TEST SCORES AND REPEATED MEASURES ANALYSIS OF VARIANCE RESULTS FOR THE "PEOPLE-IN-GENERAL" SCALE (FROM THE ENVIRONMENTAL ASSESSMENT INVENTORY) FOR FRESHMEN IN THE CLASSES OF 1980, 1981, and 1982

	n[1]	Mean Pre-test Score	Mean Post-test Score
Class of 1980			
all males[2]	41	54.10	53.17
all females	32	57.47	55.38
Class of 1981			
all males	26	52.27	51.65
all females	49	54.71	51.67
Class of 1982			
all males	52	51.63	50.15
all females	57	56.35	52.51
ALL GROUPS $\bar{X}$	257	54.45	52.25

Repeated Measures Analysis of Variance

	Degrees of Freedom	F Value	Significance
Class	2	1.96	ns[3]
Sex	1	5.02	.0259
Class x Sex	2	.37	ns
Change over Time	1	9.82	.0019
Change over Time x Class	2	.33	ns
Change over Time x Sex	1	2.42	ns
Change over Time x Class x Sex	2	.10	ns

[1] n's are smaller than reported elsewhere because the repeated-measures-analysis-of-variance requires that complete data (all testing times) be available for all subjects used; hence, subjects on whom we have incomplete data are not used in this analysis.
[2] For this analysis, males and females from all groups are combined.
[3] ns = not significant at the .05 level of confidence.

scale, but the sex differences were not found to be significant on the Femininity scale. There were cohort differences between the women in the Class of 1980 and other classes studied on the Masculinity scale (p<.004) but not on the Femininity scale. The analysis failed to find differences related to time of test administration.

Discussion of Question 1

In terms of principled thinking (as reflected in the p-score of the Defining Issues Test), the freshman year turned out to be a period of moderately significant growth in moral reasoning; the mean pre- and post-test scores for the three classes changed from 38.12 to 42.20. There were some cohort differences, the Class of 1981 entering and leaving with higher scores than those of other classes. The women of the Class of 1981 entered with a mean score of 45.29 and left with a comparable mean score of 45.21, thereby scoring higher than students in the other classes — either upon entering or upon completing their freshman years.

A second important finding was the difference between the psychological sense of community anticipated by entering freshmen and that which they reported actually experiencing at the university. Entering freshmen in all three classes had very high expectations that their freshman years would be a time for the development and enhancement of community, expectations which were not met. Since, as we have assumed, a psychological sense of community facilitates personal development, the discrepancy between anticipated and actual sense of community is noteworthy. The perception of our freshmen may reflect the failure of the college community to provide students with the nurturance they sought. On the other hand, students' pre-test expectations may simply reflect the problems of transition as they moved from family, old friends, and a high school environment successfully traversed to new friends and associates and the more demanding college environment.

There was a slight increase on the Rotter Internality-Externality dimension which could reflect situational circumstances and/or psychological development. The situational circumstances are obvious: students could have increased in externality (become less inner-directed) because the impact of the freshman year made them less sure of themselves. Perhaps students were reaching out to help both themselves and others cope with the greater interpersonal stress and academic demands of the freshman year.

The stage of moral reasoning predominant for our sample (Stage 3) may have contributed to this increase in externality. At

Stage 3, the viewpoints of the external interpersonal world are the basis for making one's own moral judgments; essentially, the orientation is to "what the neighbors think." Upon entering the university environment, our freshmen moved to a "new neighborhood" and reached out to re-establish or re-anchor their beliefs. The increased externality of the freshman year could reflect the needs of Stage 3 adolescents to interact intensely with the orientations of their fellow students. Unfortunately, the homogeneity of our sample did not allow us to examine pre-conventional or post-conventional students to determine whether they experienced different changes in internality-externality during their freshman year.

On the Attitude Toward People scale, students showed a less positive attitude at the end of the year; on the Alienation scale, these changes were inconsistent; on the Self-esteem measure, there were no general changes.

Essentially, there seemed to be few major changes during the freshman year on the dimensions we studied except for moderate growth in moral reasoning defined as percent of principled thinking. While the proportion of principled reasoning increased during this period, a number of other psychological attitudes remained unchanged or altered in the direction of more negative perceptions of self or others. We expect that a major transition such as that of moving from high school to college is difficult; the transition includes establishing a new basis for relationships with parents, forming new friendships, intensifying intimacy and sexuality with peers, adjusting to new and more demanding academic work assignments, and generally relocating oneself in a new and strenuous environment. The evidence from our study indicates the importance of the problems encountered in the freshman year and the need for educational programs that help counteract the trends toward more negative attitudes.

2. ARE THERE CHANGES DURING THE FRESHMAN YEAR WHICH ARE DIFFERENT FOR THE SIERRA GROUP AND THE TWO CONTROL GROUPS?

The purpose of this section is to identify how the students in

Sierra Hall (the experimental group) differed in their response to the freshman year when compared to students in Lago Hall (Control Group I) and to the randomly selected population of freshmen (Control Group II). The Survey Design provides one methodological approach to determining what differential effects, if any, were produced by the Sierra curriculum and living environment. In analyzing group differences between pre-test scores and post-test scores, we chose to adjust for initial differences among the groups. We chose this statistical technique because our goal was to understand differences among the three groups in *patterns of change* evinced over the course of the freshman year, not to assess their *initial* differences or the final result. If we simply examined the difference between pre-test and post-test scores, our analysis would be affected by regression towards the mean. If we examined only the post-test scores of the three groups, our analysis would not be responsive to initial differences among the groups.

In order to examine differences in change from pre- to post-testing related to treatment condition, we employed the analysis of covariance, using the pre- to post-test gain score as the dependent variable and the pre-test score as the co-variate (Hendrix, Carter, & Hintze, 1978, p. 101). This method of analysis allows us to examine differences in degree of change among the three treatment groups while controlling for initial differences among groups. We need this technique to compare three groups at two test administrations so as to distinguish the variance accounted for by variations in treatment.

Self-Esteem (J&FPQ) and Moral Reasoning (Defining Issues Test)

The adjusted gain scores on the measures of moral reasoning (as percent of principled thinking), locus of control, alienation, self-esteem, and attitude toward people were subjected to the analysis of covariance. Results of this analysis are displayed in Table 8-7.

Inspection of Table 8-7 reveals that there were some statistically significant differences among the three groups on the measures of self-esteem and principled thinking.

For all three years Sierra students increased in their sense of

TABLE 8-7

ANALYSIS OF COVARIANCE USING ADJUSTED GAIN SCORES FOR EACH YEAR ON MORAL REASONING, LOCUS OF CONTROL, ALIENATION, SELF-ESTEEM AND ATTITUDE TOWARD PEOPLE FOR FRESHMEN IN THE CLASSES OF 1980, 1981, AND 1982 COMPARING SIERRA, CONTROL GROUP I, AND CONTROL GROUP II

Instrument	Mean Gain Scores				
	Sierra (Experimental Group)	Control Group I (Lago)	Control Group II (Random Control)	F Value	Significance
Class of 1980					
Moral Reasoning (DIT)	11.9224	3.0458	4.9085	2.9456	ns (.0596)
Locus of Control	-.5918	-.3351	1.1879	1.9847	ns
Alienation	-4.8734	-5.5707	-5.0777	.0428	ns
Self-Esteem	-2.0072	.1329	1.1471	.7894	ns
Attitude Toward People[1]	-.2857	-2.3050	-1.9407	.4339	ns
Class of 1981					
Moral Reasoning (DIT)	2.8989	6.8531	-6.4511	8.3459	.0009
Locus of Control	.3700	.6441	-.0521	.3074	ns
Alienation	1.7693	1.0325	-.4955	.5537	ns
Self-Esteem	-3.4824	-1.1428	-2.0200	.6066	ns
Attitude Toward People[1]	-1.8597	-4.2668	-.2473	1.2488	ns
Class of 1982					
Moral Reasoning (DIT)	2.9597	1.8065	3.7244	.1852	ns
Locus of Control	.8699	1.9135	1.0553	.8089	ns
Alienation	1.7713	4.7194	3.1542	1.7656	ns
Self-Esteem	-.2657	-2.8630	8.5304	10.6314	.0001
Attitude Toward People[1]	-1.1692	-3.8803	-3.7205	1.3608	ns

[1]These Attitude Toward People figures represent results of a straight analysis-of-variance of the *Attitude Toward People Scale* performed on post-test scores. Because the data from the *Attitude Toward People Scale* did not meet the requirement for covariance analysis (homogeneity of slopes), and because the pre-test showed no significant differences between groups, the analysis-of-variance was done instead of analysis-of-covariance.

self-esteem (a negative score reflects an increase in self-esteem). Students in Control Group I (Lago) increased in self-esteem for two of the three years. Students in Control Group II (Random Control) showed an increase in their self-esteem only one year (the Class of 1981), experienced a moderate decline in self-esteem one year (the Class of 1980), and had a major decline in self-esteem a third year (the Class of 1982). The general decline in self-esteem for members of Control Group II (Random Control) may be based on their different living arrangements. Sierra and Lago residents lived only with other freshmen in their residence halls, while members of Control Group II did not. There are differences between freshmen and upperclassmen in their status and in their competence for completing college level work. Given these differences, it is probable that freshmen living with other freshmen would have generally positive experiences in comparing themselves to others — leading to a higher sense of self-esteem. Being less aware of their "inferior" status and skills, they would be less likely to take a negative view of their place in college life.

With respect to group differences in moral reasoning (as reflected by percentage of principled thinking), Table 8-7 reveals that Sierra residents in the Class of 1980 experienced a major increase in moral reasoning (a mean adjusted gain score of 11.9224). This is in contrast to increases of 3.0458 for Control Group I (Lago) and 4.9085 for Control Group II (Random Control). When the analysis of covariance was performed, the differences among adjusted gain scores approached significance (p < .0596). For the Class of 1981, the differences among the three groups on moral reasoning were more pronounced, reaching statistical significance (p < .0009) largely because Control Group II scores declined sharply, with a loss of 6.4511. In the case of the Class of 1982, scores for all three groups increased, with no significant differences among them.

Since the analysis of covariance for the adjusted gain scores showed a significant difference for the Class of 1981 (p < .0009), it was permissible to employ a post hoc analysis to identify the location of that difference. The results of this analysis are presented in Table 8-8.

The post hoc analysis revealed that both Sierra and Control Group I scores differed from those of Control Group II (Random

TABLE 8-8
DIFFERENCES IN MORAL REASONING USING COVARIANCE ANALYSIS OF ADJUSTED GAIN SCORES, AND PLANNED CONTRAST AND POST HOC ANALYSIS FOR THE DEFINING ISSUES TEST MEASURE OF MORAL REASONING FOR FRESHMEN IN THE CLASSES OF 1980, 1981, 1982 COMPARING SIERRA, LAGO (CONTROL GROUP I), AND CONTROL GROUP II

Adjusted Gain Scores:

Class	Sierra	Lago	Control II	F Value	Significance
1980	11.9224	3.0458	4.9085	2.9456	ns (.0596)
1981[1]	2.8989	6.8531	−6.4511	8.3459	.0009*
1982	2.9597	1.8065	3.7244	.1852	ns

Planned Contrasts: "t" test

Class	Contrast	"t" value	"t" probability
1980	Sierra vs. Lago & Control II	2.3634	.0211
	Lago vs. Control II	.4129	ns
1981	Sierra vs. Lago & Control II	1.0399	ns
	Lago vs. Control II	3.8984	.0004
1982	Sierra vs. Lago & Control II	.0805	ns
	Lago vs. Control II	.5669	ns

*Post Hoc Analysis (For Class of 1981):

Contrasted Groups	Degrees of Freedom	F Value	Significance
Sierra vs. Lago	59	1.0329	ns
Sierra vs. Control II	59	6.4657	.01
Lago vs. Control II	59	12.7259	.01

[1]The Class of 1981 met the requirements for post hoc analysis; no other group met the requirements.

Control) for the Class of 1981 (p<.01 for each). Control Group II declined in percentage of principled thinking, registering an adjusted gain score of −6.4511, while Sierra and Control Group I (Lago) increased, registering adjusted gain scores of +2.8989 for Sierra and +6.8531 for Control Group I.

Another way to explore the differential changes in principled thinking among Sierra and the control groups is to compare the amount of growth in moral reasoning for all years combined. This analysis is presented in Table 8-9.

TABLE 8-9
ADJUSTED GAIN SCORE ANALYSIS OF COVARIANCE OF PER-CENT OF PRINCIPLED THINKING FROM THE DEFINING ISSUES TEST COMPARING ALL SIERRA CLASSES FROM THE CLASSES OF 1980, 1981, and 1982 WITH ALL CONTROL GROUP I (LAGO) SUBJECTS FROM THE CLASSES OF 1980, 1981, and 1982 WITH ALL CONTROL GROUP II (RANDOM CONTROL) SUBJECTS FROM THE CLASSES OF 1980, 1981, and 1982 FOLLOWED BY PLANNED COMPARISON "T" TEST CONTRASTS OF SIERRA (THE EXPERIMENTAL GROUP) VERSUS ALL CONTROL GROUPS (CONTROL GROUP I AND CONTROL GROUP II), AND CONTROL GROUP I VERSUS CONTROL GROUP II

Adjusted gain score analysis of covariance

	Sierra (All classes combined)	Control Group I (All classes combined)	Control Group II (All classes combined)
Principled thinking adjusted gain score	+ 6.2662 n = 83	+ 3.1606 n = 58	+1.2887 n = 46

F value = 3.0080
Degrees of freedom = 2
$p < .05$

Planned comparison contrast: "t" test

Sierra versus All Control Groups
"t" = 2.3720 $p = < .0188$

Control Group I (Lago) versus Control Group II (Random Control)
"t" = .8236   p = ns

A review of Table 8-9 reveals that there were differences in the amount of change among the groups. Combining all Sierra classes, we find an adjusted gain score change of +6.2662 in percent of principled thinking. The corresponding increases in principled thinking were +3.1606 for Control Group I and +1.2887 for Control Group II.[3] This difference was statistically significant ($p<.05$). The planned comparison of the Sierra group to the combined control groups revealed that the group which

[3]The unadjusted mean change scores from pre- to post-test scores for all classes combined were Sierra, +6.9675; Control Group I, +3.1862; and Control Group II, −.0087.

received the experimental treatment (Sierra) was found to differ significantly from the aggregated control treatments (p<.0188).

In terms of our overall evaluation of the psychological intervention provided through the Sierra Project, this is an extremely important finding. Principled thinking was the only measure of character (the others being moral maturity and ego development) which we were able to collect on the entire sample—the two control groups as well as the Sierra group. On this measure, Sierra residents exhibited greater change toward a higher level of moral reasoning than students in both control groups. The differences were moderate in size, one class (the Class of 1980) accounting for a large proportion of the positive change in Sierra scores. The conclusion we draw, however, is that the Sierra curriculum can make a moderate contribution toward furthering character development in college freshmen during a period in their lives which would normally include a small but persistent gain in level of moral reasoning.

Ego Development
(Washington University Sentence Completion Test)

Except with the Class of 1981, it was not possible for us to measure the ego development of the control groups. Table 8-10 provides the analysis of the data collected on the Class of 1981, comparing Sierra and Control Group II.

Examining Table 8-10, we see that the initial level of ego development was significantly lower in the Sierra group than in Control Group II for the Class of 1981 (p<.05). However, the Sierra group had greater growth between fall and spring testing (p<.0019). Sex and the interaction of sex and group were also found to exert effects on student change (p<.0141 and p<.0026 respectively). Sierra men from the Class of 1981 increased in ego level (from I-3 to I-3/4), while Sierra women and students of both sexes in Control Group II declined slightly.

Psychological Sense of Community
(Environmental Assessment Inventory)

Table 8-11 displays the results of the analysis of covariance

TABLE 8-10
MEAN TEST SCORES AND REPEATED MEASURES ANALYSIS OF
VARIANCE FOR THE WASHINGTON UNIVERSITY SENTENCE
COMPLETION TEST FOR MEASURING EGO DEVELOPMENT
FOR THE CLASS OF 1981 COMPARING SIERRA AND CONTROL
GROUP II

	n[1]	Mean Pre-test Score	Mean Post-test Score
Class of 1981			
Sierra Males	16	4.19[2]	5.13
Control Males	13	5.31	5.00
Sierra Females	18	5.06	4.89
Control Females	16	5.38	5.19

Repeated Measures Analysis of Variance

	Degrees of Freedom	F Value	Significance
Group	1	4.23	.0442
Sex	1	1.28	ns[3]
Group x Sex	1	.23	ns
Change over Time	1	.50	ns
Change over Time x Group	1	10.60	.0019
Change over Time x Sex	1	6.40	.0141
Change over Time x Group x Sex	1	9.92	.0026

[1]n's are smaller than reported elsewhere because the repeated-measures-analysis-of-variance requires that complete data (all testing times) be available for all subjects used; hence, subjects on whom we have incomplete data are not used in this analysis.
[2]Key to numbers:

1 = I-2	6 = I-4
2 = Δ	7 = I-4/5
3 = Δ/3	8 = I-5
4 = I-3	9 = I-5/6
5 = I-3/4	10 = I-6

[3]ns = not significant at the .05 level of confidence.

(utilizing adjusted gain scores) to compare the three groups on the measure of psychological sense of community.

Information presented on this table indicates that Sierra and Lago students both reported experiencing less of a psychological sense of community than they had anticipated. There were significant cohort (class) differences ($p < .0001$), with the Class of

TABLE 8-11
ANALYSIS OF COVARIANCE USING ADJUSTED GAIN SCORES[1]
FOR THE PSYCHOLOGICAL SENSE OF COMMUNITY (FROM
THE ENVIRONMENTAL ASSESSMENT INVENTORY) FOR
FRESHMEN IN THE CLASSES OF 1980, 1981, AND 1982
COMPARING SIERRA AND CONTROL GROUP I

	n	Adjusted Gain Score
Class of 1980		
Sierra Males	12	- 0.32951
Lago Males	10	- 3.63170
Sierra Females	14	3.28518
Lago Females	9	- 2.59982
Class of 1981		
Sierra Males	13	- 5.08495
Lago Males	9	-11.30879
Sierra Females	21	- 9.12185
Lago Females	15	-11.05665
Class of 1982		
Sierra Males	21	- 6.26681
Lago Males	15	- 7.35021
Sierra Females	24	- 5.40796
Lago Females	18	- 9.24355

Analysis of Covariance

	Degrees of Freedom	F Value	Significance
Group	1	7.85	.0057
Sex	1	.00	ns[2]
Class	2	12.53	.000
Group x Sex	1	.02	ns
Group x Class	2	.28	ns
Sex x Class	2	.80	ns
Group x Sex x Class	2	.81	ns

---

[1]Gain scores are adjusted for initial differences as measured by pre-test scores.
[2]ns refers to not significant at the .05 level of confidence.

1980 reporting the least discrepancy between anticipated and experienced community. Men in Sierra that year reported a decrease of only −0.33, and women reported an actual increase of +3.29. As noted earlier, it was the Sierra Class of 1980 which demonstrated the greatest increase (+11.9224) in use of principled moral reasoning (see Tables 8-7 and 8-8). For all classes combined, Sierra residents reported a significantly smaller gap ($p < .0057$) between what they expected and what they found. This difference may well reflect our deliberate attempts to achieve a high level of community within Sierra. These results, taken together, indicate that the supportive environment provided by Sierra may enhance the effect of a psychological education curriculum which attempts to raise the level of students' moral reasoning.

Discussion of Question 2

An examination of the differential effects of the Sierra treatment indicates that Sierra students accounted for most of the increase in moral reasoning (defined as percentage of principled thinking) of the combined sample. The effect of the Sierra curriculum in this respect is particularly striking because Control Group I (Lago) had a high attrition rate at post-testing; those Lago students who did complete the post-tests may not have been representative of that control group as a whole. Thus, it may well be that the difference in growth in moral reasoning between Sierra and the two control groups is underestimated.

It is not possible to comment definitively on differences in ego development among the three groups. The measure of ego development was administered to only one control group (Control Group II) with one class of students (the Class of 1981). Women in the Sierra Class of 1981 were clustered around Stage I-3/4, as were both sexes of Control Group II. That year, however, the male residents of Sierra experienced a complete stage shift from I-3 to I-3/4, a shift which is quite significant both statistically and theoretically.

These findings set the stage for a more focused look at changes occurring in the Sierra group on dimensions of character development, including moral reasoning (as percentage of principled thinking from the DIT), moral maturity (as assessed by the MJI), and ego development (as measured by the WUSCT).

3. WHAT IS THE INTERRELATIONSHIP OF THE THREE DIFFERENT MEASURES OF CHARACTER DEVELOPMENT IN COLLEGE STUDENTS?

There is no validated and reliable measurement of character development in college students. In the absence of such an instrument, we chose to administer three separate instruments which are theoretically related to character development: the Moral Judgment Interview, the Defining Issues Test, and the Washington University Sentence Completion Test. Information about them far exceeds the scientific validity and reliability of any new instrument we could have constructed as part of the Sierra Project.

We chose to use multiple proximate criteria of our central construct for two reasons: first, the reliability and validity have been established to a satisfactory level for all three proximate measures. Our second reason for using these three measures is that we expected (on theoretical grounds) a moderate degree of correlation between them, indicating that we were measuring related but not identical constructs.

Tables 8-12 and 8-13 present intercorrelation matrices reflecting the relationships among all the instruments in the Survey Design. These intercorrelations are based on the combined data from the Classes of 1980, 1981, and 1982. Table 8-12 presents the intercorrelations of the fall battery, and Table 8-13, the spring.

As inspection of Tables 8-12 and 8-13 reveals, the intercorrelations at pre-test and at post-test administrations are consistent. Moral reasoning as measured by the Defining Issues Test was correlated with moral reasoning as measured by the Moral Judgment Interview: .3927 at the pre-test and .3489 at the post-test; both correlations were significant ($p < .001$). Moral reasoning as measured by the Defining Issues Test was correlated with ego development as measured by the Washington University Sentence Completion Test: .2810 at pre-test ($p < .001$) and .2510 at the post-test ($p < .002$). The Moral Judgment Interview and the Washington University Sentence Completion Test were correlated .2512 at the pre-test ($p < .003$) and .2315 at the post-test ($p < .006$). Taken together, these modest but statistically signifi-

TABLE 8-12
INTERCORRELATIONS[1] OF ALL INSTRUMENTS
AT FALL PRE-TEST FOR ALL YEARS (CLASS OF 1980, 1981, AND 1982) COMBINED

Instruments	Rotter I-E Scale	Defining Issues Test (Rest)	Moral Judgment Interview (Kohlberg)	Bem Sex-Role Inventory -Fem. Scale	Bem Sex-Role Inventory -Masc. Scale	Wash. U. Sent. Compl. Test (Loevinger)	Keniston Alienation Scale	Janis & Field Personal. Question.	People-in-General Scale
Rotter I-E Scale	1.000 (0) s=.001	-.066 (273) s=.140	-.1058 (104) s=.143	-.0168 (300) s=.386	-.1503 (300) s=.005	-.0233 (188) s=.395	-.2122 (270) s=.001	.2527 (259) s=.001	-.2214 (267) s=.001
Defining Issues Test (Rest)		1.000 (0) s=.001	.3927 (102) s=.001	-.0686 (303) s=.117	-.0540 (303) s=.174	.2801 (136) s=.001	.0590 (267) s=.168	.0867 (257) s=.083	-.1220 (266) s=.023
Moral Judgment Interview (Kohlberg)			1.000 (0) s=.001	.1267 (115) s=.089	.1635 (115) s=.040	.2512 (119) s=.003	-.0817 (103) s=.206	.0063 (97) s=.476	-.0725 (99) s=.238
Bem Sex-Role Inventory -Fem. Scale				1.000 (0) s=.001	.0572 (336) s=.148	.0419 (154) s=.303	-.2616 (293) s=.001	.1011 (279) s=.046	.2076 (289) s=.001
Bem Sex-Role Inventory -Masc. Scale					1.000 (0) s=.001	.0155 154 .424	-.1404 (293) s=.008	-.4474 (279) s=.001	.0822 (289) s=.082
Wash. U. Sent. Compl. Test (Loevinger)						1.000 (0) s=.001	-.0467 (139) s=.293	-.0585 (128) s=.256	.0378 (134) s=.332
Keniston Alienation Scale							1.000 (0) s=.001	.1229 (279) s=.020	-.4768 (289) s=.001
Janis & Field Personality Questionnaire								1.0000 (0) s=.001	.1238 (275) s=.020
People-in-General Scale									1.000 (0) s=.001

[1]Format for each cell is as follows: Pearson correlation/(n)/significance.

cant interrelations reflect a degree of overlap on an empirical level which is consistent with the measures' overlap on a theoretical level.

TABLE 8-13
INTERCORRELATIONS' OF ALL INSTRUMENTS
AT SPRING POST-TEST FOR ALL YEARS (CLASS OF 1980, 1981, AND 1982) COMBINED

Instruments	Rotter I-E Scale	Defining Issues Test (Rest)	Moral Judgment Interview (Kohlberg)	Bem Sex-Role Inventory -Fem. Scale	Bem Sex-Role Inventory -Masc. Scale	Wash. U. Sent. Compl. Test (Loevinger)	Keniston Alienation Scale	Janis & Field Personal. Question.	People-In-General Scale
Rotter I-E Scale	1.000 (0) s=.001	-.1442 (266) s=.009	-.2292 (119) s=.006	.0847 (290) s=.075	-.2611 (290) s=.001	-.0536 (144) s=.262	.1686 (258) s=.003	.2790 (254) s=.001	-.1238 (254) s=.024
Defining Issues Test (Rest)		1.000 (0) s=.001	.3489 (112) s=.001	-.0088 (284) s=.442	-.0198 (284) s=.370	.2510 (131) s=.002	-.0671 (250) s=.145	.0626 (248) s=.163	-.0606 (248) s=.171
Moral Judgment Interview (Kohlberg)			1.0000 (0) s=.001	-.0464 (123) s=.305	.2148 (123) s=.009	.2315 (118) s=.006	.1150 (107) s=.119	-.1113 (105) s=.129	.0352 (106) s=.360
Bem Sex-Role Inventory -Fem. Scale				1.000 (0) s=.001	.0149 (312) s=.397	.0727 (148) s=.190	-.3063 (274) s=.001	.0987 (270) s=.053	.3126 (270) s=.001
Bem Sex-Role Inventory -Masc. Scale					1.000 (0) s=.001	-.0321 (148) s=.349	-.0670 (274) s=.135	-.5369 (270) s=.001	.0512 (270) s=.201
Wash. U. Sent. Compl. Test (Loevinger)						1.000 (0) s=.001	-.0855 (132) s=.165	.0802 (131) s=.181	.1966 (130) s=.012
Keniston Alienation Scale							1.000 (0) s=.001	.1509 (275) s=.006	-.5916 (275) s=.001
Janis & Field Personality Questionnaire								1.0000 (0) s=.001	-.1074 (271) s=.039
People-In-General Scale									1.0000 (0) s=.001

'Format for each cell is as follows: Pearson correlation/(n)/significance.

4. WITHIN THE SIERRA HALL GROUP, WHAT CHANGES OCCURRED DURING THE FRESHMAN YEAR ON THE MEASURES OF CHARACTER DEVELOPMENT?

Due to fiscal constraints, the experimental group was the only group to receive the Moral Judgment Interview and the Washington University Sentence Completion Test.[4] Consequently, we do not have adequate data about some patterns of character development to make comparisons among the three groups or to generalize beyond the Sierra group.

Ego Development in Sierra Hall (WUSCT)

The results from our testing with the measures of ego development and moral maturity (MJI) give us a greater understanding of the character development in Sierra Hall students. Table 8-14 presents the pre- and post-test measurement of ego development in Sierra freshmen.

Examining Table 8-14, we see the mean scores for all three Sierra freshman classes clustered between Stages I-3 and I-3/4. The levels of these Sierra students would therefore be described in the following terms:

I-3: Conformist Stage

Acceptance by group (defined narrowly) is very important, with disapproval a powerful punishment. Compliance with rules is the basis for right and wrong. Individual differences are not perceived. Conformity is the norm. Sex roles are stereotyped.

I-3/4: Self-aware Level

(Transition from conformist to conscientious stages). Awareness of self is perceived in relation to the group, with the recognition that one does not always live up to group norms. Inner life is recognized but still stereotypically viewed. Alternatives and exceptions are allowed, but in terms of stereo-

---

[4]The only exception was the administration of the Washington University Sentence Completion Test to Control Group II (Random Control) in the Class of 1981 when resources were available (see Table 8-10).

> types, not in terms of individual differences (Modal level for adults in this society).
> (Adapted from Loevinger & Wessler, 1970 and Loevinger, 1976)

In both Stage I-3 and Level I-3/4, internalized rule-making (which involves evaluation and choice) has not yet been established. In other words, neither stage provides the mature ego development necessary for full transition from conventional to post-conventional moral reasoning.

There were no cohort differences in ego development within Sierra Hall. There was, however, a significant increase in ego development between the pre-test and the post-test ($p < .001$). The amount of change was not great, but there was a consistent pattern of gradual growth for both men and women, with the exception of women in the Class of 1981. This increase was somewhat greater for men ($p < .0184$).

Moral Maturity in Sierra Hall (MJI)

Table 8-15 indicates the mean test scores and summarizes the results of the RMAV exploring moral reasoning (using the Moral Judgment Interview) for each Sierra Class.

Table 8-15 discloses that the mean scores for all three classes clustered around a Moral Maturity Score (MMS) of 300, or Stage 3, on both testing occasions. According to the results of this measurement of moral reasoning, Sierra freshmen spent their first year of college study solidly rooted in a conventional mode of thinking which places heavy emphasis on the opinions of those around them.

While there was a consistent and significant finding that moral maturity as measured by the MJI increased during the freshman year ($p < .0001$), the amount of change was not great. There was also a significant interaction between year (class) and sex ($p < .0356$), though effects for factors of year or sex alone failed to reach significance. This small but consistent pattern of upward growth is similar to the trends exhibited by the DIT measure of moral reasoning.

TABLE 8-14
MEAN TEST SCORES AND REPEATED MEASURES ANALYSIS OF VARIANCE FOR THE WASHINGTON UNIVERSITY SENTENCE COMPLETION TEST FOR MEASURING EGO DEVELOPMENT[1] FOR THE SIERRA CLASSES OF 1980, 1981, AND 1982

	n^2	Mean Pre-test Score	Mean Post-test Score
Class of 1980			
Sierra Males	19	4.63[3]	4.90
Sierra Females	20	4.55	4.70
Class of 1981			
Sierra Males	16	4.19	5.13
Sierra Females	18	5.06	4.89
Class of 1982			
Sierra Males	21	4.14	4.62
Sierra Females	25	4.48	4.76
ALL GROUPS $\overline{X}$	119	4.50	4.82

Repeated Measures Analysis of Variance

	Degrees of Freedom	F Value	Significance
Class	2	1.23	ns[4]
Sex	1	.69	ns
Class x Sex	2	.69	ns
Change over Time	1	10.78	.0014
Change over Time x Class	2	.35	ns
Change over Time x Sex	1	5.72	.0184
Change over Time x Class x Sex	2	2.41	(.09) ns

---

[1]Given to Sierra Hall (experimental group) only except for the Control Group II (Random Control) of the Class of 1981 (see table 8-10).

[2]n's are smaller than reported elsewhere because the repeated-measures-analysis-of-variance requires that complete data (all testing times) be available for all subjects used; hence, subjects on whom we have incomplete data are not used in this analysis.

[3] Key to numbers:

1 = I-2	6 = I-4
2 = Δ	7 = I-4/5
3 = Δ/3	8 = I-5
4 = I-3	9 = I-5/6
5 = I-3/4	10 = I-6

[4]ns = not significant at the .05 level of confidence.

TABLE 8-15
MEAN SCALES SCORES AND REPEATED MEASURES ANALYSIS OF VARIANCE RESULTS FOR THE MORAL JUDGMENT INTERVIEW MEASURE OF MORAL REASONING [1] FOR THE SIERRA HALL CLASSES OF 1980, 1981, and 1982

	n[2]	Mean Pre-test Score	Mean Post-test Score
Class of 1980			
Sierra Males	22	322.64	329.09
Sierra Females	19	298.32	311.37
Class of 1981			
Sierra Males	17	307.47	327.59
Sierra Females	23	322.00	329.44
Class of 1982			
Sierra Males	18	309.83	322.44
Sierra Females	21	316.24	316.29
ALL GROUPS $\overline{X}$	120	313.48	322.90

Repeated Measures Analysis of Variance

	Degrees of Freedom	F Value	Significance
Class	2	.69	ns[3]
Sex	1	.80	ns
Class x Sex	2	3.44	.0356
Change over Time	1	19.84	.000
Change over Time x Class	2	.91	ns
Change over Time x Sex	1	1.91	ns
Change over Time x Class x Sex	2	2.09	ns

[1]Given to Sierra Hall (experimental group) only.
[2]n's are smaller than reported elsewhere because the repeated-measures-analysis-of-variance requires that complete data (all testing times) be available for all subjects used; hence, subjects on whom we have incomplete data are not used in this analysis.
[3]ns = not significant at the .05 level of confidence.

Principled Thinking in Sierra Hall (DIT)

Earlier we presented the results of the principled thinking scores on the Defining Issues Test (DIT)—see Tables 8-1, 8-7, 8-8, and 8-9. The Sierra classes increased their percent of principled thinking over the course of the freshman year as follows: the Class of 1980 increased 11.9224; the Class of 1981, 2.8989; and the Class of 1982, 2.9597. The average increase for the three Sierra classes combined was 6.2662.

Discussion of Question 4

The increase in principled thinking among Sierra students closely parallels their increase in moral maturity as assessed by our other measure of moral reasoning, the MJI. Taken together, these two measures confirm a pattern also reflected in Sierra students' growth in ego: the freshman year in Sierra produced moderate, consistent increases on all three dimensions of character development.

5. ARE THERE PATTERNS OF DEVELOPMENTAL CHANGE DURING THE FRESHMAN YEAR WHICH ARE RELATED TO LEVEL OF MORAL REASONING OR EGO DEVELOPMENT?

The results presented in this section will be based on the three measures of character administered to the Sierra students: the two measures of moral reasoning (the Defining Issues Test and the Moral Judgment Interview) and the measure of ego development (the Washington University Sentence Completion Test).

Rest outlines several strategies for using the Defining Issues Test to analyze developmental change in longitudinal studies. In an earlier section, we discussed our use of one of these methods — namely, that of looking for differences in average P-score, both by group and by sex. Another method is to examine the distribution of scores at the various stages and determine how these distributions shift from pre- to post-test for each group. We have taken three approaches to examining shifts in distributions. The first approach is to design a simple visual representation illustrating the percentage of thinking at each stage at the pre-test and at the post-test. As an example, Tables 8-16, 8-17, and 8-18 provide this visual representation for the 1980 Sierra, Control Group I, and Control Group II populations.

TABLE 8.16
SHIFT IN MORAL REASONING STAGE DISTRIBUTION AS
MEASURED BY THE DEFINING ISSUES TEST FOR SIERRA
RESIDENTS IN THE CLASS OF 1980

Stage	Pre-test	Post-test
2	6.85	6.56
3	15.83	13.58
4	30.95	27.33
5A	22.74	26.87
5B	5.65	8.39
6	5.83	7.03
A	5.89	5.36
M	4.11	4.88

Solid — pre-test
Dotted — post-test   n = 28

TABLE 8.17
**SHIFT IN MORAL REASONING STAGE DISTRIBUTION AS
MEASURED BY THE DEFINING ISSUES TEST FOR CONTROL
GROUP I IN THE CLASS OF 1980**

Stage	Pre-test	Post-test
2	5.60	5.88
3	14.26	12.99
4	33.47	31.17
5A	25.04	27.48
5B	7.31	6.32
6	4.72	4.39
A	5.35	6.32
M	4.24	5.44

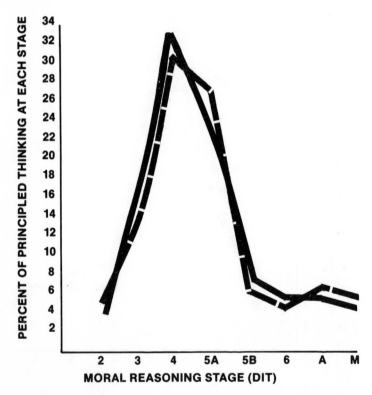

Solid — pre-test
Dotted — post-test   n = 19

TABLE 8-18
**SHIFT IN MORAL REASONING STAGE DISTRIBUTION AS MEA-
SURED BY THE DEFINING ISSUES TEST FOR CONTROL GROUP
II (RANDOM CONTROL) IN THE CLASS OF 1980**

Stage	Pre-test	Post-test
2	9.44	9.57
3	15.74	14.80
4	29.44	26.47
5A	27.41	27.54
5B	4.72	7.19
6	3.89	4.68
A	4.63	4.74
M	4.72	5.01

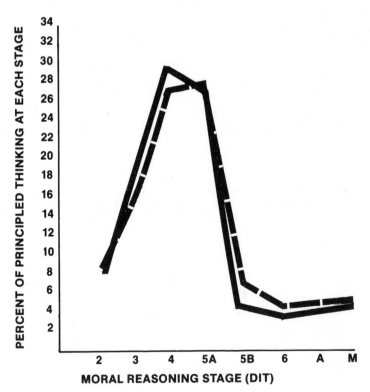

Solid — pre-test
Dotted — post-test   n = 18

These tables reveal a pattern of declining use of Stage 4 and increasing use of Stage 5 moral reasoning. A similar trend is illustrated in the second approach which indicates the direction of change in percentage of moral reasoning at each stage for each group. Table 8-19 shows the change at each stage for each group and class.

Table 8-19 reveals no consistent pattern of change in percentage of moral reasoning at Stages 2, 3, 6, and A, though there is a consistent decline in use of moral reasoning at Stage 4 (morality of law-and-order) for most freshmen. (The exception is Control Group II for 1981 and 1982). Sierra Hall residents showed an increase in the use of principled moral reasoning at both Stage 5A (social contract-voluntary commitments) and Stage 5B (social contract-procedural justice). Such a consistent pattern of change did not appear in the two control groups, though Lago residents did increase in percent of Stage 5A (social contract-voluntary commitments) thinking each year.

Tables 8-16 through 8-19 simply illustrate changes in percentage of moral reasoning at each stage. We can also analyze shifts in distribution statistically. It was not possible to use the repeated measures analysis of variance or analysis of

TABLE 8-19
INCREASES (+) (-) IN PERCENT OF THINKING AT DIFFERENT STAGES ON THE DEFINING ISSUES TEST, GROUPED BY THE CLASSES OF 1980, 1981, AND 1982

n = 28

Stage	Sierra			Control I (Lago)			Control II (Random Control)		
	1980	1981	1982	1980	1981	1982	1980	1981	1982
2	-	+	-	+	-	-	+	-	-
3	-	+	-	-	-	+	-	+	-
4	-	-	-	-	-	-	-	+	+
5A	+	+	+	+	+	+	+	-	-
5B	+	+	+	-	+	nc	+	-	+
6	+	-	+	-	-	+	+	-	+
A	-	nc	-	+	+	-	+	-	+

[1]nc indicates no change.

TABLE 8-20
MEAN STAGE SCORES[1] AND MULTIPLE ANALYSIS OF VARIANCE RESULTS FOR THE SHIFT IN DISTRIBUTION OF PERCENTAGE OF MORAL REASONING AT DIFFERENT STAGES, USING THE DEFINING ISSUES TEST, FOR THE CLASSES OF 1980, 1981, AND 1982 BY GROUP

	n[2]	Stage 2 change	Stage 3 change	Stage 4 change	Stage 5A change	Stage 5B change	Stage 6 change	Stage A[3] change
Class of 1980								
Sierra	28	-.29	-2.25	-5.77	4.13	2.74	1.19	-.53
Lago	19	.27	-1.27	-2.29	2.44	-.99	-.34	.97
Control II	18	.13	-.94	-2.98	.13	2.47	.80	-1.09
Class of 1981								
Sierra	16	1.46	1.56	-6.46	2.92	1.45	-1.56	.00
Lago	12	-.28	-1.53	-7.50	7.08	2.08	-1.95	.42
Control II	13	-.26	3.08	3.33	-3.21	-1.03	-3.33	-1.28
Class of 1982								
Sierra	25	-.27	-2.07	-.53	2.00	1.07	.20	-.87
Lago	20	-.67	.08	-1.58	.67	.00	2.75	-.83
Control II	22	-1.71	-1.98	1.35	-3.69	2.22	.62	.23

Multiple Analysis of Variance:

	df	F	Significance
Class	14	1.388	ns[4]
Group	14	1.420	ns
Class x Group	28	.894	ns

[1]Scores shown reflect the changes between pre-test and post-test.

[2]n's are smaller than reported elsewhere because persons for whom we had incomplete data were deleted; also deleted were persons who had high M (inconsistency check) scores.

[3]Stage A scores were included in this analysis because of their potential theoretical importance; on a practical level, on some subjects' protocols, Stage A contributed as much as 25%.

[4]ns = not significant at the .05 level of confidence.

covariance using adjusted gain scores to examine these changes because comparisons between non-independent stages violate assumptions necessary to properly interpret the results of these statistical procedures. We performed a multiple analysis of variance (Cramer, 1974) to analyze changes from pre- to post-test. Table 8-20 presents the results of the multiple analysis of variance (MANOVA) by group and by class. Consideration of Table 8-20 indicates that the degree to which different stages of moral reasoning are used, based on analysis by class, group, or interaction of class and group, failed to reach significance.

Descriptive and statistical analyses of the distribution of class and group scores at the various stages have not revealed conclusive differences. It is clear that the freshmen in our sample use less Stage 4 reasoning and more Stage 5 reasoning after a year of college, and that Sierra residents use consistently more 5A and 5B reasoning than students in the control groups. The one statistical approach we employed (MANOVA) may not have had all of its assumptions met (independence of variables), since the percent of moral reasoning at one stage is not independent from the percent of moral reasoning at another. This area of research needs further inquiry.

Our final approach to detecting patterns of change in our three measures of character involves relating initial levels of character development to the subsequent post-test scores on the Defining Issues Test, the Moral Judgment Interview, and the Washington University Sentence Completion Test. For illustrative purposes, the following tables displaying the data from these analyses refer to the combined scores of the Sierra Classes of 1980, 1981, and 1982. Table 8-21 shows change in moral reasoning as measured by the Moral Maturity Score (MMS) of the Moral Judgment Interview (MJI) when subjects are grouped by their initial levels of ego development.

These data illustrate a general, consistent upward growth in students' moral reasoning, irrespective of initial ego stage. However, students at a lower ego stage tend to have lower scores on moral reasoning (defined as moral maturity).

Change in moral reasoning (as measured by the P-score, reflecting percentage of principled reasoning, on the Defining Issues Test) can also be investigated in relation to initial level of

TABLE 8-21
CHANGES IN MORAL MATURITY (MJI) SCORES FROM PRE-TEST TO POST-TEST WHEN SUBJECTS ARE GROUPED BY INITIAL STAGES OF EGO DEVELOPMENT (WUSCT) FOR THE SIERRA CLASSES OF 1980, 1981, and 1982

	EGO STAGES	MJI	
n	pre	pre $\overline{x}$	post $\overline{x}$
2	2	260.0	280.0
5	Δ	310.2	324.2
10	Δ/3	292.1	321.3
25	3	319.6	318.5
62	3/4	315.2	325.2
13	4	315.9	326.4
1	5	344.0	367.0

118 = n Total
8 missing cases

TABLE 8-22
**CHANGES IN DIT PERCENT OF PRINCIPLED REASONING FROM
PRE-TEST TO POST-TEST WHEN SUBJECTS ARE GROUPED BY
INITIAL STAGES OF EGO DEVELOPMENT (WUSCT) FOR THE
SIERRA CLASSES OF 1980, 1981, and 1982**

	EGO STAGES	DIT	
n	pre	pre $\bar{x}$	post $\bar{x}$
2	2	22.5	37.5
4	Δ	39.1	36.3
7	Δ/3	30.0	31.9
19	3	29.7	31.0
57	3/4	36.4	42.9
15	4	43.3	44.7
1	5	57.0	72.0

105 = n Total
31 missing cases

TABLE 8-23
CHANGES IN EGO DEVELOPMENT (WUSCT) SCORES FROM PRE-TEST TO POST-TEST WHEN SUBJECTS ARE GROUPED BY INITIAL MORAL MATURITY SCORE (MJI) FOR THE SIERRA CLASSES OF 1980, 1981, and 1982

	MJI	EGO DEVELOPMENT	
n	pre	pre $\bar{x}$	post $\bar{x}$
1	211-230	5.00	5.00
4	231-250	3.25	3.50
3	251-270	1.67	4.33
8	271-290	4.63	5.13
38	291-310	4.53	4.87
36	311-330	4.53	4.64
15	331-350	5.07	5.33
5	351-370	4.20	4.40
1	371-390	5.00	5.00
1	>390	5.00	5.00

112 Valid
24 missing

TABLE 8.24
**CHANGES IN EGO DEVELOPMENT (WUSCT) SCORES FROM
PRE-TEST TO POST-TEST WHEN SUBJECTS ARE GROUPED BY
INITIAL PERCENTAGE OF PRINCIPLED THINKING (DIT) FOR
THE SIERRA CLASSES OF 1980, 1981, and 1982**

n	DIT pre	EGO DEVELOPMENT pre $\bar{x}$	post $\bar{x}$
11	<20	4.27	4.27
14	$20 \leqslant x < 25$	4.57	4.57
15	$25 \leqslant x < 30$	4.40	4.80
13	$30 \leqslant x < 35$	4.00	4.23
14	$35 \leqslant x < 40$	4.71	5.07
8	$40 \leqslant x < 45$	5.00	5.50
10	$45 \leqslant x < 50$	4.70	5.10
18	>50	4.90	5.20

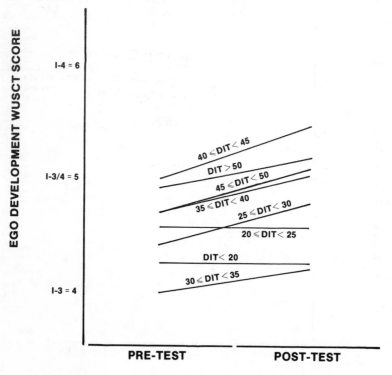

103 Valid
33 missing

ego development. Table 8-22 presents the data for the Sierra freshmen in the Classes of 1980, 1981, and 1982. This table identifies for principled thinking the same general upward trend we observed for moral maturity when students were grouped by initial levels of ego development. The rare exceptions to this were the four individuals in the Classes of 1980 and 1982 who scored at the Delta (δ) stage on ego development at the pre-test and who declined during the year on moral reasoning. The small number (4) of these individuals in our sample for the Classes of 1980, 1981, and 1982, who have completed pre-test and post-test DIT's, precludes generalization.

As a final analysis, we studied change in ego development, when students are grouped by initial level of moral reasoning, first using moral maturity (MJI) then principled thinking (DIT). Tables 8-23 and 8-24 present the data for the Sierra freshman Classes of 1980, 1981, and 1982.

Except when cell sizes were too small for generalization, there did seem to be a persistent relationship between ego development and moral reasoning. There was moderate upward movement in ego development when subjects were grouped by initial level of moral reasoning—irrespective of whether the measure of moral reasoning was moral maturity (MJI) or principled thinking (DIT).

SUMMARY

This chapter, presenting the results of our analysis of the data collected as part of the Survey Design, was organized around two different sets of questions. We will now summarize our results in the same format.

1. Are there changes during the freshman year which appear common to all of the groups sampled?

Yes. Freshmen as a whole made moderate gains in moral reasoning as reflected in their increasing use of principled thinking over the course of their first year of study. On the other measures collected, we also found a pattern over the course of the freshman year:

- · Psychological Sense of Community — students perceived less community than they had expected.
- · Alienation — female students were less alienated than male students, but there were no differences between cohorts or test administrations. Results were generally inconclusive.
- · Self-esteem — there were no significant cohort, sex, or test administration differences.
- · Attitude toward People — freshmen became less positive toward people over the course of their first year in college.
- · Sex Roles — there were no changes on this measure.

2. Are there changes during the freshman year which are different for students in Sierra Hall (the experimental group) than for students in the two control groups?

The analysis of covariance of the adjusted gain scores from the measures administered as part of the Survey Design indicates that there were differences in self-esteem and in moral reasoning (percent of principled thinking) but no further differences between Sierra and the two control groups. The Sierra group and Control Group I (Lago) increased in self-esteem while Control Group II (Random Control) declined markedly.

In percent of principled thinking, there was an adjusted gain score change of +6.2662 when all Sierra classes were combined. In comparison, Control Group I changed +3.1606 and Control Group II +1.2887. The Sierra scores were significantly different than the scores of the control groups ($p < .02$). Apparently, the psychological intervention moderately facilitated the character development of these college freshmen during a period in their lives which would otherwise already have included a small but persistent improvement in level of moral reasoning.

3. What is the empirical interrelationship of the three different measures of character development in college students?

There is a moderate correlation (.39 at the pre-test and .35 at the post-test) between the two measures of moral reasoning.

Ego development also correlates moderately with moral maturity as measured by the MJI (.25 at the pre-test and .23 at the post-test), and with percent of principled thinking in moral reasoning as measured by the DIT (.28 at the pre-test and .25 at the post-test).

4. Within the Sierra Hall group, what changes occurred during the freshman year on the measures of character development?

The three measures of character development (principled thinking, moral maturity, and ego development) all indicate that Sierra freshmen grew during the year. In terms of their ego development stage, the residents of Sierra clustered between I-3 and I-3/4. The stage clustering represents a range from conformity (compliance with rules and stereotypic sex roles) to a transition state in which alternatives and exceptions are allowed but remain stereotypic. Taken together, Sierra students increased their mean level of ego development from 4.50 to 4.82 (when 4.0 = Stage I-3 and 5.0 = Level I-3/4). This increase was significant (p<.0014). However, neither Stage I-3 nor Level I-3/4 represents the level of ego development necessary for students to make a complete transition from conventional to post-conventional moral reasoning.

On both testing occasions, the mean moral maturity (MJI) scores for all three classes clustered at 300, or Stage 3. Throughout the freshman year, students relied on conventional thinking, focusing on the opinions of those around them. While moral maturity was consistently greater by the end of the freshman year (p<.0001), the improvement was quite small in absolute terms—from 313.45 to 322.90. A small but consistent pattern of moral growth was also found by the principled thinking assessment of the DIT.

5. Are there patterns of developmental change during the freshman year which are related to the level of moral reasoning or ego development?

Freshmen as a group consistently declined in the percentage of Stage 4 thinking they exhibited when completing the DIT. Some groups increased their percentage of thinking at higher levels — at Stage 5A (social contract-voluntary commitments and

Stage 5B (social contract-procedural justice) — with the Sierra group increasing the most consistently.

Exploring the relationship between initial levels on specific dimensions of character and growth in other aspects of character we find that, when subjects are grouped by initial level of ego development, there are consistent patterns of growth during the freshman year in both principled thinking (DIT) and moral maturity (MJI); when subjects are grouped by initial level of moral reasoning (either principled thinking or moral maturity), there is an apparent pattern of growth discernible in ego development as well.

References

Bem, S. L. The measurement of psychological androgyny. *Journal of Counseling and Clinical Psychology*, 1974, *42*(2), 155-162.

Cramer, E. M. *Revised MANOVA program*. Chapel Hill, NC: L. L. Thurstone Psychometric Laboratory, University of North Carolina at Chapel Hill, 1974.

Hendrix, L. J., Carter, M. W., & Hintze, J. L. A comparison of five statistical methods of analyzing pretest-posttest designs. *Journal of Experimental Education*, 1978, *47*(2), 96-102.

Jenrich, R., & Sampson, P. Analysis of variance and covariance including repeated measures. In W. J. Dixon & M. B. Brown (Eds.), *BMDP-79: Biomedical computer programs p-series*. Berkeley: University of California Press, 1979, 540-580.

Kaplan, A. G. Psychological androgyny: Further considerations. *Psychology of Women*, 1979, *3*(3), 221-319.

Loevinger, J. *Ego development: Conceptions and theories*. San Francisco: Jossey-Bass, 1976.

Loevinger, J., & Wessler, R. *Measuring ego development* (Vol. I): *Construction of a sentence completion test*. San Francisco: Jossey-Bass, 1970.

Chapter 9

AN EVALUATION OF THE DIFFERENTIAL IMPACT OF A DEVELOPMENTAL CURRICULUM ON STUDENTS WITH VARYING PERSONALITY PROFILES

Holly Axtelle Magaña

In most evaluation studies, the evaluator examines the effect of a particular curriculum or intervention on an aggregated group of individuals. Rarely does the investigator analyze whether the intervention has had a different impact on different types of individuals. The present study is an attempt to do just this. By separating students into four clusters, based on differences in their personality profiles before participating in the curriculum, this study can then explore whether there are significant differences among the groups in the type of change displayed after their involvement in the curriculum.

The students in this study are separated into four clusters on the basis of differences in their pattern of scores on a series of developmental and personality measures. These measures were administered at the beginning of the academic year, before the students' involvement in the Sierra Project curriculum had begun, and again at the end of the academic year, after the completion of their involvement in the curriculum. The students are separated into clusters on the basis of their scores at the beginning of the year. A statistical procedure (hierarchical clustering analysis) is used to generate the four clusters, such that each cluster contains individuals who display a distinct pattern of scores on the personality measures. Data on the students' degree

173

of change after their year-long involvement in the developmental curriculum is then analyzed in order to test for differences among the clusters of students. These results reveal significant differences in degree of growth in moral reasoning skills. This chapter attempts to explain these differences in light of the original differences in the personality profiles of students in each of the four clusters.

SUBJECTS

The subjects of this study were 48 freshmen at the University of California, Irvine: 18 males and 30 females. The 48 students in this study come from two sub-samples of 24 students each. The first sub-sample consists of Sierra students from the Class of 1980, while the second consists of Sierra students from the Class of 1981.

MEASURES

The students were administered a series of psychological measures in the fall before the term began, and again in the spring at the end of the academic year. These measures were designed to assess a variety of dimensions which have been considered important in the character development of young adults (Whiteley, 1980). The measures used in this study are as follows:[1]

1. Moral Judgment Interview (Kohlberg, 1973);

2. Defining Issues Test (Rest, 1973);

3. Washington University Sentence Completion Test for Measuring Ego Development (Loevinger, 1966; Loevinger & Wessler, 1970);

[1]A description of these instruments appears in Chapter 7 and in a paper deposited in the Henry Murray Research Center, Radcliffe College, 10 Garden Street, Cambridge, MA 02138. This paper, written by Holly Axtelle Magaña, describes each of the measures and provides a discussion of current reliability and validity studies of these measures.

4. Bem Sex-Role Inventory (Bem, 1974): Masculine Scale, Feminine Scale;

5. Rotter Internal-External Control Scale (Rotter, 1966);

6. "People in General" Scale (Stokols, 1975);

7. Janis and Field Personality Questionnaire (Hovland & Janis, 1959); and

8. Keniston Alienation Scale (Keniston, 1965).

THE PROCEDURE FOR SEPARATING STUDENTS INTO CLUSTERS

The first step in the analysis was to separate the students into subgroups, each having a distinct pattern of scores on the personality measures which were administered at the beginning of the year. This was done using Johnson's hierarchical clustering analysis (Johnson, 1967). However, before submitting the data to the clustering procedure, it was necessary to standardize the scores and to compute a similarity matrix.

The data was standardized using a normalization procedure developed by Mosteller (1968). The raw data was placed in a matrix where the rows represented each of the 48 subjects and the columns represented each of the eight psychological measures. This matrix was then normalized using the Mosteller procedure which equalizes the row and column marginals in data matrices.

It was necessary to equalize the column marginals in order that scores on each of the instruments would be on equal scales. The row marginals were also equalized because it has been suggested that when analyzing profile data, the overall level of a subject's profile is only interpretable if all of the measures in the profile concern the same domain of behavior and are pointed in the same direction, i.e., a high score is always positive (Nunnally, 1978). The measures used in this study concern somewhat different domains of behavior and, in some cases, are not clearly pointed in one direction or the other; that is, for some of the measures, such as the locus of control scale and the feminine and masculine scores of the sex-role scale, one end of the continuum is not necessarily more positive or negative than the other end. Since this is the case, it is necessary to equalize the overall level of each profile which, in effect, means equalizing the row totals of the data matrix. Mosteller's normalization procedure was chosen since it appeared to be the best method to use for standardizing both the rows and the columns of the subject-by-instrument data matrix. The applicability of this normalization procedure to various problems in the social sciences has been demonstrated by Romney (1971, 1976) and Romney, Kieffer, and Klein (1973).

Before submitting the data to the clustering analysis, it was necessary to compute a measure of the similarity between all possible pairs of profiles. It has been widely concluded that the best measure of profile similarity is the distance score (Cronbach & Gleser, 1953; Nunnally, 1962; Osgood & Suci, 1952; Sawrey, Keller, & Conger, 1960). Using this measure, the k scores of an individual's profile are considered as the coordinates of a point in k-dimensional space. The similarity between the profiles of any two individuals is simply the linear distance between their respective points. This distance is most commonly computed by taking the square root of the sum of the squared differences between scores on each instrument. By using the distance score as a measure of dissimilarity among all possible pairs of subjects' profiles, a new subject-by-subject dissimilarity matrix is computed, and this matrix is used as the input to the clustering program.

The primary function of hierarchical clustering analysis is to display the natural clustering of objects (or, in this case, subjects) into groups. The clustering procedure works by examining the dissimilarity matrix in search of the smallest distance between any two objects. When it finds the smallest distance, it joins the two objects connected by that distance into the first cluster. Then the distance matrix is recomputed using the new cluster as if it were one object in the matrix, again searching for the smallest distance and thereby forming the next cluster. The next cluster may be formed either by joining the previously made cluster to another object or by joining together two other objects or clusters of objects. This method of clustering analysis is hierarchical in nature because each clustering is obtained through the merging of clusters at the previous level. In the first step, each object defines a cluster. In the last step, the entire group of objects defines the largest cluster.

RESULTS OF SUBJECT CLUSTERING

The cluster analysis produced a hierarchical tree structure (see Figure 9-1) which first divided subjects into two distinct groups, and then divided each of these two groups into two approximately equal subgroups. Each of these four groups was then further subdivided into smaller divisions until, at the lowest level, each subject represented a separate unit. For the purpose of this study only the four main clusters will be examined. The subjects were divided almost evenly between these four clusters, which had n's of 11, 11, 14, and 12.

A series of one-way analyses of variance were performed in order to determine whether the clusters differed significantly on each of the nine measures. The results from this analysis are reported in Table 9-1. Significant differences among the clusters were found on the Defining Issues Test (DIT) of moral reasoning, the Keniston Alienation Scale, the I-E locus of control scale, the "People in General" Scale on attitudes toward people, the moral maturity score on the Moral Judgment Interview, and the Washington University Sentence Completion Test. There were no significant inter-cluster differences on the Janis and Field Personality Inventory, the Bem Femininity Scale, or the Bem Masculinity Scale.

Table 9-2 shows the mean scores for each cluster on each of the six instruments on which significant intercluster differences had been found in the previous analysis. In addition, the overall mean for each instrument is reported at the bottom of Table 9-2. Individuals in cluster one have slightly higher than average moral reasoning and ego development scores. Their attitude toward people score is extremely high and they are very low on the alienation scale. Cluster two subjects are differentiated by their extremely high moral reasoning and ego development scores and their extreme internality on the locus of control measure. Individuals in cluster three are highly alienated and have an extremely negative attitude toward people. The remainder of their scores are average with the exception of their moral maturity score which is well below the mean. Cluster four individuals are distinguished by their low moral reasoning and ego development scores and their extremely external locus of control.

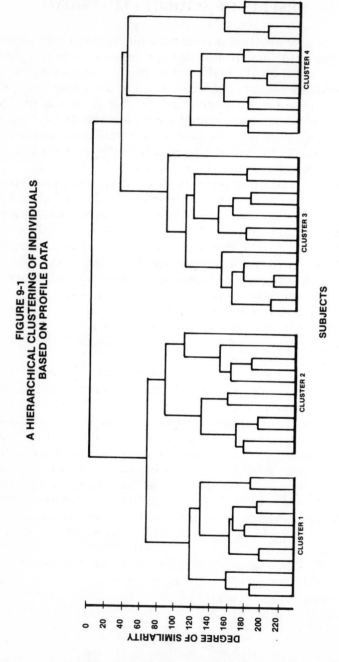

FIGURE 9-1
A HIERARCHICAL CLUSTERING OF INDIVIDUALS
BASED ON PROFILE DATA

TABLE 9-1
DIFFERENCES AMONG THE CLUSTERS ON PRE-TEST
MEANS ON EACH INSTRUMENT

	Cluster (N)			
	1 (11)	2 (11)	3 (14)	4 (12)
DIT—Moral Reasoning				
mean	40.6	55.7	35.3	22.3
s.d.	8.7	8.2	11.6	7.6
$F = 25.44***$				
Alienation				
mean	18.7	28.2	40.3	29.6
s.d.	3.6	7.3	5.0	9.5
$F = 21.57***$				
Locus of Control				
mean	10.3	5.6	12.0	15.2
s.d.	3.3	2.2	3.5	2.7
$F = 20.43***$				
"People in General" Scale				
mean	63.36	50.27	48.07	54.42
s.d.	6.77	8.67	7.04	9.46
$F = 8.29***$				
Ego Development				
mean	176.45	177.73	164.64	161.33
s.d.	13.34	19.65	13.67	15.43
$F = 3.30*$				
Kohlberg Moral Judgment Interview				
mean	323.91	336.82	307.14	306.25
s.d.	26.90	31.99	26.51	26.47
$F = 3.24*$				
Sex Roles (masculine scale)				
mean	4.63	4.88	4.34	5.00
s.d.	.74	.83	.51	.91
$F = 2.00$ n.s.				
Sex Roles (feminine scale)				
mean	5.29	5.01	4.76	5.11
s.d.	.43	.46	.67	.64
$F = 1.87$ n.s.				
Self-esteem[1]				
mean	37.7	39.0	45.4	42.4
s.d.	10.9	15.4	14.9	19.2
$F = .62$ n.s.				

---

*p less than .05
**p less than .01
***p less than .001
n.s. not significant
[1]a high score indicates low self esteem

TABLE 9-2
PROFILE OF CLUSTER MEANS ON THE SIX MEASURES
ON WHICH THERE WERE SIGNIFICANT INTERCLUSTER DIFFERENCES

Cluster 1 (n = 11)

measure	mean	characterization
DIT	40.6	slightly high moral reasoning
Alien.	18.7	low alienation
Locus	10.3	average
People	63.4	highly positive attitude toward people
Ego	176.5	high ego development
Kohl.	323.9	slightly high moral reasoning

Cluster 2 (n = 11)

measure	mean	characterization
DIT	55.7	high moral reasoning
Alien.	28.2	average
Locus	5.6	internal control
People	50.3	average
Ego	177.7	high ego development
Kohl.	336.8	high moral reasoning

Cluster 3 (n = 14)

measure	mean	characterization
DIT	35.3	average
Alien.	40.3	highly alienated
Locus	12.0	average
People	48.0	negative attitude toward people
Ego	164.6	average
Kohl.	307.1	low moral reasoning

Cluster 4 (n = 12)

measure	mean	characterization
DIT	22.3	low moral reasoning
Alien.	29.6	average
Locus	15.2	external control
People	54.4	average
Ego	161.3	low ego development
Kohl.	306.3	low moral reasoning

(Overall Means: DIT 37.9; Alien.: 29.9; Locus: 10.9; People, 53.7; Ego, 169.5; Kohl., 317.6.)

In summary, the differences among the clusters can be discussed in terms of two dimensions: developmental maturity and attitudes toward life. Clusters two and four differ on the dimension of developmental maturity. Cluster two individuals have very high scores on the measures of moral reasoning and ego development while individuals in cluster four have very low scores on these measures. The students in clusters one and three differ primarily on the dimension of attitudes toward life. Cluster one individuals have a very positive attitude toward people and show very low levels of alienation, while the students in cluster three are very alienated and have a very negative attitude toward people.

THE ANALYSIS OF INTER-CLUSTER DIFFERENCES IN CHANGE PATTERNS

The next step was to discover whether there were significant differences among the clusters in the degree to which they changed on each of the measures over the course of the students' year-long involvement in the Sierra Project's developmental curriculum. All of the instruments had been administered to the students at the beginning and the end of their freshman year involvement in the curriculum. Table 9-3 reports the mean scores for each cluster on each instrument at pre-testing and post-testing.

In order to examine change over the year, two types of analyses are reported. A paired t-test on time one versus time two scores reports the degree of change for each cluster independently (see Table 9-4). An analysis of covariance on the gain scores using the pre-test score as a covariate (Hendrix, Carter, & Hintze, 1978) is used to report the level of significance of differences in degree of change among the clusters (see Table 9-5).

The most notable changes are on the Defining Issues Test (DIT) measurement of moral reasoning. Two clusters (numbers two and four) made significant gains on the DIT as reported in the paired t-tests in Table 9-4. However, a certain degree of the cluster four change may be accounted for by regression to the

TABLE 9-3
PRE- AND POST-TEST MEAN SCORES FOR EACH CLUSTER ON EACH INSTRUMENT*

Cluster 1 (n = 11)

measure	Pre-test mean	Post-test mean
DIT	40.6	44.6
Alienation	18.7	22.5
Locus of Control	10.3	9.2
"People in General"	63.4	60.4
Ego Development	176.4	177.0
Kohlberg	323.9	330.9
Sex Roles (fem)	5.3	5.4
Sex Roles (masc)	4.6	4.7
Self-esteem	37.7	36.5

Cluster 2 (n = 11)

measure	Pre-test mean	Post-test mean
DIT	55.7	63.4
Alienation	28.2	26.8
Locus of Control	5.6	6.4
"People in General"	50.3	56.4
Ego Development	177.7	181.6
Kohlberg	336.9	344.9
Sex Roles (fem)	5.0	4.9
Sex Roles (masc)	4.9	5.0
Self-esteem	39.0	34.7

Cluster 3 (n = 14)

measure	Pre-test mean	Post-test mean
DIT	35.3	35.4
Alienation	40.3	36.3
Locus of Control	12.0	12.2
"People in General"	48.1	46.9
Ego Development	164.6	167.6
Kohlberg	307.1	320.7
Sex Roles (fem)	4.8	5.1
Sex Roles (masc)	4.3	4.3
Self-esteem	45.4	45.4

Cluster 4 (n = 12)

measure	Pre-test mean	Post-test mean
DIT	22.3	37.0
Alienation	29.6	30.9
Locus of Control	15.2	14.8
"People in General"	54.4	53.0
Ego Development	161.3	167.4
Kohlberg	306.2	317.5
Sex Roles (fem)	5.1	5.0
Sex Roles (masc)	5.0	4.8
Self-esteem	42.4	38.2

*A low score indicates high self-esteem.

TABLE 9-4
PAIRED T-TESTS ON PRE-TEST TO POST-TEST CHANGE
FOR EACH CLUSTER

	Cluster 1 d.f. = 10	Cluster 2 d.f. = 10
DIT-moral reasoning	t = 1.00	t = 3.14*
Alienation	t = -2.12	t = .53
Locus of Control	t = 1.04	t = - .85
"People in General"	t = -1.42	t = 2.40*
Ego Development	t = .15	t = 1.09
Kohlberg-moral reasoning	t = 1.15	t = 1.11
Sex Roles (masc)	t = .25	t = .48
Sex Roles (fem)	t = .68	t = - .76
Self-esteem	t = .45	t = 2.03

	Cluster 3 d.f. = 13	Cluster 4 d.f. = 11
DIT-moral reasoning		
Alienation		
Locus of Control	t = .02	t = 3.42**
"People in General"	t = 1.77	t = - .51
Ego Development	t = - .22	t = .41
Kohlberg-moral reasoning	t = - .60	t = - .62
Sex Roles (masc)	t = .73	t = 1.96
Sex Roles (fem)	t = 2.40*	t = 1.61
Self-esteem	t = - .74	t = -1.14
	t = 3.14**	t = -1.22
	t = - .03	t = 1.02

*p less than .05
**p less than .01

mean[2] since subjects in this cluster started off with the lowest DIT scores. This conclusion appears to be justified when one examines the mean gain scores which have been adjusted by using pre-test scores as a covariate (see Table 9-5). While cluster four subjects have an adjusted gain score which is considerably higher than that of subjects in either cluster one or three, cluster

[2]The term "regression to mean" refers to the phenomenon whereby any time that an individual or a subset of individuals scores unusually low (or unusually high) in relationship to the overall mean for the group or population of which they are members, one can expect that, if the measure is repeated, their subsequent scores will be closer to the overall mean for that group. This means that a subgroup that scores particularly low on an initial testing would be expected, just by chance, to score higher on a subsequent testing.

TABLE 9-5
**ANALYSIS OF COVARIANCE ON CLUSTER DIFFERENCES IN GAIN
SCORES USING THE PRE-TEST SCORE AS A COVARIATE**

	Cluster (N)			
	1 (11)	2 (11)	3 (14)	4 (12)

DIT—Moral Reasoning

Gain Scores				
Unadjusted mean	3.73	7.72	.07	14.66
Adjusted mean	4.57	13.32	- .77	9.74

$F = 3.236^*$

Ego Development

Gain Scores				
Unadusted mean	.55	3.91	3.00	6.09
Adjusted mean	3.01	6.83	1.27	3.18

$F = .440$ n.s.

Sex Roles (feminine scale)

Gain Scores				
Unadjusted mean	7.73	-14.36	30.86	-12.08
Adjusted mean	16.40	-14.99	22.06	- 9.19

$F = 2.568$ n.s.

Sex Roles (masculine scale)

Gain Scores				
Unadjusted mean	4.09	12.45	- 6.92	-20.08
Adjusted mean	1.34	20.40	-22.34	- 6.86

$F = 1.37$ n.s.

Kohlberg Moral Judgment Interview

Gain Scores				
Unadjusted mean	7.00	8.09	13.57	11.25
Adjusted mean	10.16	17.67	8.39	5.62

$F = .801$ n.s.

Locus of Control

Gain Scores				
Unadjusted mean	- 1.09	.73	.21	.42
Adjusted mean	- 1.24	- .49	.45	.56

$F = .593$

Alienation

Gain Scores				
Unadjusted mean	3.82	- 1.36	- 4.00	1.33
Adjusted mean	- .56	- 2.03	.08	1.21

$F = .333$ n.s.

"People in General" Scale

Gain Scores				
Unadjusted mean	- .29	6.09	- 1.21	- 1.41
Adjusted mean	.98	4.72	- 3.46	- 1.11

$F = 2.88^*$

Self-esteem[1]

Gain Scores				
Unadjusted mean	- .54	- 4.26	.07	- 4.16
Adjusted mean	- 1.05	- 5.24	1.64	- 3.76

$F = 1.857$ n.s.

---

*p less than .05
n.s. not significant
[1]a negative gain score indicates an increase in self-esteem.

two subjects now have the highest adjusted gain score. This suggests that, while both clusters two and four changed significantly on the DIT, change was more significant for subjects in cluster two despite the fact that the absolute quantity of change is greater in cluster four.

On the "People in General" Scale, which measures general attitudes toward people, there was significant positive change for subjects in cluster two (see Table 9-4). In fact, cluster two is the only cluster for which there was positive change (see Tables 9-3 and 9-5). In addition, there was a significant difference among the clusters in degree of change on the "People in General" Scale (see Table 9-5).

On the Bem Feminine Scale, cluster three made a significant positive change (see Table 9-4). However, when the inter-cluster differences in change on this measure are analyzed using the analysis of covariance procedure, no significant difference is found (see Table 9-5). This discrepancy probably means that the significant change reported in Table 9-4 is a result of the fact that cluster three started out considerably lower on this measure than the other clusters (see Table 9-3) and then regressed to the mean at the second testing.

DISCUSSION

This analysis differentiates among four groups of individuals who have markedly different personality profiles. The results of the cluster analysis suggest that (at least for this sample of individuals) there are four groups of people who display distinct combinations of the personality characteristics which were measured in this study.

This clustering separates subjects, at the most basic level, according to their scores on the developmental measures. The cluster analysis makes the first separation between subjects with high developmental scores (clusters one and two) and those with lower developmental scores (clusters three and four). In considering this finding, it is important to remember that the profiles had been normalized so that the overall level of scores in all of the profiles were equal. This means that the distinctions made among individuals in this analysis were made only on the basis of the pattern of scores across the various measures.

Therefore, the fact that the clusters are now found to differ significantly in terms of developmental level means that the developmental level is related to the overall pattern of scores exhibited by an individual, and does not mean that these differences in level determined the cluster separation.

Within each of these two larger groups, which are separated on the basis of developmental level, three other variables play important roles in making further distinctions. Two of these variables, degree of alienation and attitude toward people, appear to vary together to define a general dimension consisting of an individual's overall attitude toward life. Within the group of subjects who have high developmental scores, there is one subgroup (cluster one) which displays an extremely positive attitude toward life. It is the other sub-group (cluster two), however, which has the most positive developmental scores. This extremely high developmental group is also distinguished by their high degree of internality on the locus of control measure. At first glance, this finding may be counter-intuitive. Why would not the most developmentally advanced individuals have the most favorable attitude toward life?

The answer to this question may lie in the fact that an extremely positive attitude toward life may not be part of the world view held by extremely mature individuals. A moderate degree of skepticism may be more realistic and thus more adaptive and more mature. By the same token, an extremely positive. attitude toward life may reflect a certain degree of naiveté – and, therefore, might be associated with slightly less mature developmental scores. For example, Greenberger and Sorensen (1973) have posited that enlightened trust is an important aspect of psychosocial maturity. They state that while enlightened trust incorporates a general belief that one can trust others, it also includes a rejection of simplistic notions of good and bad and a recognition of the "individual and situational factors that might curtail trust" (Greenberger & Sorensen, 1973, p. 23). In regard to the present study, this may suggest that the extremely positive attitude toward life displayed by cluster one individuals reflects, in part, a reliance on simplistic notions of good and bad. This would explain why these subjects are not the most developmentally advanced group, although they have generally high developmental scores.

Among the other half of the subjects with lower developmental scores, the attitude toward life dimension also plays an important role in distinguishing between the two subgroups. Here the subgroup (cluster three) whose developmental scores are higher has extremely low scores on the attitude toward life measures, while the group with the lowest developmental scores (cluster four) has average attitude toward life scores. Here, it is the lowest developmental group whose attitude toward life scores are in the average range, while the group which is slightly more advanced developmentally has an extremely negative attitude. One possible explanation is that this negative attitude is a phase in the developmental process.

Elkind (1974) has stated that an important aspect of the adolescent experience is the newfound capacity to conceive of ideals in the form of ideal families, religions, and societies. Elkind states that much of adolescent rebellion against adult society occurs when the adolescent realizes that there is a large gap between these ideals and the reality of adult society. This realization may also prompt feelings of alienation and the negative attitudes toward people which are in evidence for the cluster three subjects in this study. Such an explanation might explain why the cluster three individuals score slightly higher on the developmental instruments than do the cluster four subjects. The negativity displayed by the cluster three subjects in this study may be part of the developmental process for some individuals.

Another important aspect of the mean profile scores for cluster three is that one of the developmental scores, the moral maturity score on the Moral Judgment Interview, is well below the mean while the other developmental scores are average. This finding is interesting because the Moral Judgment Interview is the measure which requires the most involvement and cooperation from the subject. It is the only measure which is not a paper-and-pencil test. Perhaps the overall negativism of these subjects interfered with their performance in the interview situation.

Still another aspect of the differences among the four clusters concerns the differences in locus of control. The cluster which exhibited the highest developmental scores also had the most internal scores on the control measure, while the subjects in the cluster with the lowest developmental scores had the most external scores on the control scale. This finding may be due to a difference in the degree to which these two types of individuals attempt to take control of their lives and/or in the degree to which they are successful when they make such an attempt. It should be noted here that Rotter's control scale is meant only as a measure of the degree to which individuals believe that they control the reinforcers in their lives. However, this does not deny the strong possibility that one's belief in the control of reinforcers may be associated with one's ability to control reinforcers. In this case, it seems more plausible to assume that the developmentally advanced group is more successful at controlling the relevant reinforcers in their lives, than to assume that they only differ in the extent to which they believe that they control those reinforcers.

Other studies have also found a relationship between moral reasoning and locus of control. Alker and Poppen (1973) found a significant positive correlation between the personal control dimension of Rotter's control scale and moral reasoning. Bloomberg (1974) found that internal subjects used more stage six moral reasoning. Another study suggests that there may be a relationship between psychosocial maturity and the degree to which individuals take control of their lives (Josselson, Greenberger, & McConochie, 1975).

Josselson et al. (1975) performed in-depth interviews with high school students who had scored either extremely high or extremely low on their measure of psychosocial maturity. They report that low maturity boys "exhibit great reliance on external forces to guide their lives" (p. 18). They tend to wait for things to happen and show a disinclination to make decisions. Similarly, for low maturity girls "responsibility for control of their lives – and their impulses – generally lies outside of themselves" (p. 41). They are inclined to attribute things that happen to them to fate. High maturity boys, on the other hand, have an orientation toward the future and exhibit a sense of control over their lives, while high maturity girls are introspective and do not exhibit a pronounced sense of control as much as they do a sense of independence.

While the results reported here, those reported by Alker and Poppen (1973), and those reported by Bloomberg (1974) suggest a relationship between developmental level and belief in control of reinforcers, the study by Josselson et al. (1975) suggests that more mature individuals actually tend to be more likely to take control of the events in their lives. One plausible reason for this finding might be that the developmentally advanced individual is more capable of successfully controlling the events in his or her life. If this were true, one might expect that greater maturity would be accompanied by more internal scores on the locus of control measure. However, the analyses of change do not indicate that changes in developmental level are accompanied by changes in degree of internality. In fact, there were no significant changes in degree of internality (see Tables 9-4 and 9-5).

The most striking finding regarding change over time was that the clusters differed significantly in the amount of principled thinking (as measured by the DIT) which they exhibit. Clusters two and four changed significantly in a positive direction while clusters one and three did not show considerable change. The two clusters that made the gains in principled thinking had been at opposite ends of the spectrum in regard to their initial developmental level. The changes in cluster four do not appear to be merely the result of regression to the mean, since the results of the analysis of covariance (which used the pretest scores as a covariate) still indicate that the cluster four changes were substantially greater than those of cluster one or cluster three.

It is of interest here that the two groups which made the developmental gains (clusters two and four) did not have extreme scores in either direction on the measures of alienation and attitudes toward people. This finding may suggest that extremely negative or positive attitudes toward life distort one's perception of reality, and thus interfere with the psychological growth and development of the individual. One possible implication of this finding is that it may be advantageous for educators who are interested in promoting personal growth and development to work first on bringing their students' attitudes toward life into line with reality before attempting to promote developmental change. In doing this, it would be important for the educator to focus on reducing both the naiveté of the overly positive individual and the cynicism of the overly negative individual.

Keniston (1965) has made some observations in regard to the alienation construct which have implications for this discussion.

In particular, he makes the distinction between articulate and inarticulate alienation. Articulate alienation occurs when the alienated individual is "able to communicate his discontented vision of his society" (p. 415) and can "articulate the principles from which he rejects and the changes to which he aspires" (p. 416). The inarticulately alienated individual is not able to communicate these sentiments, experiencing scorn for politics, withdrawal from society, and feelings of powerlessness. Keniston states that it is the articulate form of alienation which is most likely to lead to individual fulfillment and social improvement.

If this is the case, then a useful type of intervention with the cluster three individuals might be to encourage them to understand and articulate their feelings of alienation as well as to explore solutions to the conditions which they feel are responsible for these feelings. It may be that developmental change will not occur for these individuals until such issues are resolved. Conversely, cluster one individuals might benefit from an intervention which focuses on increasing their awareness of the existence of various social and human problems.

The finding that individuals change differently according to their cluster membership also has implications for longitudinal research in general. Most longitudinal research examines growth trends for an aggregated group of subjects in an attempt to find one growth trend which describes development for all individuals. Had all subjects been pooled together in the present study, it is likely that no significant changes in moral reasoning would have been uncovered. The fact that significant differences in amount of change were found for individuals who exhibited differences at the time of the initial testing indicates that a priori individual differences may govern, to a substantial extent, the course of developmental change. If this is the case, the practice of aggregating all subjects and looking for one growth trend may obscure a great deal of information about the nature of development.

There are a number of limitations to the interpretations which can be made from these results. The first regards the generalizability of the personality types which emerged from this analysis. The nature of the clusters which emerge from any analysis of this type will be determined to some extent by the nature of the sample which is used (including the point in the life cycle at which it is tested) and the particular types of measures which make up the profile. The nature of the sample in this study limits the generalizability of the findings since the subjects were all college freshmen enrolled in a personal growth curriculum. However, the finding that marked individual differences exist even within such a relatively homogeneous group may make the findings even more noteworthy.

The second limitation regards the interpretation of the change findings. Because all of the subjects in the study had been involved in a developmental curriculum, it is impossible to know whether the changes made by individuals in clusters two and four were a result of the curriculum, or whether these individuals would have made sizable gains on their own without the intervention.

Despite these limitations, the results do indicate that members of a relatively homogeneous group, exposed to a very similar environment, demonstrate substantial individual differences in degree of development subsequent to this exposure. Furthermore, these differences in rate of development can be predicted from knowledge of the individual's initial personality make-up.

These findings seem to indicate that the practice of examining growth trends for an aggregated group of subjects, without considering individual differences, may conceal a great deal of information about the developmental process. In addition, these results suggest a fruitful method for examining more closely the issue of stability of psychological qualities.

Recent evidence suggests that there is very little stability in psychological characteristics over the first few years of life (Kagan, 1971; Kagan, Kearsley, & Zelazo, 1978). This issue of stability is also of interest when discussing any age group, and is characteristically examined by looking at normative evidence: that is, "the degree to which children [or other individuals] retain their relative rank on two distributions over time" (Kagan et al., 1978, p. 272). If, for example, one or two subgroups within a sample change markedly while the other groups remain stable (as was the case with the results reported here) the relative rank of all subjects will change on the second distribution. This would make it appear to the psychologist that there is no stability of the characteristics being measured when, in fact, there is stability for some subjects and marked change for others. The practice of separating subjects into groups which later exhibit differing degrees of stability may be a productive method for gaining information which can contribute to a better understanding of stability and change throughout the life cycle.

This study suggests that the Sierra curriculum may have had a greater impact on certain types of individuals than on others. While it is not clear whether the clusters of students who changed did so as a direct result of the curriculum, or if they would have changed under any circumstances, the findings do suggest that individual differences in personality profiles are associated with differences in growth trends. Professionals interested in designing curricula and/or environments which will promote development may find it fruitful to pay attention to individual differences in personality profiles and to the degree to which such differences are associated with differences in responsiveness to various types of interventions. Hopefully, such an orientation would eventually lead to the ability to successfully design varying types of educational environments and experiences capable of meeting the needs of different types of individuals.

References

Alker, H. A., & Poppen, P. J. Personality and ideology in university students. *Journal of Personality*, 1973, *41*, 653-671.

Bem, S. L. The measurement of psychological androgyny. *Journal of Consulting and Clinical Psychology*, 1974, *42*(2), 155-162.

Bloomberg, M. On the relationship between internal-external control and morality. *Psychological Reports*, 1974, *35*(3), 1077-1078.

Cronbach, L. J., & Gleser, G. C. Assessing similarity between profiles. *Psychological Bulletin*, 1953, *50*, 456-473.

Elkind, D. *Children and adolescents: Interpretive essays on Jean Piaget* (2nd ed.). New York: Oxford University Press, 1974.

Greenberger, E., & Sorensen, A. B. *Educating children for adulthood: A concept of psychosocial maturity* (Report No. 159). Baltimore, MD: Center for Social Organization of Schools, The Johns Hopkins University, 1973.

Hendrix, L. J., Carter, M. W., & Hintze, J. L. A comparison of five statistical methods for analyzing pretest-posttest designs. *Journal of Experimental Education,* 1978, *47*(2), 96-102.

Hovland, C. I., & Janis, I. L. (Eds.). *Personality and persuasibility.* New Haven, CT: Yale University Press, 1959.

Johnson, S. C. Hierarchical clustering schemes. *Psychometrika,* 1967, *32*(3), 241-254.

Josselson, R., Greenberger, E., & McConochie, D. *Phenomenological aspects of psychosocial maturity in adolescence,* Report No. 198. Baltimore, MD: Center for Social Organization of Schools, the Johns Hopkins University, 1975.

Kagan, J. *Change and continuity in infancy.* New York: Wiley, 1971.

Kagan, J., Kearsley, R. B., & Zelazo, P. R. *Infancy: Its place in human development.* Cambridge, MA: Harvard University Press, 1978.

Keniston, K. *The uncommitted: Alienated youth in American society* (1st ed.). New York: Harcourt, Brace, 1965.

Kohlberg, L. *Standard scoring manual.* Unpublished manuscript, Harvard University, 1973.

Loevinger, J. The meaning and measurement of ego development. *American Psychologist,* 1966, *21,* 195-206.

Loevinger, J., & Wessler, R. *Measuring ego development* Volume I: *Construction and use of a sentence completion test.* San Francisco: Jossey-Bass, 1970.

Mosteller, F. Association and estimation in contingency tables. *Journal of the American Statistical Association,* 1968, *63,* 1-28.

Nunnally, J. The analysis of profile data. *Psychological Bulletin,* 1962, *59,* 311-319.

Nunnally, J. *Psychometric theory.* New York: McGraw-Hill, 1978.

Osgood, C. E., & Suci, G. J. A measure of relation determined by both mean differences and profile information. *Psychological Bulletin,* 1952, *49,* 251-262.

Rest, J. R. The hierarchical nature of moral judgment: A study of patterns of comprehension and preferences of moral stages. *Journal of Personality,* 1973, *41,* 86-109.

Romney, A. K. Measuring endogamy. In P. Kay (Ed.), *Explorations in mathematical anthropology.* Cambridge, MA: The MIT Press, 1971, 191-213.

Romney, A. K. *The "bulk" problem and correcting for unequal marginals.* Unpublished paper, University of California, Irvine, 1976.

Romney, A. K., Kieffer, M., & Klein, R. E. A normalization procedure for correcting biased response data. *Social Science Research*, 1973, *2*, 307-320.

Rotter, J. B. Generalized expectancies for internal versus external control of reinforcement. *Psychological Monographs: General and Applied*, 1966, *80* (1, Whole No. 609), 1-28.

Sawrey, W. L., Keller, L., & Conger, J. J. An objective method of grouping profiles by distance functions and its relation to factor analysis. *Educational and Psychological Measurement*, 1960, *20*, 651-673.

Stokols, D. Toward a psychological theory of alienation. *Psychological Review*, 1975, *82*(1), 26-44.

Whiteley, J. M. A developmental intervention in higher education. In V. L. Erickson & J. M. Whiteley (Eds.), *Developmental counseling and teaching*. Monterey, CA: Brooks/Cole, 1980, 236-261.

Chapter 10

THE VIEW FROM WITHIN: PERSPECTIVES FROM THE INTENSIVE CASE STUDY

Arthur Resnikoff and J. Steven Jennings

Freshmen at the University of California, Irvine enter an environment characterized by a complex interplay of personal, family, and cultural backgrounds. These students face the new challenges of rigorous academic demands and social pressures while living away from home for the first time. The multiplicity of these variables, coupled with the developmental expectations of the Sierra Project, contribute to our difficulty in identifying those changes in students' thoughts and behavior attributable, at least in part, to the formal and informal curricula of Sierra. We have attempted to identify the Sierra influence through the phenomenological approach of an "intensive case study" design. Our study examines the effects of both planned and unplanned interventions by gathering and analyzing the personal reactions of seven Sierra participants. These students, from the Class of 1982, were studied throughout their year-long involvement in the Sierra Project.

In Section I, we present our rationale for employing the intensive case study design; in Section II we describe our methodology, its procedures, its participants and our criteria for interpretation; in Section III, we provide brief biographical sketches of each of our seven student participants; in Section IV, we discuss our findings in terms of general trends and individual changes; and in Section V, we summarize our interpretations of the data and the major common factors of the freshman experience.

SECTION I: THE INTENSIVE CASE STUDY DESIGN

The intensive case study methodology utilizes information reported by the subject as data. Since this design is primarily phenomenological, it is also subject to the inconsistencies inherent in an intervention analysis which uses self-report as a gauge. While there are obvious drawbacks to an analysis of this type, it can supply information beyond that provided by statistical analysis.

There are two general theoretical rationales for this methodological approach. The first is the "naturalistic-ecological perspective" (Wilson, 1977). Proponents of this perspective maintain that the setting of research has been shown to be an important influence on findings; different findings result when the same phemomena are studied in the laboratory and in the field (Barker, 1968; Willems & Raush, 1969).

Proponents of the naturalistic-ecological approach contend that in order to generalize research findings to the everyday world, the research must be conducted in a natural setting similar to that within which individuals who are not subjects of research function—since they are the group to which we wish to generalize research findings. Both the emotive and physical properties of these settings exert influences on the internalized notions of the people in them, on their perceptions of their own expectations and the expectations of others. These influences may be extraneous to the focus of the research, yet influence its results. Rosenthal and Rosnow (1969) concluded that there are multiple influences on a subject in a social-psychological study beyond those which might be intended: a suspiciousness of the intent of the research; a sense of the behavior which is appropriate or expected; a special interpersonal relationship with the experimenter; the desire to be evaluated positively.

A second rationale for more naturalistic research, congruent with the approach taken in this study, is that of the "qualitative-phenomenological approach" (Wilson, 1977). This tradition maintains that one "cannot understand human behavior without understanding the framework within which the subjects interpret their thoughts, feelings and actions" (Wilson, 1977, p. 249). To objectify the gathering and manipulation of data, the "natural science approach" requires researchers to limit themselves, to put a priori restrictions on the data. For example, a coding scheme may quantify information so that it can be manipulated statistically. But such schema are arbitrary; they impose only one set of meaning upon data and thereby eliminate other, perhaps more viable, options. Such restrictions of perspective may lead some researchers to be concerned about irrelevant variables or to overlook unexpected results. Seeking to be objective, traditional "natural science" approaches may simply fail to recognize and address their own form of subjectivity.

There is a richness in individuals' experiences which cannot be assessed by traditional paper-and-pencil tests. Such measurements are valuable in assessing change of a trait or state, but simply cannot capture the means by which an intervention has affected individuals, the process of change within individuals, and the assumptions, beliefs, and/or attitudes influenced during that change. Tests cannot monitor the thinking processes occuring during the intervention; they can only monitor a limited range of the outcomes of the processes.

In our evaluation of the Sierra Project, we are exploring a range of effects on a number of individuals as they experience the full set of activities involved in their freshman year. Over that time, there were a myriad of planned and unplanned influences having an impact upon each individual. Traditional statistical analyses show some statistical differences over that time period —indicating a link between intervention and effect—but they fail to distinguish the meaning behind the differences, the discrete experiences resulting in changes in students' thinking. In other words, the analytical scope of a traditional methodology must be widened by an evaluation procedure examining *how* events may have affected students' reasoning, attitudes, and behavior.

In any experiment, there is variation among individuals— some individuals change on a given dimension, whereas others do not. When statistical analyses indicate that a group has changed when compared to another group, we have little information about the behaviors characterizing the group change, about differences among individuals. When we discuss interventions and their effects, we want to know the specific events leading to particular outcomes, as well as how these events affected different individuals under different circumstances.

While the intensive case study as an evaluation tool provides a solution to many limitations of other methodologies, it does not have the element of control that one may find in an experimental design. There are no baseline data of any sort; there is a limited sample, no control group, and no objective definition of variables. It is, therefore, not possible to posit cause-and-effect relationships on the basis of this data. However, this study does explore intensively the reports of a variety of individuals over a nine-month period. It attempts to relate these reports to events documented from a number of sources in order to develop a rich base of information to further reveal the Sierra experience.

SECTION II: METHODOLOGY

Choosing the Sample. Letters sent to all prospective participants in the Sierra Project for the Class of 1982 offered them the opportunity to participate in an intensive case study. Study participants were guaranteed two academic credits for winter and for spring quarters—four credits for the entire year. After a number of students volunteered for the study, prospective subjects were divided by sex; the final subjects' names were then drawn randomly from these two pools of students. Our final sample consisted of seven students[1]: two Chicano students, one male and one female; two Anglo students, one male and one female; two Asian students, one male of Japanese descent and one female of Filipino descent; and one Black female student.

The Interviewers. To limit a potential source of bias, interviewers had no role in determining the curriculum of the Sierra Project during the course of the study, though they were familiar with its general content and purpose. They therefore had no investment in the specifics of the intervention which would predispose them to view the data in a particular way. There were two interviewers, one a psychologist and one an undergraduate student—Dr. Arthur Resnikoff, counseling psychologist and Director of the UCI Counseling Center, and J. Steven Jennings, a senior at UCI who subsequently entered graduate

---

[1]One student, who had been in the United States for only one year, was dropped from the study because of language difficulties.

study at Pennsylvania State University. Students met with each individually, alternating interviewers each session. The two interviewers met monthly in order to share and compare their perceptions and to discover any discrepancies in the factual statements being reported.

Interview Schedule and Format. Students were interviewed weekly for the first four weeks of the study, then bimonthly for the remainder of the entire academic year. The interviews lasted 30-45 minutes and were audiotaped.

Initially, the students participating in the study were made aware of its purposes and the type of information required of them. They were asked to express their thoughts and feelings about their day-to-day experiences and interactions while at the university, and to attend to changes in their thinking about themselves and others over the course of the year. The interviews were semi-structured; the interviewers posed open-ended questions, then paraphrased the students' comments to encourage them to elaborate on their experiences. After rapport had been established between student and interviewer and all parties were familiar with the procedures, one or two open-ended questions sufficed to stimulate students to provide specific descriptions of events in their lives. At the end of the year, students were asked to sum up their experiences, identifying the events or situations which had influenced their lives.

Reporting the Data. The basic data gathered consisted of a complete set of taped interviews (and the corresponding interview summaries) with seven students collected over their freshman year. The interviewers' summaries were descriptive accounts of the interview sessions, occasionally including interpretations of students' reports, which were clearly identified as added comments. In addition, each participating student kept a journal during the year, generally making one or more rather detailed entries each week. Curriculum plans and instructors' notes on events which took place in class were also made available to us. The qualitative data thus consisted of both written and oral information supplied by the students interviewed and other outside information supplied by instructors and live-in staff of Sierra Hall. We attempted to integrate and interpret these data in order to draw conclusions about student growth during the Sierra experience.

The Process of Interpretation. The biographical summaries which appear in the next section of this chapter were generated from information gained within the first four interviews. Using these and other subsequent data obtained, we first noted common occurrences — those outcomes which seemed to affect the entire sample. We then identified individual experiences which seemed to reflect or catalyze student growth. We attempted to set student reports of specific concerns within a time frame to determine trends. Although the Sierra Project attempts to influence ego development and moral reasoning, this intensive case study is designed to discover whether the curriculum or any other events had an impact upon these students' thoughts, feelings, and behavior. Prior to the beginning of the study, we assumed that effects would come from seven possible dimensions:

1. The social structure of the dormitory;
2. the physical structure of the dormitory;
3. the pressure of academic and social relations;
4. the developmental stage of each student studied;
5. the pressure of leaving home;
6. the testing of one's adequacy academically, socially and sexually; and
7. the individual history which each student brought to the study.

These seven factors provided a guide for observation, but we attempted to be open to any other changes in attitude and behavior revealed or reported.

SECTION III:
BIOGRAPHICAL SKETCHES OF PARTICIPANTS

In order to give life to the very real people who participated in this study, the following brief biographical summaries were prepared from the first month's interviews and journal entries. Referring to these summaries while reading the latter portion of this chapter, which discusses changes in particular individuals, may be helpful.

Julian

Julian is a Mexican-American who grew up in a barrio of Los Angeles. His family, large but close, held rather traditional values, though his mother worked to help support the family. Julian felt that there were clear differences in the manner in which he, the youngest child, was treated by his siblings and parents: Julian felt that his sisters tended to order him around, while his brothers treated him with more respect. Julian perceived his father as rather strong minded and not very sensitive.

Julian's family played a major part in his decision-making process concerning college in general and UCI in particular; one of his older sisters provided specific information about UCI from personal experience. Julian indicated during his initial interviews that having respect for one's elders was very important, and it was clear that his feeling of respect was a critical influence on his decisions about college. Yet it was equally clear that the decision to attend UCI was Julian's own and that he expected his family to support and trust him.

Julian's desire for a college education made him unlike many of his peers. After he had made his decision about college, he began to feel distanced from his high school friends. Despite these social problems, Julian felt that education is valuable because it opens up greater opportunities for an individual.

Julian was quite concerned about establishing and maintaining an environment in which he'd be able to study effectively. He was at first hesitant about moving into Sierra, having formed an impression from a summer orientation program that the dorm atmosphere would encourage distraction from his school work. Once in the dorm—while retaining concerns about the environment's effect on his studies—he cultivated new friends with great confidence and energy.

While he had some definite ideas about his future when he entered UCI, Julian did not value investing a lot of time and energy toward planning and, especially, *counting* on the future. He enjoyed talking over old times with his friends and discussing past experiences with newer acquaintances. Julian seemed to use this discussion technique to establish and maintain friendships rather than focusing on experiences currently being shared with friends.

Gloria

Gloria (pseudonym) grew up in Los Angeles in a Mexican-American family. Her father left the family the year before Gloria entered high school. During her freshman year in high school, her mother died. Some of Gloria's six older siblings and her younger brother and sister remained in the house and maintained the immediate family. Gloria had been very close to her mother; when she entered UCI four years after her mother's death, she still drew upon her memories of her mother when thinking through her own behaviors.

In her first interview with us, Gloria indicated that she felt her distrust of men's honesty and sincerity stemmed from her father having left the family. She saw her younger siblings as spoiled and irresponsible and her older siblings as rather hypocritical in the advice they gave in attempting to fill the role of their absent parents. She said that she would generally sit and listen to what her older brothers and sisters had to say, but in the end, very quietly, would make up her own mind about what she wanted to do. Although Gloria saw that her family had begun rearranging the household once she had decided to leave — so that she would soon have no space of her own — she regarded her home as a safe place to return to and planned to do so for part of the coming academic year.

Gloria was still very preoccupied with thoughts and feelings about her ex-boyfriend, Raul. Many of Gloria's feelings about the loss of her mother and boyfriend were connected to her lack of someone to turn to with problems and concerns. The feelings of distrust toward men Gloria had formed when considering her father's actions were strengthened by her experiences with Raul. She was wary of becoming involved with any of her male peers at UCI. She viewed obtaining a college degree as a means of independence from male support. She therefore wanted to get a good education so that she would be able to obtain a job providing her with financial security. She planned to have children but wanted the means to provide for their needs by herself.

Gloria was concerned about her hesitancy in speaking out in front of others — especially in classroom situations — and hoped to overcome it. Although she frequently had a better understanding of situations than others did, she felt that no one was aware of this because of her quiet demeanor. Gloria also evidenced a marked deference to adults and authority figures, and seemed to think she generally had little influence on the possible outcomes of situations affecting her.

Mark

Mark grew up in San Marino, a predominately white, upper middle class community in the greater Los Angeles area. His immediate family included his parents and two older half-brothers. Although his brothers were several years older than he, Mark felt that they got along well. Mark and his father maintained a close relationship, although Mark felt that his parents may have pampered him as he was growing up. Mark spent a good deal of his senior year in high school socializing with a group of about a dozen male peers, and appears to have had several girlfriends throughout his high school career. His studies were geared toward college, where he planned to continue his track activities.

The reputation of the track team, academic majors, and size and location were factors which influenced Mark's decision to enter UCI. Doing well academically was his most important priority; Mark was confident and excited about beginning his course-work. He felt he would need to discipline himself strictly in order to achieve his academic goals, and therefore planned to limit any potential involvement with a girlfriend.

Mark also hoped to join a fraternity at UCI. Our impression was that his desire for the social life provided by a fraternity was not based on a disappointment with the social life of the residence hall; he saw the dorm environment also provided opportunities to establish college friendships. The curriculum component of Sierra had especially appealed to Mark, who saw a relationship betweem some of the curricular topics to be covered and his own interest in psychology. He felt that the class would be an interesting and undemanding four units of credits.

Mark was quite conscious of the differences among his fellow students and discerned shifts in the general mood of the residents during the first few weeks of school. His interest in psychology may be related to his being more conscious, or at least more expressive, of these variables than the other participants in the research.

Kathy

Kathy is an Anglo student who grew up in Oxnard, California, a small town north of Los Angeles, where she attended a small, private Catholic high school. Her mother had died six years prior to Kathy's admission to UCI, her father remarrying before she finished high school. Kathy reported that as an adolescent she had gone through frequent periods of depression which often coincided with the start of a school year. Overall, however, Kathy presented herself as a stable, sensitive individual.

The relationship between Kathy and her father was very close and mutually supportive. His frequent praise of her—of her attendance at UCI, and of her scholastic accomplishments— added to Kathy's motivation to perform well in her academic endeavors; she enjoyed making her father happy and proud of her by being academically successful.

Kathy wished to maintain close ties with several individuals at home, particularly with her boyfriend, Donnie. Kathy anticipated their relationship continuing during her first year of college. Interestingly, during the summer prior to her freshman year at UCI, she had become concerned about her ability to initiate and maintain relationships beyond those with her family and boyfriend. She noted that she spent most of her time during the summer either with Donnie or alone.

Kathy preferred having activities in her day-to-day life well organized and planned out and seemed quite systematic in her thinking. She appeared to possess the intellectual capacity to succeed—and perhaps excel—in her studies at UCI, but concluded that she needed to devote substantial time to studying (perhaps more than most of her peers) if she was to do well in her courses.

Roy

Roy is a Japanese-American whose family lives 35 minutes from UCI in Carson. His parents encouraged Roy to live away from home during the academic year, though he was hesitant to take this step. In fact, Roy moved into Sierra several days later than most of the other residents, delaying the move for as long as possible. Perhaps part of his reluctance stems from his position as the only member of his group of male peers from high school to have moved away from home to attend a university, the majority of friends having chosen to attend junior college and/or work close to home. Roy reported that a group of his friends had engaged in a number of burglaries while they were all in high school, but said that he had ended his involvement before his high school graduation.

At the beginning of his freshman year, Roy was concerned with his ability to do well academically at UCI. He wanted to carry a light academic schedule his first quarter, hoping this would help him be successful and gain confidence in his capabilities as a student. He was also apprehensive about the social climate of the campus, particularly of Sierra. Roy liked to take time out from his studies to relax and enjoy himself but expected his fellow students to have a more serious, studious frame of mind. Despite his late arrival, Roy presented himself as having a calm and realistic attitude about entering UCI and beginning a new academic and social life. Upon realizing that he had been assigned what he described as a "colored" roommate, Roy reacted with some trepidation. He was concerned that he and his roommate would not have much in common, and might have trouble getting along because they were of different races. Relating to and getting along well with his peers was a central concern in Roy's life.

Roy had a close relationship with a girlfriend during and after high school. He described the relationship as exclusive and possessive, at least on his part, openly admitting that he behaved in a jealous manner toward his girlfriend. While attending UCI, he apparently intended to continue their relationship, both by phone and through visits home on weekends.

Jogie

While attending public high school, Jogie lived with her family in Carson, a city between Irvine and Los Angeles. She is of Filipino descent and the second of six children. Jogie viewed her family as a close one and was concerned about maintaining this closeness. She said that she had never held a part-time job in high school and that she planned to go home each weekend to have her mother do her laundry.

During high school, Jogie's social activities centered around a small group of males roughly her own age. While she did form close friendships with several female peers, she described her interactions with the group of male students as similar to those that a sister might have with her brothers. Jogie reported her parents to be neutral about her selection of UCI, neither raising objections nor being particularly supportive. Her decision to attend UCI seemed to have been based on its location close to her home, its low cost, and the availability of financial aid. She chose Sierra Hall as her residence largely because of its all freshman composition.

We felt that Jogie was friendly and outgoing during our meetings with her, and the most dynamic of our subjects. However, she persistently discounted herself and her abilities. She also reported feeling scared and uncomfortable about moving into Sierra and beginning her college career at UCI. She was initially concerned about meeting and getting to know her male peers, but found this process took less time than she had expected once she moved into Sierra.

Lavada

Lavada spent her childhood living with her family in Watts, the area of Los Angeles known as the location of rioting in 1965. Later, the family moved to Carson. One of seven children in a black family, she was the first to move away from home to go to a four-year university. Lavada felt that growing up in Watts was an experience that had "prepared her for anything."

The stressful environment of Watts, in combination with a difficult home environment, affected Lavada's interests and behavior as a child. She became highly motivated in school, finding personal satisfaction in academic accomplishment. She felt very close to her family and felt that she worked hard at school in order to gain recognition and attention from her brothers and sisters. Because of her high GPA in high school, her family grew to expect that she would go to college. Nonetheless, Lavada says she made her own decision about going to college and about which college to attend.

Lavada noted several specific goals she expected to accomplish by the time she graduated from UCI: to become an expert in her major (psychology), to be independent, to know her direction in life, to do some good for others, to make a lot of friends, to be herself. She said that she tended to study too much, feeling guilty if she didn't study a certain amount. She hoped that at UCI she could begin to take her grades and her studying a bit less seriously than she had in high school, perhaps moving more toward social activities. Once she arrived at UCI, Lavada found the adjustment to college less difficult than she had expected. She found that she enjoyed living in a dorm and that the academic load was much easier to handle than she had anticipated.

Unlike the majority of Sierra residents who are assigned roommates they do not know, Lavada had known her roommate since junior high school. Although conflicts based on differences in lifestyles surfaced soon after they began sharing their dorm room, Lavada appeared to possess some of the skills necessary to open a discussion about the problems they were facing and methods of dealing with those problems.

SECTION IV: TRENDS ACROSS THE SAMPLE

We noted two trends that characterized our sample. First was a common sense of cohesiveness, each individual having a sense of being a part of that group. The second was a growing sense of self-assurance experienced by each of the individuals in this sample. More often than not, these trends were influenced by events in the Sierra class curriculum; students discussed many of the concepts addressed in class on an informal, practical level.

Group Change: The "Honeymoon" Effect

To many of these students, the beginning of the academic year brought with it all the glamour and excitement of new friends and freedoms. Upon meeting their new roommates, many students were unhesitatingly friendly and uncritical. An excerpt from Kathy's journal illustrates this point:

9/27 I enjoy UCI. . . . The people here are so fantastic! Friendly,
helpful, and down to earth . . . . My roommate is super!
We get along so very well, such a sweet girl . . . so bubbly
and alive; she always seems to cheer me up. And she's
so caring and unselfish . . . . We have a lot in common,
and we enjoy each other's company.

Unfortunately, this was to a great degree a "honeymoon" effect
which soon dissipated, leaving these students with a more critical view of Sierra life and of their roommates in particular.
Contrast Kathy's earlier statement to these later comments:

1/31 I'm kind of disillusioned with my roommate tonight. At
times she's so cruel to people here in the dorm . . . she's
so caught up in her own world. I try to be interested in
her life; I wish she would do the same for me. She has
no feelings for others at times . . . at times I think she
uses people for all she can get from them and if they
have nothing to give her, she wants nothing to do with
them.

This disillusionment seemed to be common; students found the
actual outcomes of relationships incompatible with their expectations. Many students initially invested time and effort in their
roommates and new friends, but later tended to withdraw.

A Sense of Cohesiveness

The excitement and interest in developing new relationships
within the dorm—and the subsequent disillusionment and withdrawal from those attachments—can be seen as reflective of a
broader shift in group feeling about relationships with others in
the dorm. The desire to meet and get to know the others in the
dorm peaked early in the year as students anticipated the
SIMSOC weekend, which involved a simulation of society requiring participation of the entire group. Students in the sample
clearly expected that this weekend would provide an opportunity to become acquainted with others and to establish new
relationships. Most individuals reported that they did accomplish these goals as a result of this weekend.

However, as time passed and conflicts between students developed, this group feeling seemed to ebb, perhaps hitting its lowest point early in the winter at the Mammoth retreat. There were feelings of resentment toward those students who did not share in the group's chores on the weekend trip. The sense of unfairness which resulted led a number of students to mistrust others' intentions.

The degree to which students felt cohesiveness, a sense of being a part of the group, influenced the impact of their various experiences. Subjects tended to be willing to enter into new behaviors as a function of their sense of "belonging to the group." Two subjects in this study, Mark and Kathy, adopted a more reserved stance toward the activities and curriculum within the Sierra dorm. Mark considered his studies, track, and fraternity affiliations to be his most important priorities. Though he did attempt to make contact with others in the dorm, the investment of time and energy which Mark was willing to make toward this end was limited.

Kathy, on the other hand, was directly influenced by certain events which took place at the beginning of the year. Like many others in the sample, Kathy wanted to get to know her roommate and dormmates while, at the same time, maintaining important ties with those at home. The SIMSOC weekend, a turning point for many in their establishment of new relationships, triggered in Kathy a desire to distance herself from the group as a whole (although not from any specific individuals). While Kathy's feelings about others in the dorm vacillated as the year progressed, the general trend was toward lessening her participation.

In the interview following the SIMSOC weekend, Kathy reported that she was going to be wary of others, that she would not enter into an experience as openly as she had that weekend. The following excerpt comes from that interview:

> 10/20 I didn't like that. I hated it. Oh, it was the worst! I just wanted to come home . . . . I didn't learn anything from it . . . . I just couldn't see the point in it . . . . One good thing about it was that we got closer as a dorm, but that's the only good thing. I wouldn't do it again . . . . People yelling all night long . . . really inconsiderate . . . .

> [During the game] I had to go around to all the dif-
> ferent regions . . . everybody was being so greedy! . . .
> they'd just kick me out and I felt so rejected. I guess I
> took it too personally.

Although this weekend had a strong effect on Kathy's subsequent behavior, her anxiety about doing well academically and
her desire to maintain her relationships with her father and
boyfriend also contributed to Kathy's decision to reduce her
involvement. Despite this decision, however, Kathy continued to
waver between feelings of commitment and belonging and feelings of estrangement:

> 12/1 The dorm isn't really, you know, you don't feel like, at
> least I don't feel like, "Oh, this is home." . . . It's getting
> better, but it's just more like a place to stay, a place to
> sleep, to shower . . . . I think with time we'll get closer . . .
> [but] I do feel close to them . . . . maybe if we could all
> get together and do more things together, it would be
> better, but now it's kinda like a passing acquaintance,
> more or less . . . there's just not enough time . . . people
> *want* to become closer . . . you feel comfortable around
> 'em, and you feel like they like you and they want you
> there, and they're concerned about you . . . because you're
> a part of their dorm. And that's a real good feeling.

> 2/27 I don't know what it is, but lately I just dread coming
> back to school after a weekend home more than ever.
> I've always not really cherished the idea of leaving home
> to come back, but lately I'm beginning to hate coming
> back. Once I get here it's really not bad, I'm not unhappy.
> I just do my work and that's about it.

Unlike many students in the sample, Mark and Kathy did not
see themselves as closely linked to the rest of the "group" and,
because of this, did not experience many of the same effects as
others in our sample. Individuals' stances toward the events,
the degree to which they were open toward the intervention —
and their conscious decisions about engaging in activities —
influenced the degree to which they experienced a sense of
cohesion in the dorm.

Subgroup Formation: Racial Identification

As the year progressed, the "honeymoon" effect began to ebb, and group cohesiveness moved from the dorm or suite level to smaller subgroupings. The students reported formation of racial and ethnic subgroups, despite curricular topics aimed at reducing reliance on racial stereotypes. The development of these subgroups intensified after the winter quarter retreat. Non-Anglos suggested that it was the Anglo students who were the first to group together.

In the following excerpts from interviews, three students describe their views about a particular session of the dorm class, a session which had sparked a great deal of discussion. Julian, Lavada, and Kathy expressed differing opinions on the nature and importance of the session and ensuing discussions. Julian found that the session made him more aware of racial differences and of his own racial stereotypes:

> 2/22 (Julian) It was pretty interesting . . . each group tried to show what the sterotypes were . . . . I really realized that people's values were all different, and there's variations within the racial groups . . . . You just had to, I guess you had to accept that they thought that way [about other races], or they saw it that way 'cause that's just the way they were brought up . . . . I sort of have stereotypes on the blacks, the whites, and all the other minorities . . . . For me, [I've gained] a little more respect for each other's culture.

Lavada reacted differently to the session, focusing particularly on what she considered a poor response by Anglo students to the class discussion.

> 2/22 (Lavada) It wasn't as bad as I thought it would be . . . . I thought the whole class was good, except some people wouldn't say what they really felt . . . . The whites got kinda upset, like we were attacking them personally . . . . The people who are so "open-minded" are the ones who really, really got upset . . . . Everybody else took it pretty good except for them [Anglos] . . . I don't know. I guess they're just not used to hearing it [stereotypes of

Anglos] . . . but it was fun! . . . I guess they never thought we had stereotypes for them!

Kathy rejected the entire discussion of race and race relations as divisive and ineffective:

2/21 (Kathy) I really can't understand why we are going through all this stuff in dorm class. It doesn't help us at all. In fact, it makes things six times as bad. It causes hurt and resentment between the different races in the dorm and I really don't see any worthwhile purpose in it whatsoever. It causes dissention among the races. Blacks against whites, whites against Mexicans, Mexicans against whites, etc. It's all so ugly! I HATE IT! Everyone is forced into this stupid category that was never so important before . . . [the R.A.] has gone through these classes before and it's very obvious that she still possesses a great deal of prejudices and hostilities. Shouldn't that be an indication that this aspect of the class isn't useful?

Some students in the sample achieved a broadened acceptance of those of other races, some remained fixed in their beliefs, and some grew more defensive about their differences. The trend, however, was for students to form subgroups based on common racial and ethnic identification as a source of security and identity against the pressures they saw in the university.

Individual Differences:
Self-Disclosure and its Effects

In a previous section, we discussed the movement from a "honeymoon stage," during which students felt the joy of meeting and getting to know others, to a more realistic stage, wherein students recognized their own and others' personal limitations and the problems of relationships. This recognition eventually led most students to want to "work on" their relationships with others, particularly to call upon the new skills they were learning in the areas of communication, conflict resolution, and assertion training. Among the skills they had learned that enhance communication was self-disclosure, the sharing of personal information with another individual, which a number of students used to resolve conflicts.

Two examples illustrate the use of self-disclosure for conflict resolution, in one case by a group, in the other with individuals. Two suites, one male and one female, were considered "brother and sister" suites because of their location. After an initial period of friendship, there were a number of disagreeable incidents between members of these suites, particularly exacerbated by two males who seemed to instigate a large number of rather annoying practical jokes. A state of irritation seemed to develop; the two suites began to engage in constant bickering. Finally, the male suite decided to have "nothing to do" with its sister suite.

As the year progressed, individuals from these two suites began to relate to each other on a tentative basis, gradually increasing in friendliness. However, toward the end of the spring quarter, the practical jokes resumed. Calling on their understanding of self-disclosure, the women made a conscious effort to talk frankly with the male suite members in order to come to a more satisfying solution. The members of the female suite wanted to express their anger about a particular incident, describing their feelings without destroying the friendship which was developing again between the suites. Their self-disclosure resulted in an agreement to reduce the jokes and to establish friendlier relations.

The second example of the use of self-disclosure involves a one-on-one situation. Early in the year, one of the individuals in our sample, Jogie, established a close relationship with a male from her "brother" suite, Kevin. During the fall, Jogie and Kevin had a disagreement which led to the breaking off of their relationship. Jogie, like the women in the suite discussed above, asked Kevin to talk with her in order to try to resolve their differences. Their talk was characterized by some self-disclosure; they attempted to express their feelings about one another, and to review and discuss the events in their relationship. The following excerpts from Jogie's journal demonstrate the status of their relationship over the course of the year, and the increasing trend toward greater frankness and self-disclosure.

10/11 I don't even know why we weren't talking much . . . Kevin didn't tell me anything about what was going on and he made me feel like I shouldn't even ask because I

should know or something like that . . . . [My room-
mate] made him come talk to me about it . . . we got
talking and after a long and uncomfortable conversation or quarrel or whatever we found out that it was a
big misunderstanding.

10/16 . . . he just started to ignore me . . . I really wanted to
find out what was the matter, but he never gave me the
chance to talk to him.

4/19 All week, we've been talking about how everything
stands between us as of now . . . he talked about how
he thinks that we're really not truthful to each other
about the things we tell each other. It's just that we
hold back a lot of things . . . I think that whatever I hold
back from him, I have a reason for doing so.

4/24 Everything between me and Kevin has been straight-
ened out . . . again [but] this time is so different . . .
Kevin came up to me [at a party] and said "Let's dance!"
. . . . I thought maybe he would start talking to me
about something he wanted to know or get straight-
ened out! But, boy—was I wrong! After about 10 sec-
onds . . . he goes, "You know what? . . . You're fucked!!!"
It just blew my mind! He started to walk away, but I
chased after him in the hallway and grabbed him hard
by the arm! . . . I didn't let him talk until I got everything
out . . . we went to talk outside . . . . We must have
discussed everything there is in a relationship. We were
very truthful about the things we said because . . . I
made it clear that this was it! If it doesn't work out
now it never will! But it did work out . . . for the very
first time, I felt like I was in control of the whole conversation . . . . Everything is going to be alright, after all
this time.

The use of self-disclosure can indicate a growth in confidence.
In this respect, Lavada's case may serve as an example. Lavada
spent her youth in the Watts community of Los Angeles. While
she wanted to share her background with other students in the
dorm, she was also somewhat embarrassed by it. However, when
the structure of the Sierra curriculum gave her the opportunity

to discuss her background (in the Triple I-D group[2] and else-where), Lavada began to describe her past to others. She appreciated the acceptance and interest which she found. The reaction to her self-disclosure made her feel more open to others throughout the remainder of the year, much more confident. The following interview summaries touched upon these changes:

3/19 I [the interviewer] remarked about how I see [Lavada] as being somewhat more open, and willing to talk about her background, for example. She responded that she had wanted to get to know me better before she became so disclosive, and now feels comfortable in the interview and journal situation. She generalized this to her inter-actions with people in Sierra. In the Triple I-D group, she noticed that some people were having trouble asking her about her background—they seemed to be a bit overwhelmed . . . . However, she reports that she likes to "get things out" . . . . Interestingly, she has read psy-chology books, newspapers, etc., with a critical eye: based on her experience, do they really know what they are talking about? In terms of her development over the year, she sees herself as being much more open, more able to talk in the Triple I-D group and class. At first, she wouldn't even think about speaking up in class.

5/17 In response to my asking what she had learned this year, Lavada mentioned that she is much more able to talk with people, letting them know the kinds of things she is thinking and feeling. She reports being much more open and able to talk about all kinds of topics, including personal ones. In the past, she spent a good deal of time worrying about what someone might be thinking or feeling about what she has to say. She feels that the Sierra experience has provided her the permis-sion to say things that she might not have said in the past. This has occurred both in the regular classes and in the Triple I-D groups. She has modeled the behavior of others in their talking about themselves and because of that felt permission to talk about herself. The experi-

[2]See Chapter 6 for a description of Triple I-D groups.

ence of being able to talk with other people without undue concern about their reactions has been extremely helpful.

Generally, the process of change (or a particular outcome) cannot be attributed to any specific event which occurred as part of the Sierra Project. However, the value of self-disclosure as a means of communication and conflict resolution, and as an index of self-confidence, was reiterated by a number of students in our sample.

Development of Competency

A number of students reported becoming more competent and confident in their own abilities. While this is a common reaction in college students, which White (1966) and Chickering (1969) have discussed, it could be seen very clearly within the sample. For example, Roy felt more competent with respect to his psychological development and independence; he saw himself as having developed maturity. Though he was still impulsive, he felt that he valued some degree of impulsiveness. Roy also reported feeling new confidence in his relationship with his parents; they seemed to recognize this and to take his opinions seriously. Although Roy noted that his attitude was not entirely different from past attitudes, he felt his father, in particular, showed a greater respect for his point of view. It made him feel confident that the independence he felt was perceived by his family as well.

Mark felt more competent with respect to both psychological and academic areas. He was very satisfied with his success in reaching the goals he had set for the year pertaining to his school work, fraternity, and track. He was able to manage what was clearly a heavy workload, balancing the responsibilities he had set for himself. He was proud of his performance in track and felt that he had the potential to be a national competitor in the triple jump. He did mention that not all his goals had been adhered to: he had developed a relationship with a woman during the latter part of the year, despite his plans not to do so in his freshman year. Unfortunately, while Mark saw himself as a competent adult, he felt that this change in him would not be recognized by his family upon his return home, that they would continue to "pamper" and restrict him.

Kathy's sense of competence was enhanced, and her confidence increased, by seeing her own capacity for hard work and perseverance. She was impressed with her own ability to handle hard academic work and achieve good grades at UCI. She had become enmeshed in her studies, both to prove to herself that she could succeed and to demonstrate her success to her father. She remarked that he would have been extremely disappointed had she not done well in her work, and that she would have felt guilty because of the wasted expense of her éducation. These factors motivated her to develop competence.

Gloria's case illustrates how hard-won such a sense of competence is, the uncomfortable feelings which accompany its development, and the satisfaction it can bring. Gloria's personal concerns made her freshman year very difficult; she wondered about whether she could "hang in there." These personal issues, which had concerned her for some years, continued to plague her; after being depressed for some time, she reported herself as "hitting bottom" during the winter quarter. Nonetheless, she was able to prove to herself that she could "make it," that she could "last" in the university. While she said in the fall that she wasn't sure she could survive at UCI, she reported in the spring that she had known all along that she had the ability to survive and succeed. The following excerpt from her journal was written at the end of the spring quarter.

> 6/4 I know next year will bring new experiences and friends, but it's just that sometimes I don't like changing so much. I know life would be boring if we didn't have change, but it's not the easiest thing to handle. Steve,[3] it feels weird, but I feel so much more sure of myself now after this year. I do still have self-doubt within me, but it's not as much as before. College life has done something to me which is making me more responsible. As you know, sometimes I wish I didn't have such responsibilities, but I know it's just a part of maturing. When I go back to my old school for my brother's graduation, I know I'm going to feel so old. But it's like I don't care because I know the

[3]J. Steven Jennings is the interviewer addressed in this journal entry.

maturing I've done this year is beneficial to me and my future. I realize now that the fear I had at the beginning of the year was there because of all the tremendous self-doubt in me. . . . But now that I've succeeded in my first year, Steve, I can't tell you what a boost this is for my self-confidence. I feel like screaming and saying I've done it, I've done it, I've put in one year at UCI and come out with a B+ GPA (I hope). Oh, Steve, my mom would have been proud. I know my family will be. The most important thing is that I've proven to myself that, Steve, I can do it, I can do it, by darn, I can do it. If I sound excited it's because I am. This is only my first year and I feel great. Just imagine when I get my degree; I'll advertise it!

In many ways, Gloria's words capsulize the new-found sense of competence reported by many students.

SECTION V:
FURTHER INTERPRETATIONS AND CONCLUSIONS

The perceptions of the seven students in our sample — perceptions of their environment, of those around them, and of themselves — gave us a view of their varied evolutions during their freshman year. Although change in these individuals was not uniform, three attitudinal or behavioral changes were repeatedly reported by students in the sample. The first related to a sense of cohesiveness: students chose either to belong to one large group or to divide into smaller, more specialized and even more cohesive sub-groups. Our data indicate that a sense of cohesiveness or attachment was an important element students in the Sierra Project felt.

The second trend reflected a growing ability to establish personal identity and personal values with regard to relationships. As part of the development of personal identity, some students moved from a rather uncritical acceptance of others to a more critical view of their dormmates. Perhaps it could be called a growing distrust; perhaps it could be called seeing the world in more realistic terms. But the sample, across the board, said that — as a result of the living situation in Sierra — they were able to know individuals rather extensively, recognizing in them qualities which they enjoyed, as well as qualities which they disliked or found frustrating.

We observed a third trend which indicated the influence of the teaching style used in the intervention on student attitudes and thinking. The Sierra curriculum involved both structured and unstructured activities. Some sessions followed a structured format which allowed students to become involved with a specific theme. First, students were presented with the theme, then with information and ideas introducing them to important issues of that theme. They took part in an activity and/or discussion relating to the theme before they were provided with a brief summing up of the session.

Students in our sample talked in their interviews about the ideas they had learned. They generally did not report specific ideas about the material presented when there was little structure to the learning activity. A clear implication was that some structure was necessary for students to focus their thinking about a theme. Conclusions reached within a structured format were more salient for the student than those which resulted from a looser format. Furthermore, after unfocused discussion sessions, students reported interest in the subject but generally did not arrive at specific conclusions about their own thinking and attitudes relating to the theme. Since these students were college freshmen accustomed to the structured teaching strategies of high school, perhaps the most effective teaching method may be this structured discussion format — a compromise between lectures designed to expound a determined theory and "free" discussion which apparently does not focus their thinking or provide closure on content.

A final developmental change occurring in the students of our sample is also related to curriculum. The Sierra experience was designed to provide a mix of challenges to students' thinking in order to encourage their movement toward higher stages of character development. Therefore, classes and discussion sessions frequently involved staff or students presenting ideas which were in direct conflict with the values or information which some students possessed. These conflicting ideas, presented logically and cogently, could not be casually dismissed; the students were presented with this predicament: could they respect others without agreeing with (and perhaps even without respecting) their ideas? From observation of our sample, it seems that these discrepancies led to an ability to disassociate values and individuals, thereby allowing disagreement with other students without loss of mutual respect. Students did not necessarily grow to find each other's ideas more acceptable, however. What they did learn was that they could feel free to express their opinions whether or not they felt that those opinions would be acceptable to their peers. This movement toward increased tolerance was directly related to the intervention within the class.

Our chapter has attempted to cover aspects of the Sierra curriculum specifically influencing individuals in our sample, as well as to trace the substance of changes occurring during the year which may or may not be evidenced in the results of paper-and-pencil or structured interview tests. It is clear that the content discussed in the Sierra class often provided an impetus leading students to reaction and reflection. When examining the effects of an event or curriculum intervention upon individuals, we often assume that the intervention influences subjects in differential ways, depending upon a large number of situational and personality variables. In most studies, we know how the intervention was conducted, we know the outcome, but we often have little or no knowledge of the subjects' perceptions of their experiences and the process by which they may change, important information about the effect of that intervention. This chapter has attempted to show how such information can be culled from the rich source of student self-report — from intensive interviews and journal-keeping — to further describe student growth and some of the impact of Sierra on that growth.

The attitudinal and behavioral changes we have discussed occurred across our sample. Clearly, these individuals changed and grew during their year in Sierra — in their thinking processes, in their feelings about themselves, in their ways of dealing with others. We hope that our limited description of the changes in thoughts, feelings, and behavior occurring in these students leads to a better understanding of the life of college freshmen in general and, in particular, of the life of freshmen in the Sierra Project.

References

Barker, R. *Ecological psychology*. Stanford, CA: Stanford University Press, 1968.

Chickering, A. W. *Education and identity*. San Francisco: Jossey-Bass, 1969.

Rosenthal, R., & Rosnow, R. (Eds.). *Artifact in behavioral research*. New York: Academic Press, 1969.

White, R. W. *Lives in progress: A study of the natural growth of personality* (2nd ed.). New York: Holt, Rinehart & Winston, 1966.

Willems, E., & Raush, H. (Eds.). *Naturalistic viewpoints in psychological research*. New York: Holt, Rinehart & Winston, 1969.

Wilson, S. The use of ethnographic techniques in educational research. *Review of Educational Research*, 1977, 47, 245-265.

Chapter 11

FIVE YEARS LATER:
RETROSPECTIVE COMMENTARY
ON A MORAL COMMUNITY

Loren Lee

Statements from the heart carry meaning more rapidly than statistics. Or so I've found. When interviewing ex-Sierrans, I requested that they be "gut-level" honest — and they were. Their disclosures, five years after being in the program, speak uniquely for its impact.

My method was to select 14 Sierrans from the group that entered in 1975. I attempted to gather a cross-section of the class — students of differing value orientations, backgrounds, and levels of involvement in the program — looking for students whom I remembered as being "on the outskirts," as well as those deeply involved in the life of Sierra. I interviewed ten of the students in depth, usually at their homes in northern or southern California. The remainder were interviewed briefly, usually over the telephone.

In order not to bias their responses, I used an approach to questioning which "funneled" students' responses from broader to more specific areas. First, ex-Sierrans were asked simply to talk at length about Sierra — what things had been important to them or had made an impression, what areas of the project benefited them the most and the least. Next, as they began to speak about certain topics, I asked them more specific questions to elicit clarified impressions. Finally, I briefly described particular aspects of the class and the curricular modules on which students were asked to comment, discussing any impact these modules had upon their lives and presenting any criticisms they had of them. These interviews were transcribed, organized, and edited for presentation in this section. To all this information I have readily added my own recollections as a participant in Sierra.

Despite my attempts to sample a range of students, however, there are several limitations to the material presented here. The students questioned came from one "class" of Sierra; thus, some of their impressions may be unique only to that year of the intervention. Also, over a five-year span, it can be expected that some students will have forgotten some of their freshman experiences; I am assuming that their more lasting impressions were of their most important experiences. Finally, students were asked to give their honest and "heartfelt" impressions; had they been asked to give a formal critique of the Sierra program, their answers probably would have been different. Nonetheless, the comments acquired should provide a valuable glimpse of student opinion about Sierra. This is particularly true since, five years later, ex-Sierrans are in a better position to judge the longitudinal impact of Sierra upon their lives, and to assess this impact in relation to other factors of their college experience.

In addition to its long-range perspective, this assessment will differ from other evaluative instruments used in the Sierra Project in at least two ways. First, it is primarily an analysis of student opinion focused through one person's eyes; to that extent, it differs from the more empirical, test-based results of the investigation. Second, I did not attempt to produce a quantitative evaluation, but rather a representative slice of student feelings; little claim is made as to exactly how many students felt one way or another. My purpose was to elicit as broad-based and "normative" a response as I could from the students with whom I spoke. Therefore, the nature of this evaluation is subjective and indicative as opposed to objective and comprehensive.

MORAL GROWTH: THE STUDENTS' PERCEPTIONS

What was it that Sierra did (or didn't do) to cause us to grow? In what ways were our values and methods of valuing affected? What are the lasting changes that Sierra has made upon us as moral beings? Are there better ways to induce moral maturity?

Students I spoke with gave a wide range of answers to the above questions; I developed an overriding sense that each student's impression of that Sierra year was different. For example, in assessing their own moral growth, students do not perceive themselves within the framework that is being used by the investigators (i.e., a Kohlbergian schema). Their internal models of morality vary, and any attempts to assess their reactions to growth experiences must flow from a knowledge of these models. Thus, it is helpful to understand the students' organization of "moral realities" when formulating our own, often theoretical conclusions.

From the start, I began to realize two things from my interviews with ex-Sierrans. The first is that there exists no general agreement among students as to what constitutes a higher plane of morality. They make little distinction between principled morality and law-based morality, or between "good boy/good girl" and hedonistic orientations. That is to be expected, since only a small portion of the students are familiar with Kohlberg. As it happened, none of the students I spoke with who were familiar with Kohlberg accepted the framework as wholly valid or descriptive of their own moral growth. One Sierran, now a law student, voiced the following:

> My general feeling on Kohlberg is that it's an inconsistent doctrine and . . . built around a "holier than thou" attitude. If you accept his theory and someone attempts to argue against it saying, "I think the highest level of moral reasoning is to obey the law of the land (which would be Stage 4, I seem to recall, right?), and I think this is the level most people should strive for, and if everyone reached that level then the world would be a better place to live," then I think the answer to that by a Kohlbergian is, "Ahha, here we have a Stage 4 person." In other words, you can't really give and take against his theory. It can't be disproven. . . .
>
> Discussions about Kohlberg's theory are like discussions on religion with people who come from opposite ends of the spectrum and are talking at each other and never hearing each other, and neither person having the instruments to take what the other person says and apply it. No, they have their two beliefs. And that's what always struck me about this

Kohlberg stuff. There's no way to disprove it and you have to accept it on blind faith and go forward from there. And anyone who would put forward an opposing theory—which I always thought social sciences was about—the people who back Kohlberg will just always say, "Well, of course you don't understand . . . you don't understand Stage 6 thinking cuz you're only a Stage 4—naturally you don't think Stage 6 is superior. But it is."

Another Sierran, now a teacher, commented on the validity of the testing and her feelings toward the theory:

G: I didn't care for the whole battery of tests. Like the moral development: it was so easy—like you could just mold your answers. I could be a Stage 6 myself or a Stage 2.

L: How did you know about that, G? You're apparently familiar with Kohlberg.

G: Yeah. I had always read *Psychology Today* . . . . And weren't we instructed in Kohlberg in class?

L: I forget. At any rate, you knew about the theory.

G: Yes. I've taken social psychology and educational psychology and I think it (Kohlberg's theory) is a lot of bunk.

L: And the testing itself—what did you feel about that?

G: I don't think people took it seriously.

While other students' comments varied, the overwhelming tide of opinion was that they could accept neither the testing nor the theory as valid (at least for themselves).

What Models Did the Students Use?

Upon interviewing students further, I found that many do not differentiate content and structure of moral reasoning. To grow in the moral sense is not simply to voice one's values with a new framework (i.e., orientation or epistemology), but to change one's sense about what the relevant values are. Hence, moral growth means coming to grips with the values that pertain most closely to one's identity, and learning to incorporate those values effectively into one's behavior. The primary direction is toward wiser discrimination between values and a personalization of those values. That the students rejected Kohlberg's theoretical framework does not indicate that their understanding of moral growth was better or more sophisticated. Most held fairly traditional concepts. Though they had different notions of the way morality develops, their views converged in several respects:

1. Growth in moral reasoning means learning to differentiate right from wrong and good from poor decisions based upon a value set that is uniquely one's own.

2. Morals are not something one can readily teach post-adolescent teenagers. They are inculcated only once, during childhood, and after that they are changed mostly through experience.

3. Moral reasoning is, in some ways, connected both to profound topics, such as life philosophies, and to more pragmatic topics, such as lifestyles. For instance, students did not draw fine distinctions between holding a fundamental tenet that all life is sacred, maintaining a wartime pacifist ideology, and marching in anti-draft demonstrations. (While students are capable of drawing the distinctions between levels of belief and action, they are more likely to see the whole as an unbroken stream — general philosophies leading to moral values, which then become prescriptions for everyday living.)

4. Moral growth is more a product of environment than of internal maturation. However, as powerful as the environment is, it is the individual's own choice how he or she will develop morally. Thus, in order of influence, causative factors in moral growth are: the person, the environment, and maturation processes.

5. There are no sequences to moral development that enough people agree upon to be considered universal. Some order exists, but most of it is "individually mapped"; i.e., the person decides how he/she will morally progress.

As to the particular models that the students hold concerning moral development, there were several:

Modified Social Learning Models. Some students believe that people's moral natures reflect those of the important individuals around them; i.e., behavioral decisions are based on modeling that friends, relatives, and particularly parents provide. Some feel that both normative behaviors and particular situational behaviors are results of the models available in the environment at a specific time. Some seem to believe that the stimulus is a negative one—for example, whatever the parents model, the child will do the opposite. Most students having social learning conceptions obviously do not adhere completely to the ordering of causative factors shown in #4 above; the adamant, in particular, felt that the environment was the most influential factor most of the time. Others believe that individual choice enters the picture when one selects models for imitation.

Character Approaches. Moral maturity is understood by many students to mean the valuing of specific moral virtues such as patience and self-sacrifice. The emphasis on the application of those virtues, increasing and improving over time, is what constitutes moral development. For some, this means that virtue is recognized through suffering, through committed relationships, and through the facing of death. For others, moral development allows the refinement of whatever portion of virtue the individual already possesses; for instance, the virtue of generosity might be refined by giving frequently to charitable organizations.

Behaviorist Models. While few students actually accept behaviorist (reinforcement) explanations of morality, some recognize it as a tenable explanation for some people choosing to act as they do. Most students feel the notion that all moral decisions are a function of rewards and punishments is too extreme.

Cognitive Discrimination Perspectives. Many students envisage moral development as a gradual accumulation of reasoning strategies by which one can answer questions of right and wrong. Becoming morally mature means having the capacity to consider alternatives soundly and to reason from a premise. It means knowing how to draw the relevant data from a situation, applying principles when judging that data.

Shaping of the Will or Spirit Thesis. Several of the students with religious backgrounds consider moral development as a process that one goes through in learning to conquer temptation more effectively. Moral maturity is viewed as the ability to "stare wrongful desires in the face" and to refuse them. Making the will more malleable to "God's guidance" is another definition of moral maturity.

Personality Factor Models. Several students associate moral maturity with possession of adaptive qualities of personality, e.g., independence or assertiveness. Moral development is the isolation of factors of personality that best equip individuals to live effectively in their environments. This type of model is distinguished from the character approaches in that the latter emphasize traditional positive virtues, whereas personality factor models stress developing traits of personality to increase one's practical influence in the world.

Superimposed upon all of these models are varying conceptions of the direction of moral development. Some students see a linear upward growth — every individual becoming slowly better and better. Others see moral development as a process of harmonizing with one's environment, moving along the paths of least resistance. As children grow older they adopt patterns of socialization in order to avoid confrontation; throughout life, they are changing their values to "make as few waves as possible." Other individuals, particularly ones who had witnessed dramatic changes in one stage of their lives, consider the development of man's moral nature as a series of random and non-contiguous experiences; the values and methods of valuing at one stage of life have little relevance or relationship to those of another stage. Moral nature is perceived as a parade of blocks, each block containing the values and principles of that time completely separate from any other block.

The Range of Response

It is clear that creating generalizations based on direct student response is somewhat difficult considering these many differing views as to what constitutes moral growth. This part of our students' views of the success of the Sierra intervention thus cannot objectively assess the program; its most useful role is in summarizing the impact of the program as it is *perceived* by the students.

As I mentioned earlier, the range of student response five years after the Sierra Project experience was rather broad. In response to the question, "Did Sierra make any differences in your moral growth?" ex-Sierrans gave answers ranging from "no difference at all" to "important differences" in their perception of moral values, other individuals, etc. Students contending that the Sierra Project had not influenced them were often vehement in their insistence that I record their statements. Asking for a "gut-level" response to Sierra's contribution to student's moral growth, I sometimes got answers such as: "Not in the least bit. My moral growth was entirely separate from what happened in Sierra." Students typically responded that the course material was interesting but not life-changing:

L: Would you say, T, that Sierra in any way affected your moral reasoning?

T: I don't think it really had an effect. I think that situations that came up later in my life I would have resolved or not resolved in the same way with or without Sierra. But they (the discussions on moral issues) were interesting.

L: So it caused you to think about [moral issues], but didn't really change your moral reasoning processes?

T: Right.

L: Would you say that, on the whole, Sierra . . . stretched your capacity as a moral reasoner—forced you to think more broadly, etc.?

T: I don't think so. None of the stuff like the moral dilemma material [Defining Issues Test] have I ever thought back to in making decisions.

Other students stated that Sierra did change them, but only because it was a dormitory and it was their first year away from home—the program had nothing to do with it. One student commented that it was the "presentation of many different new things," such as living in close proximity to other individuals, that caused growth, but that this could have been accomplished in other dorms, also. Another student voiced the argument this way:

> Well, you see, I don't think it had anything to do with Sierra. As a whole, it could have happened to me [anyway] as a freshman in a university [placed] in a totally new environment in a dorm. There was nothing unique about Sierra that led to my changes in attitudes. It was being away from home, having more close relationships with people my own age, having observed them in every single facet of life — eating with them, sleeping with them occasionally, and just spending a lot of time together. It seemed to happen in Sierra as a place, but not because of it.

Three types of responses came from the students reporting that Sierra had made some difference in their moral growth. The first was that their experiences in Triple I-D groups,[1] class discussions, and the informal life of the community had caused them to be more aware and tolerant of other value systems:

L: Would you say, K, that Sierra helped you at all in your ability to reason morally?

K: From the many discussions of moral issues we had, yes. I would have to say my morals widened up.

L: When you say widened up, does that mean you became more liberal as far as your morals, or [that] you saw a greater spectrum of morals in other people?

K: I guess I saw the greater variety of moral values that different people have because I used to think that there's one set of morals — and mine's right — and other people's, if it's different, it's not right. That's a reflection of the narrowness I had when I was in high school because there was a limited number of individuals with whom I discussed morals. We did a lot of discussions on morals [in Sierra] — not just inside the dorm class but outside in the dorm community with friends. Through this, I think I've learned a lot about other people's morals. I don't make so many distinctions about what is wrong, yet I still have a firm set of certain moral values that I'm not going to change.

[1]See Chapter 6 for a description of Triple I-D groups.

Those who said they became more tolerant generally insisted that they had not changed any of their own values, but had accepted a wider range of values in other individuals. From one girl:

> Well, Sierra didn't really change my *inside* moral values. That I haven't changed and I don't think I will. But it's modified *outside*-wise to make me more flexible, softer. I'm not a better person or a higher person as in higher vs. lower, but I'm able to learn about other aspects of people. Instead of me, myself, being this rigid thing bouncing around and hurting people, hurting myself, I've become softer, more flexible and able to harmonize with others.

A second form of response came from those individuals who noted that Sierra had caused them to challenge their set of values. A typical response went like this:

> I think [Sierra] helped me to realize that it's okay to question. I don't remember specifics, but somehow I remember that we were shown how to question ourselves. That seems to have transpired in the learning. Somewhere, the way to question things, the way to find answers was provided.

Most individuals, however, do not credit Sierra with having produced actual changes in their value system that first year but do note that, as a result of being in a freshman dorm away from home, their values changed. Sierra was helpful to them in this respect because the discussions and environment supported open dialogue and "processing" of important value changes. One girl summarized her first sexual encounter and Sierra's role in her considerations of this encounter:

> L: Were there any particular incidents that happened that first year that really prompted you to rethink all your moral values?
>
> M: Some incident?
>
> L: Just, like something you did or someone else did to you.
>
> M: .... well, the sexual aspect I guess. That's something that really opened up. That was my first time because I never had any sexual contact in high school .... Sexuality was a "no no" ... but that's where I opened up.

L: So that was a break for you, a change for you.

M: Yeah, but there was a lot of guilt. I think probably all through the freshman year . . . .

L: So . . . it was the first time. Did Sierra encourage that for you or in any way help you process it?

M: Well, I guess situation-wise, it was easier to happen because of the co-ed living situation, more freedom away from your parents. But it [Sierra] did help me process it through understanding it . . . . At that starting time, I felt so much guilt over having sex that I didn't enjoy it. Like now, I enjoy it; I don't have any guilty conscience.

For many individuals, going to college meant cutting the parental reins for the first time. Sierra was only indirectly responsible for this emancipation and its effects on student growth; the community provided the support to aid their transitions. One student's comments reflected this perception of a supportive community:

L: Would you say that Sierra in any way affected your method or practice of moral reasoning?

P: Yeah, I began thinking my own way — as far as not always thinking what my parents were thinking, as far as what I thought was right for me to do, as far as social life went, as far as sex life went. I found I was slipping into my own more . . . .

L: You had a chance to be a little more independent in your own morality . . . . Was that a result of Sierra or just a result of being out at college?

P: I think that was just the result of being out of the home and being able to experience things for myself.

L: Did Sierra help you to process any of this new independence, i.e., was there anything in Sierra's environment that was encouraging to your new independence?

P: Yeah, because I found I was getting a lot of support for what I was learning to think myself. Instead of looking to parents all the time, I was looking to friends for support for what I wanted to do.

Thus, those individuals who felt Sierra did play a role in their moral growth mentioned three results: a) they became more tolerant in their acceptance of others' values; b) they were challenged and came to question their own set of values; and c) they were provided with a supportive environment when undergoing a change in values or a transitional phase of their life.

On the whole, however, I concluded from the comments I received that the "average" Sierran found the program helpful but not pivotal, consequential but not crucial, to moral growth. Most expressed sincere appreciation for having been able to participate in the program, but clearly hesitated to suggest that it had induced large scale revisions in their thinking or valuing processes. They felt enlightened, but not necessarily transformed.

The Delayed Response

In several cases, students felt that Sierra did make a significant difference, but that change only appeared two or three years after their freshman year. Students reported varying "long-term" effects that Sierra had on their moral development after the conclusion of that first year:

1. A few noted how their training in empathy skills and conflict resolution placed them at a distinct advantage in following years when they lived in other dorms. The result of their increased success was an enhanced self-image. However, this training also caused them to recognize a broadening of their relational values; they realized how critical the issues of trust and openness—things they had taken for granted during their first year—had now become. For these people, *leaving* Sierra had the greatest impact: they came to recognize that in the "cold, cruel world," they needed to implement for themselves the relational principles that Sierra had stood for.

2. As a result of questioning begun in Sierra, a few students reported distinct shifts in their value systems in following years. For the most part, these shifts were toward more liberal attitudes; a few students changed their views toward

sex; others became more open in their acceptance of alcohol and marijuana. No students I spoke with actually became more conservative as a result of their value exploration in Sierra.

3. During their sophomore and junior years two students made distinct changes in their sex-role behavior which they attributed partly to the study of sex-role choices during their Sierra year. One, a "closet" gay, decided to come out and openly declare his sexual preference; another, deciding she had been too long the virtuous "Mommy and Daddy's little girl," moved in with her boyfriend. While results like this are dramatic (and not necessarily beneficial), it is difficult to know precisely how much of an effect Sierra actually had on their decisions. The fact that they ascribe their behavior to things learned in Sierra is at least a partial indication that some students perceive the program as moving them in very large ways.

4. Several students reported considering communes as an alternative lifestyle after discussions generated in Sierra, but there is no information about whether any ex-Sierrans engaged in such a radical venture. On a more moderate scale, two students reported dropping out of school in later years to "find themselves." For both, the time in Sierra had produced significant questions — particularly with regard to the value of education, career choices, etc. Both eventually returned to school to successfully complete degrees.

While the reports of "post-hoc" effects were few, they suggest that more individuals may have experienced delayed effects from the Sierra program than may ever be known to the investigators.

What Other Things Made a Difference in the Students' Moral Growth?

Beyond the few cases cited, most individuals could not recall their moral values being significantly affected by their Sierra experience; they generally pointed to other factors which played a significant part in their development that first year. While students expounded on these "other factors" at length, they can generally be placed in five categories:

1. The most important single factor cited by students was the influence of a boyfriend or girlfriend. This is understandable, for college freshmen often consider that most "significant other" as the one person worth pleasing by modifying their values. One student adapted herself to the extent that she took the classes her boyfriend thought she should and chose all her extracurricular activities by the same criterion. However, not all students reported changing their values just to please mates; many changed their values during the process of experiencing an intimate relationship. For instance, one ex-Sierran noted the impact that an interracial relationship occurring in his freshman year had upon his views of marriage. Students frequently noted their realization that relationships required sacrifice—of money, time, and emotion. It is not surprising that, in a society where the "desirable" status is still to be "with somebody," freshman students find a large part of their value confrontation and growth in couple relationships.

2. A second factor commonly cited by students was membership in a tight-knit cohesive group—such as a sorority or fraternity, ethnic organization, or church fellowship. Since these groups usually provided a supportive system which sometimes lasted beyond the four years of the students' college experience, it is likely that the values students adopted were influenced by their group membership. These groups may have been perceived to be effective in producing moral growth for the individual because many such groups strive to emphasize and incorporate "noble" ideas.

3. The third factor which students perceived as influencing their moral growth might be termed "real world" experience. For some, this included holding a job during their freshman year. Sampling these vocational experiences gave students an opportunity to assess the actualities of relationships in the working world, the value of education, etc. Others found that the realities of academic competition at the university caused them to question their life priorities

—a large salary, a prestigious degree, etc. Since this factor of real world experience is related to students' eventual adjustment to life outside the university, it is easy to see why it also played a large role in their value selection.

4. Study in humanistic disciplines affected a wide number of students. Students who took the Humanities Core course series — and classes in history in particular — reported that their perspectives were changed vastly by their academic coursework. This effect may have occurred because a portion of the Humanities Core course literature is designed to expose societal fallacies or "thought traps." For instance, readings from George Bernard Shaw argue against the proposition that "greed is evil"; readings from Sartre discuss society from an existential point of view, an orientation with which many of the students were previously unfamiliar. The result was that many students lodged their feelings of conflict and disillusionment in a new housing — one which is given expression by Nietzsche and Kierkegaard, Malraux and Camus. This finding — that students perceive humanistic study to have influenced their moral judgments — suggests that substantial change in values may occur from conventional processes of education.

5. The final factor which students reported as modifying their moral growth was their experience with drugs. A small number of ex-Sierrans reported that experience with hallucinogens and barbiturates radically altered their perspectives and systems of valuing. Whether such results were lasting, whether they were actually due to the drugs or the culture associated with them, are questions I am not able to answer. The major effects that students reported were a liberation and an expansion of awareness, both in a physical and social sense. None of the students that I spoke with were able to relate their changed perspectives to actual changes in behavior — except that their experiences led them to want to experiment further.

Why Didn't Sierra Make More Differences in the Students' Moral Growth?

When we attempt to critically assess the impact of Sierra, there is always room for the possibility that we are failing to see effects which actually did occur—particularly given the complex structures Sierra was attempting to influence. Effect on student growth may not show directly in testing nor on observed behavioral indices. Some effects, as previously mentioned, are delayed. Finally, and I suspect most importantly, even students may be unaware on a conscious level of what changes the intervention produced.

However, within these constraints, it must still be concluded —at least in the students' eyes—that Sierra had limited impact on their moral development in comparison to other factors. Why? Some reasons were offered by the students themselves when interviewed:

1. An obvious reason Sierra may have had a limited impact is simply the proportion of time that Sierra took in comparison to classes, boyfriends and girlfriends, extracurricular involvements, etc. Even if Sierra had an impact equal to the fraction of time allotted to it by the freshman students, its meaningfulness would be restricted because of the significance of other activities dominating a student's life. Moreover, in comparison to the influence of forces across the span of an individual's life—even an 18 year old's—the magnitude and span of Sierra were too small and too short to hold a candle to morally shaping forces like ten years of childhood, six years in the Boy Scouts, four years in a high school peer group, etc.

2. A second reason may be that the theoretical framework for moral development was too narrowly constructed; it may have assessed the wrong factors or stressed inappropriate types of skill development.

3. A third reason cited by students was the inapplicability of moral issues commonly used in Sierra class discussion. The moral dilemma material (e.g., the Kohlberg-Rest issues or games like "Lifeboat") and the discussions of contemporary moral issues (such as euthanasia, abortion, etc.) were

not specifically related to the kinds of moral issues with which college freshmen were then being confronted, e.g., value choices in relationships, values pertinent to academic endeavor (like cheating on Chem 1 midterms), etc. Those more relevant issues were usually discussed informally, in after-dinner conversations or in late-night marathon talks. The times that pertinent issues were discussed in class, e.g., after the "Alligator River" exercise or following the dance where sex roles were reversed, the talks often stopped short of individual application. Students were left with thought-provoking psychological exercises, but little notion of how these exercises could be translated to their every-day reality. Finally, regarding the benefits of using highly artificial dilemmas, one student's remark encapsulated feelings in this area:

> I have yet to be stuck in an eight-man lifeboat with 12 people—or be found in need of a wonder drug to cure my wife which no one will sell me—or [be] on the wrong side of the river with no way to get across but to sell my body . . . . Real life just doesn't happen that way!

4. Another related reason is that the emphasis in the program is placed on moral conflict induction rather than on resolution. While moral conflict may be the factor that causes students to make the jumps from Stage 3 to 4 to Stage 5, resolution is the behavior which causes them to feel that they have grown or matured. Sierrans from '75-'76 noted that there was a lack of explicit resolution strategies —for value reasoning, for conflict resolution, for practical decision-making. In later years of the Sierra Project, several modes of decision making were explored; perhaps students from those years felt more secure because they were given those strategies to resolve issues.

5. A final reason that the Sierra program may have produced limited moral growth was its failure to provide many models of "mature moral reasoning." While a few of the staff were no doubt Stage 6 thinkers, most of us were simply rein-forced for whatever kind of thinking we were doing because all of our peers were doing it also. This is not to say that the mere presence of "higher level" thinkers is sufficient

to induce moral growth (cf. Rest, 1974), but even for traditional notions of moral development, some form of modeling is important. Several students noted that having the resident staff present was very helpful as an example; however, it would have been nice to have other individuals available for additional models. One Sierran suggested that the best formula would have been to pair up each student with a mature adult of his choosing. Each student would then spend some time during the week with the adult to discuss issues of lifestyle and growth. While the feasibility of such an endeavor is questionable, it points out the type of activity that might be utilized to provide adequate modeling.

Other Ways to Catalyze Moral Development: The Students Do the Thinking

I thought that after a year in a course designed to aid their moral growth, ex-Sierrans would have some strong notions of how they would induce development in this area. While some did, many did not. One student thought that Sierra had done a good job in this regard but couldn't say how: "Something they did in class helped, but I can't put my finger on it."

When actually asked the question, "How would you teach or promote moral reasoning?" several students replied it was impossible for anyone to make headway in influencing the moral values of an individual after 18 years of previous shaping. As one student put it:

Instilling an open mind is something that you do at a very young age. Certainly by the time someone comes to Sierra, their moral background and their moral reasoning are entrenched to such a degree that nothing could significantly change them. Moral reasoning is much more innate, and might be affected by any number of things from their background—be it religious training, their family background, just the bundle of characteristics that goes into making them . . . . And by the time you reach puberty, many of the ways you morally reason, I believe, are pretty well decided.

Most students agreed it was impossible to "teach" moral values to a college-age person; the best that might be expected is that an individual could be given many options from which to choose, or could be compelled to filter moral questions, to formally "process" them.

Other students felt that the only way persons grew morally was to observe carefully the "moral milestones" in their lives — those times when they were facing real value choices. By watching their own reactions, decisions, and the consequence of decisions, they learn about appropriate value choices. These students held the basic belief that experience is the best teacher; all that an educational program can do is help students inductively feel out their own reactions to events. From this form of "guided discovery," the students can learn to develop a hierarchy of desirable outcomes which would lead to a corresponding value set.

Yet another student felt that the key to moral growth lay in the age-old adage, "Know thyself." She advocated a greater emphasis on formal tools for introspection, e.g., self-exploration exercises, etc.

Finally, one student, now a teacher, suggested a four-plank strategy: (a) role-play, combined with (b) examination of historical examples of moral decisions, (c) investigation of childhood morality patterns as a prelude to analysis of adult morality, and (d) investigation of the various moral conceptions of different sociological groups, e.g., coal miners, the aged, Muslim men, etc.

The Instruction of Opposing Perspectives: A Critical Challenge?

A constant theme which has emerged from talks with ex-Sierrans is the notion of "subtle persuasion." While none of the students felt they were being force-fed particular ideologies or value systems, many indicated that the atmosphere of Sierra served as "liberal indoctrination."

It is important to clarify what is meant in this regard. While the Sierra staff was concerned with fostering post-conventional moral reasoning, the students often inferred that conventional value systems were unacceptable. The reason for this inference is clear: it was the traditional values that were continually placed under question in dorm discussions. Traditional sex roles were analyzed, as were traditional relational patterns, occupations, lifestyles, etc. The reason for these analyses, of course, was to encourage students to question the bases of their values. However, it was specifically stated that the traditional roles and patterns might actually be okay—if people understood them and chose them freely. It was assumed that if students questioned their conventional values, some would naturally remain traditional and some might move to more liberal mores. There was no attempt made to question the validity of the contemporary (i.e., liberal) sex and relational roles; for instance, after showing the inadequacies of traditional male-female division of labor, it was naturally assumed by everyone that the "best" way to run a house is to divide all tasks equally. This may or may not be true—but it was subtly assumed to be true. Conservative values were never placed under direct attack or liberal values explicitly advocated; however, it was always the traditional values that were questioned and the liberal ideas that were offered as alternatives. One student comments about this:

> It seemed like in Social Ecology [the academic program offering credit for Sierra], most of the stuff of the profs is really liberal, not conservative. It seemed like they were preaching and teaching the word "free will." You know—you had free will to do as you wish. If you wanted to take drugs and commit suicide, you're dead . . . because that's where you want to be.

This critical comment is particularly compelling because the student making it was considered by many of his peers to be a liberal. He is joined by a handful of students from the conservative side who clearly distinguished their position from the one they felt was being advocated in dorm class:

L: What kinds of things in Sierra made the biggest difference in how you reasoned morally?

S: In the Sierra class itself, the most significant thing was my morals vs. their morals. As far as sex roles, as far as a married family—I totally disagreed with them. The ideas that the husband and wife should do everything independently and should share everything equally . . . I still find myself being traditional.

L: I have a question now that's important. Would you say that Sierra allowed you to maintain those traditional values? Did it cause you to challenge them and/or did it channel you towards more liberal values?

S: A lot of it was challenging. I changed some of them. Now that we're married, there's a lot of things that we do jointly, whereas before it used to be men shouldn't wash the dishes, shouldn't cook, etc.

L: So you found it was a challenge but it wasn't them [the Sierra staff] necessarily advocating one or the other?

S: Well, sometimes it was advocating their [own liberal point of view] . . . .

And another girl answered it this way:

L: So did being in Sierra cause you to move toward the liberal pole in later years?

W: Um . . . I think I've tried now all the things I thought were so evil!

Thus, while few students felt dragged toward the liberal end of the spectrum, there can be little doubt that most reported a gentle tug in that direction. Perhaps that was good, for a number of students came to the university feeling constricted by patterns of behavior and belief systems; they thought and acted in the ways they did simply because their parents or teachers or ministers had told them they should. Sierra liberated them to think independently about their values and to make decisions as individuals.

On the other hand, there is a real danger whenever educators, while claiming to present a value-free curriculum, actually implicitly defend a portion of the value spectrum. Maurice Broady speaks of this difficulty for educators:

But neutrality is not possible. Every relationship with another person, to the degree that it entails some choice of conduct, embodies a view of how people ought to relate to one another. Even the effort to remain neutral, impossible though it is, is itself to adopt a moral stance. Therefore the teacher faces the dilemma that, while he is inevitably engaged in a moral relationship with his students, he is committed to a principle that he should not moralize at them (Broady, 1974, p. 58).

Thus, to be neutral, as Broady contends, is impossible; even not to take a stance is to take one. Belief in this contention may leave planners of projects like Sierra with three options:

1. A value stance can be taken implicitly, without telling students directly "where you're coming from."

2. A value stance can be taken, but it can be explicitly stated to the students that this is the position of the staff only and does not necessarily have to be adopted by the students.

3. Multiple alternatives, particularly from differing perspectives, can be presented and given equal "air time."

I have already noted that Option 1 is dangerous because a value-oriented curriculum is conveyed as value-free knowledge; the subtle advocation of one set of values easily leads to well-meaning indoctrination. The implicit suggestion of values bypasses the individuals' rights to choose for themselves; they cannot choose if they are only vaguely aware of the range of choices at hand.

These problems made Option 2 attractive. This option restores free choice because it allows individuals to realize the alternatives before them. However, Option 2, because it is the presentation of one particular view, also is in danger of becoming a one-sided persuasion. I believe, therefore, that the safest position is a combination of Options 2 and 3. Educators cannot help transmitting values in the process of communicating, but they can aid students by being explicit about what values they are assuming. Additionally, they can reduce the possibility of one-sided indoctrination by presenting a variety of value options. The need for divergent perspectives is voiced by Broady:

> In developing curricula, and in seminars especially, it is important to incorporate two elements which have their analogue in Mannheim's ideas. First of all, there must be a dialectic. By this I mean that divergent approaches to the same problem need to be studied. These divergencies of view must be sufficiently sharp to require the student not only to under-

stand them, but also to induce him to puzzle out his own opinion. Second, each argument must initially be studied in such a way that its author's reasons and justifications are properly understood (Broady, 1974, p. 67).

It is the second provision that allows for a true "dialectic" to ensue; both liberal and conservative positions must be subjected to the same level of scrutiny, given the same chance for complete explication. Only then does the individual have the chance to make up his/her mind while in possession of the fullest knowledge. But what does this suggest in practical terms for Sierra?

1. An assault on conventional morality must not be allowed to be confused with an assault on specific, currently conventional values. Rather, all values must be placed under equal scrutiny. Moral conflict can be induced, but in resolving the conflict, students should be given full recourse to liberal, conservative or moderate positions.

2. Morality must be presented as encompassing a range of philosophical and ethical perspectives. While it is impractical to give time to every possible approach to a moral question, still, the broadest strategies drawing from the widest range of perspectives are more likely to produce knowledgeable, well-defined systems of value.

3. Good use should be made of the available materials from values clarification curricula. Because such curricula are oriented toward developing in the individual a unique set of values, it fits neatly with any program attempting to foster moral development. The goals of values clarification, as presented by Raths, Harmin, and Simon (1966), seem to parallel closely these set forth by the Sierra Project. According to those authors, values clarification curricula are designed to help students learn to:

   1. choose their values freely;

   2. choose their values from alternatives;

   3. choose their values after weighing the consequences of each alternative;

   4. prize and cherish their values;

5. share and publicly affirm their values;

6. act upon their values;

7. act upon their values repeatedly and consistently.

(Adapted from Raths, Harmin, & Simon,
1966, p. 63-65)

THE TYPES OF EFFECT: MODELS AND CASE STUDIES

In this section, I attempt to answer in two ways the question, "What did Sierra *really* do to its participants?" While neither answer is sufficient to give the outsider a complete picture, they may complement other information about the project. In the first short section, I discuss several models and analogies that ex-Sierrans have used to describe their Sierra experience; in the second, I present a series of case studies to illustrate some effects that Sierra had upon its inhabitants.

Those who were never a part of Sierra have difficulty learning about it from those who were; it seems that lengthy explanations never tell all. The stranger to Sierra is left wondering what kind of group the Sierra community really was. There are the official guides to read—the developmental texts and Whiteley reprints—and unofficial memoirs, journals, and even letters, if one is lucky enough to obtain them. Still the question frequently arises—what really *did* happen to those people in Sierra? One answer comes from the stacks of tests and sets of data that have regularly poured out of the program; another comes from the staff of investigators who regularly served as observers—albeit from a particular and well-informed position. Then there are the participants. Their stories tell another angle, less complete —since the participants did not know all that the experimenters had planned—but in some sense, perhaps more accurate. The participants have attempted to tell their own story "just like it is."

The Models

The problem with models is that they are only conceptualizations. Usually they are "shorthand" for the real thing—something to remind you that something greater and more complete is out there. Still, I have found it helpful to discuss with ex-Sierrans what they felt were appropriate models of their experience. Many were skilled in analogy and immediately supplied metaphors for their time in the dorm, while others simply agreed with one of the models already proposed by the other participants. My descriptions of these models are necessarily brief, but give a taste of the ways that former Sierrans have thought about their learning and growing in the program. Eleven models emerged from the interviews with ex-Sierrans, including several that I suggested.

There are the Sierrans who believe that the major focus of the community is the distilling of thoughts, the sharing of important reasonings, and the promise of a forum for the thinkers of our generation to grind out resolutions to social issues and public policy. For these informants, the idea of a *think tank* was appropriate. This term is often used to describe ad hoc bodies in a legislative assembly that join to pound through new and high-powered suggestions for the state. Other students thought that the term "think tank" was far too official a term for the low-lying efforts of many of Sierra's thinkers. They considered much of the Sierra "thought life" as subversive, preferring to label the community as an *academic underground*, a group of highly untraditional (and potentially dangerous) thinkers, whose thoughts on "intimacy" and "bureaucracy" would never have been accepted by the greater society.

For others, the major emphasis of Sierra was upon feelings. They saw the community, particularly in forms like the Triple I-D groups, as a type of *encounter group* that allowed the venting of emotion and soothing of wounds after a hard day in the classroom. In today's jargon, the encounter group has come to be associated with such therapies as nude touching, primal screaming, etc., none of which was actually a part of the Sierra scene. However, the notion of an encounter group as a body of individuals getting together to disclose authentic feelings can be used quite accurately to describe the Sierra experience.

Other Sierrans' analogies of their Sierra experience were related to values. Sierra was seen as a *prism*, a force in their lives that helped break down the blank white light of their moral reasonings into a rainbow of component values and ideological underpinnings. They felt that their value base had been opened into many channels and hues; they saw how some of their values were inconsistent, and how their inconsistent values could be blended to become others.

The thrust of another group's analogies was ideology. They preferred to see Sierra as a meshing of the cultural and religious belief systems which people brought with them. One individual used the idea of a *microcosm* to describe the little world of ideas she saw represented in Sierra. Another said it was more like being a part of a select membership *library* where Sierrans were privileged to walk down rows containing summaries of the ideas and beliefs of the entire world — from which the librarian selected texts for consideration. While not presenting all world views, Sierra did create an atmosphere where existent pluralistic ideologies could display themselves.

Another set of Sierrans preferred to analogize at the organismic level. They talked about many people coming together, suggesting that, at times, Sierra was like an *intersection* where many different people converged for brief encounters before passing on to diverse destinations. Others felt the intersection analogy was not valid because the time frame was actually more extended; after all Sierrans were with each other for a whole year. They liked the analogy of a *zoo*, descriptive both of the range of characters found in Sierra, and of the animal ambitions of some of them.

A last group saw fit to describe Sierra in terms of what was being accomplished there. One individual said that Sierra was a *melting pot*, a place where the extremes in value and feeling could be melted down into a more congenial mixture. Other students have quickly disagreed with this model, feeling that Sierra accentuated major differences rather than diminished them. Another student, convinced that his Sierra experience was not going to lead him down a different road, suggested the analogy of taking part in a *race*: being part of Sierra was like being in a peculiar type of racing vehicle, one custom-fitted to hold many loud and reacting freshmen. The vehicle was not going to win this race; indeed, it might be slower than some of the other more pragmatic vehicles. However, its "style" would be different; its occupants would know that they had had a different sort of experience than the other racers. Finally, one ex-Sierran compared his freshman experience to a *quest*, a search for self and identity amidst the expectations provided by professors, parents, and his own personal ambitions. He stated that Sierra was a channel for that quest, a tour guide giving him pointers and tips about places to stop and look and think.

As I mentioned at the beginning of this section, these models are only suggestive. Together, they form a set of representations that can help the outsider know what we, on the inside, have experienced.

The Case Studies

In addition to these characterizations of the Sierra experience, several themes have come through consistently in my interviews with ex-Sierrans. The following case studies are designed to give these themes some context. These are not case studies in the comprehensive sense; I have not attempted to trace with precision the entire effect Sierra had upon each student. Rather, I have used portions of these students' biographies to illustrate particular facets of Sierra's influence. The selection of cases here is suggestive, not exhaustive. Names have been changed, of course, to protect the disclosers.

Sierra as Family: Tamara and Peter. Tamara, from Los Angeles, was the oldest daughter in a traditional first generation Japanese family. She landed at UCI — and consequently at Sierra — by mistake: she was following the footsteps of a close friend who signed up but later withdrew from the school. The special program of Sierra was not a particular attraction for her — Sierra simply "looked good," as did several other dorms. She submitted her name, however, and was later accepted.

Tamara knew no one when she arrived at UCI. She seldom saw her roommate — one of the more active of the resident staff. During her freshman year, Tamara was a biology major. She worked ten hours a week in a psychobiology lab in addition to taking classes. During the rest of her UCI experience, she continued as a biology major, believing that she wanted to be a doctor. However, in her junior year, she began taking art and engineering classes, and continued to pursue these two avenues while completing her biology degree. She worked part time in the intensive care units of several hospitals, finally concluding that medicine was not her forte. Graduating from UCI, she went on to work for a biology lab in the Los Angeles area, but has now decided to begin study for an architecture degree at UCLA. Tamara has taken up skiing and flying as "rewards" for her hard work in the lab. Her future plans include owning her own architecture firm, being a mother with exactly two kids, completing her Ph.D. in architecture, and teaching. She also expresses the desire someday to begin an institute which will bring together professionals from many fields to interact in a community atmosphere.

Tamara's memories of the Sierra experience are social ones. She came from a family environment which stressed respect and quiet obedience from its members, and recalls little physical affection being shown to her. Her family unit provided security; in high school, Tamara felt perfectly content to come home each day and be by herself. Coming to UCI was a lonely experience . . . until she began to meet members of her "new family":

> S was the first person I met at Sierra. He sat next to me on the left and B was there on the right. All three of us got to know each other and talk to each other. It's so interesting the way we still keep in touch—we probably will forever. Right now, people [from Sierra] are still keeping in contact with me frequently—E, S, etc., and other people here and there. I still feel quite comfortable with them. It's neat. It was a really special dorm.

She craved the affection; she began to realize that her "real self" was more "people-oriented" than she had at first suspected, that she was a more loving person than she had thought:

> Living with 50 other people was really different, since I had lived at home until this time. Meeting all those people was so exciting—it was like a big family. All those people from different backgrounds brought into one building which created —like one big family. I really enjoyed that. And M (the RA) used to say, "Five times a day you have to be hugged, or your spine will shrivel." So I used to get my hugs—from you, Ch, K, and V. I was able to get hugs from everybody. I tried to carry it out into the other dorms, but they weren't into it.

Tamara remembers that Sierra gave her the opportunity for multiple interactions. She especially appreciated the Triple I-D group where she reports hearing for the first time the "real" feelings of people, not the dressed-up versions she had been accustomed to hearing.

One of Tamara's strongest memories about Sierra was the way in which it caused her to re-think how much she actually knew about the world and other people:

> I was very sure of myself before going into Sierra. When I graduated from high school, I was really into philosophy, psychology, and I was very satisfied with myself. Like, I knew everything about life. That [attitude] broke down very quickly when I entered Sierra. That was very positive for me because I was so self-assured—falsely self-assured. Then the more I learned in Sierra, the less I was sure because there were so many possibilities and diverseness. So that really opened my eyes to some different aspects. For instance, drugs. I used to reject anyone who touched drugs. When I was in high school, I didn't have any friends who were into drugs . . . or maybe if they were, they didn't tell me cuz I had very negative views of them. But because of Sierra I met [some people] before I knew they took drugs. I liked them as friends and there was no reason to reject them just because they smoked pot or took drugs.

The biggest change Tamara recalls, however, was the opening of her life to other people. She noted that if it had not been for Sierra, she would probably still never know what it was like to have "a family away from the family." She says that she hopes always to be close to the friends she met during that special freshman year.

* * * * *

Peter grew up in Palotine, a suburb in Illinois. His high school days were spent as editor of the school paper and as a star on a local TV program featuring high school panelists. He decided upon UCI in his senior year—after realizing that USC and Occidental were too expensive. He signed into Sierra because it was an all-freshmen dorm and he knew no one. The "theme" of the dorm had little to do with his selection.

He came to UCI as a precocious prodigy. Fifty units of transferred advanced placement credit plus forty or fifty more units during that freshman year brought him to junior status by his third quarter. He started out as a math major, found he did not like the personality of mathematicians, and switched to social ecology. He swept along at a fast pace and "picked up" a second major, social science, in his third year (by this time, his accumulated units classified him as a senior).

By the end of his four years at UCI, having amassed every major academic honor (he was also a teaching assistant for a number of instructors in his two departments and published several articles), Peter was accepted by several Ivy League law schools. After hesitation, he decided upon Boalt—it was, after all, cheaper than the rest. He is presently studying there, working part time for a judge. His future plans include being part of a general practice law firm and having a family. He has no intention of becoming involved in politics ("too ugly"); he would like to work in a place where he knows he is helping people.

Peter recalls his freshman year as a difficult time for him. He was a thousand miles from home and living in a suite where the other members chose to drink more heavily than he did:

> I wasn't particularly close to the guys in my suite . . . I just didn't feel like I belonged. The first night they went out on a drinking rampage that I knew I could not keep up with. . . . I mostly just experience different feelings when I'm [drinking] but not to the point of utter oblivion. . . . My roommate was an alcoholic . . . he really needed his alcohol—which was really sad to me. Here we were taking this class [Sierra] on how to relate to people, and my roommate was never sober. I could never [relate] to him—I could never try any of what we learned on him.

When Peter went home at Christmas, he remembers not wanting to come back. He recalls one incident which helped him to conclude that Southern California is a strange place:

> I remember being in a car accident with J, a good drinking buddy. We got along really well, we were really good friends the first quarter . . . . We were just coming out of Albertson's supermarket. Irvine's wonderful because they have black streets and black curbs and black sidewalks, so someone

who's never been there before cannot tell where the street ends and the sidewalk begins. So this guy (J) missed it and went onto the curb and onto another car. And his car looked like someone had died in it — so wrecked, windows smashed, etc. . . . We were both fine; we had to go get our eyes washed out, but that was it. But a couple of months later, this insurance guy called up and said, "Were you hurt? Did you have to go to the doctor?"

"No."

"Well, I can't close out my file until I give you $25 to go to the doctor. I know it's too late, so here, go out and buy yourself a case of beer."

So after that we decided that whenever we needed money, we'd go out and stage an accident.

However, Peter says that things did not stay troubling for long. He feels that he learned a lot about living with other people. Sierra helped by providing a group of people who were also, in many ways, very much alone and looking for friends:

I think it was, in some ways, what I had originally anticipated — a lot of people looking for friends, a lot of people in the same situation saying, "I'll scratch your back if you scratch mine." There was a lot of back scratching that went on. I think that was basically it. In the dorms I lived in after Sierra, I was never quite as close, which probably had something to do with the fact that we had a class and meetings [in Sierra] . . . .

Peter found himself drawing closer to women than at any other time in his past. He felt that the search for close relationships was a response to missing the closeness of his family:

Freshman year, I remember . . . well, I definitely remember becoming much more deeply involved with a woman than I'd ever become before . . . and I think, in some ways, because I was no longer at home — and I have a very close family. I always knew I was loved. I think, in some ways, I was reaching out and seeking that . . . I got involved with absolutely no idea that it would lead to anything.

How did Sierra facilitate Peter's search for closeness? He seems to believe that the community "forced" him to be close to other students—that the natural result of frequently being placed together with other students was that he started to appreciate them:

> Emotional relationships were deeper for me [then] than at anytime before—and even with a number of friends. I never had as many friends before. It was because our lives were intertwined. We had so many common experiences that conversation became incredibly easy after the first few weeks . . . after I got over the initial fear of rejection . . . . Plus the fact that we were in this situation where we were going to live with these people for a year; it was a matter for all involved to get along with as many people as you possibly could. So it meant looking hard at everybody—I mean [with] some people you really had to look hard to see what was the redeeming quality about them, or how you could get along with them particularly.

What sort of changes happened to Peter during that first year? As he notes, he learned to draw closer to a variety of individuals, including those from different ethnic backgrounds:

> I think it would be fair to say I went to an extremely white high school. In fact, we had a black girl, but she moved junior year. So [in Sierra], I was in an environment that, culturally, was a mix of people like I had never seen before. I very much enjoyed that.

Other changes occurred, but perhaps most important was the change in his own self-esteem as he began to feel a part of his "substitute family." Peter reports that he was "a more honest and open individual" at the end of his time in Sierra because he had found people he could confide in and draw close to.

Sierra as Liberator: Judy and Cody. Judy came to Sierra fully aware of what she was getting into—her older brother had been a Sierran the year before and had given her the "complete scoop." Coming from a strict authoritarian family and eight years at a Catholic private school, she felt she was ready.

Judy began UCI as a biology major, later switching to political science, and eventually graduating with most of the classes needed for a second degree in art history. Her first years were, not surprisingly, filled with socializing and meeting people — particularly men. In her junior and senior years, she became a "hermit" and began studying feverishly. She completed her senior year with high grades.

One of her prime activities while at UCI was taking part in a sorority. Through sorority functions she met men and dated frequently. After completing her degree, she went to work in a management program of the Postal Finance Company. When I spoke to her, she had just married William, another graduate of UCI. Currently, she plans to continue in her present position and support William through law school. She feels that she "must" have her first child at 27 and her second child at 30. Following that, she wants to go back and complete her art history degree and possibly work in a museum. She has no objections, however, to just being a housewife.

Like many students, Judy recalls that Sierra was a friendly dorm:

> When I think back on Sierra, I think of a very close dorm . . . I remember that if you ever needed a friend, night or day, you could find [one]. I like the idea of having an RA and RS's — they were . . . just a year ahead — not so much that they were out of touch with what was happening.

But Judy's most important memories are of the new freedom she found as a freshman in a university dorm, especially in Sierra:

> I'm glad that I went into Sierra as a freshman because I had never been out on my own. I had been from a very close-knit family, a very strict family . . . and this was the first time I got to make my own decisions.

Judy recalls six changes she felt had occurred during that first year. First, she became more social and outgoing than she had ever been. Second, she became independent of her parents. Third, she felt she became more spontaneous in her decision making — she didn't have to plan a year in advance for a date! Fourth, she became assertive; in fact, Judy credits the assertion training from the dorm class with helping her retain her present job, a job which requires being somewhat forward and firm with strangers. The most important changes with Judy came in relationships. After eight years of going to school with girls, her source of friendships drastically changed:

> My relationships with guys in the 103 suite were really good. For the first time, I had all guys as best friends, whereas in high school, I had always been with girls . . . but I found out I was uncomfortable cuz girls'll backstab you. I decided that guys were the best thing you could have as friends. It was really easy to let yourself go . . . . If I was having problems with chemistry or something, one of them could help me — just basically the friendship with guys was really something.

The final change came in her moral values. While it is difficult to know just what part the Sierra community played in encouraging a liberalization of her values, Judy, like a large number of Sierrans, first considered "other life options" in the dorm that year.

> Well, when I came into UCI, I was very naive . . . very naive. Even in high school, I was a naive person — because I had gone to a Catholic school. And . . . when I was in high school, people were saying they were smoking dope and partying and all this. I was never into that scene, and inside I was saying, "No, people don't do this; they're just big talkers." So when I went to college, I found out it really was true. And I developed a sex life, whereas before I was just saying "No, no, no." People had said that's totally wrong, [but] I decided that that was something I did need to have before I decided to get married.

* * * * *

Cody signed up for Sierra because it "sounded good." He spent his first year as a very successful biology major, dropped out of school after the spring quarter, and subsequently spent time alternating working and "experiencing." One year later, he returned to give school another try. To his surprise, his grades improved even more; he began to spend time both in the biology lab and in the computer room. When I spoke to him, he was in the process of finishing up degrees in biology and information and computer sciences. He was also working full time in a psychobiology lab. Asked about future plans, he waved his hands in the air and said he didn't know.

Cody's impressions of Sierra, somewhat different from those of others, is of a heavily divided community facing constant tension among the staff and between groups of students. His freshman year was also rather different than that of other students since Cody was part of the "drug crew." While only having taken "light stuff" before arriving at Sierra, he decided to let his freshman year become an experimental venture, "tripping out" on LSD, amphetamines, barbiturates, and cocaine. Part of the way through the year, he became a supplier for other students on campus. He paid for his habit by shrewd dealing and by using any financial aid he could muster. He said his perspective was vastly altered; he saw society, women, culture, all differently. Cody, who recently "came out" as a proclaimed gay, said that his year in Sierra was unique because it was the first time in several years he didn't mess with sex. Too busy getting loaded, dealing, and going to school, he found no time for it.

Cody credits Sierra with making a lot of changes in his life. In some senses, every lesson on socialization learned in dorm class became a part of his collective manifesto: when traditional values were questioned, he heartily agreed; when conventional sex roles were challenged, he was ready to applaud; when staff mentioned forming a moral base based on one's own prerogatives (not someone else's), he was already in the process of drawing it up. One of the things Cody did as a result of lessons learned in Sierra was reveal his sexual preference. Another thing he decided to do was to change his last name; he didn't need the conventional association of some long lineage of people he knew little about.

Another change he claims was influenced by discussions in Sierra was his decision to give up his religion. Raised as a Catholic, Cody had for several years been a fervent independent Christian. Then, as his freshman year went on, he began to believe that Christians were caught up in "guilt trips." He decided to "put religion on the shelf;" in its place, he adopted Ayn Rand's philosophy of "selfishness as virtue." Cody is far from cruel or perverse; he simply says that he is the most important person in the universe. He says that if he doesn't take care of himself, no one will. The most important moral, he says, is honesty; if more people would just admit to their true motives, we'd find a lot of people looking out just for themselves. He states that he is ahead of them by being honest about his self-ness.

Sierra was not the only force influencing Cody during his freshman year. He names four key factors that worked to alter his perspectives — a) drugs, b) psychobiology (the understanding of the biological basis of the mechanics of feelings, thoughts and behavior), c) History 29 ("The Formation of Modern Society"), and d) the diversity of people he met at UCI. He feels that all of these forces together moved him toward being the person he thinks he should be. He appreciates the challenges that Sierra gave to him, especially what was learned, directly or indirectly, about being himself sexually.

Sierra as "Seeing It Like It Is": Sharon. In several cases, we have seen how Sierra allowed individuals to see how others live. Many had perceptions of morality crushed and reshaped; others saw a multiplicity of cultural perspectives. Sierra provided a basis for processing all this — serving as a forum for discussion of growing pains and burning issues. Sharon's case demonstrates how Sierra helped students discover what things are really like in the world.

A native Southern Californian, Sharon says she knew little about the Sierra program when she signed up, only that it was limited to freshmen. Her first year was difficult; she took biology, calculus, and English classes "just in case" she wanted to select any of those majors. Later, in her junior year (after majoring in biology for several quarters), she switched to political science and transferred to Berkeley. After finishing her bachelor's degree, she continued school for a fifth year in order to complete a teaching credential. She now teaches bilingual education in the San Francisco Bay area. Her plans include teaching a variety of grades, subjects, and students — and possibly becoming a principal.

Sharon's recitation of her memories from Sierra began with a pleasant one; like many students previously discussed, she found the dorm environment supportive:

> I had a really good impression of Sierra from the start. I thought the people were really friendly. Plus everyone was a

freshman, except for the RA [and RS's], which made it more comfortable . . . . I remember one time I was sick; it was early on. Lots of people were really nice; they kept inquiring about me. And somebody, I believe it was V, had all these drugs, and he brought me down this bag and said, "Oh here, you can have whatever you want." . . . Oh, that was another thing. The people in my suite became pretty close—we'd just get together and talk to the wee hours of the morning.

Yet Sharon remembers many shocks that first year. A somewhat traditional girl, she learned to appreciate behaviors which she had at first considered "immoral":

I found very few people those first weeks who weren't into partying. I thought, all this decadence . . . I think gradually my values [attitudes] changed . . . not that I became more decadent, but you know, I wasn't so self-righteous. Because my parents never drank, you know, I always thought drinking was wrong. It was the way I was brought up. But I found—you could have a glass of wine and not get drunk—you could appreciate some things.

The second shock came in the form of a grade. Sharon, like many students, had come to the university with high grades; she had never received a grade lower than a "B" in high school. The grades she received in the mail while she was home on Christmas break were less than a present:

Well, I got a "D" in calculus . . . what was it, Math 2B? And that was really devastating because I had never had a "D" before. And just seeing that . . . I don't know; I don't think it was totally fair because I worked hard. Thinking back, I guess I could have worked harder . . . . It caused me to re-evaluate. I had to sit back and really re-evaluate it. Because realistically, I had been getting "A's" in English and then my grades in math-science . . . and here I am thinking about being a bio-major. Like I felt I was doing it mainly because my parents wanted me to. Like I was trained to believe if you go into something in the medical or bio-sci area, it s more prestigious, more acceptable.

Sharon recalls returning to Sierra—to the waiting friends—with her sad tidings. But then she found that she was not the only one, for several other students had received low or even failing grades in some of their courses. For that moment at least, community meant commiseration.

Sharon was beset by one more challenge that first year, this one in the form of a 6'4" behemoth from the basketball team (Sharon is 5'2"). The encounter was ominously revealing, especially for a girl from a "safe and sane" neighborhood in a well-to-do suburb:

> I remember this one party. My roommate, K, had been involved, or she knew this guy, R.B., a big − − guy who was on the basketball team. And anyway, he was kind of harassing her. At that point, she didn't know how she felt about him . . . . Anyway, there was a party—one of the first Sierra parties. He was there, and he was kind of hassling her. And she didn't want . . . . He kept saying, "Step out to the balcony." He had a gun with him . . . he was kind of from a different crowd. And he was pushing her around and she was kind of worried. And I was there trying to say, "Oh, K, you have a phone call" . . . but he wouldn't buy that . . . . And a couple of times he came by and she would go to stay with a friend on the Island. And I remember one night—I was kinda scared, too—I didn't want him coming by cuz one time he had come by and she wasn't in and he kinda hung around the suite—about 6'4", a big guy. So I moved my mattresses down to J's room cuz I was worried he would come back . . . . What if he had come after me? I'd never been exposed to big guys with guns.

It may be important to note that UCI, as a whole, is not full of gruesome, firearm-toting giants. However, students like Sharon commonly came in contact with some individuals they thought had been raised on the "wrong side of town."

In retrospect, Sharon sees four things she gained from Sierra which have lasted: a) an understanding and tolerance for a really diverse range of people, b) friendships with a good number of "normal" individuals, c) a more liberal approach to issues of sex and drinking, and d) assertion techniques useful for both meeting and refusing to meet people.

Sierra as a Myth: Jack. It would be wrong to close out this section without giving some indication that there were those for whom the Sierra experience meant little. In a small number of instances, students were baffled about the meaning and purpose of Sierra. One student who felt this way during his freshman year was Jack.

Jack also came to Sierra by chance. Having trouble deciding among several "special interest" dorms, he chose Sierra because it was freshman and co-ed. During his first quarter, he worked 30 hours a week as well as attempting to carry the courseload required of a biology major. Though he tried mightily, his efforts were unsuccessful:

> That first quarter I remember studying. I think I was just overwhelmed by being there . . . Chemistry—I really think I could've done it . . . I pounded, I pounded at Chemistry.

Jack was held for Subject "A" (English Basic Requirement) and eventually had to take it three times. He changed his major to social ecology. After a little more than four years, he graduated and went to work immediately in his dad's tile business. Today he is employed there as manager of one of the branches. He plans to be married next spring to his high school sweetheart; the couple already owns a house.

In addition to being overwhelmed by his classes (particularly in combination with the demands of his part-time job), Jack was unable to fathom what the staff (or the students) of Sierra were all about. Spending a good portion of time "smoking his share" as he put it, he would commonly come to dorm class with glassy eyes. But even when perfectly sober, he never understood experiences such as SIMSOC. When asked five years later what the Sierra class meant to him, Jack replied, "Very little." He recalled some good friends he made, but thought that "sense of community" was a "myth"—something the staff tried to make us believe.

How then can we size up Sierra's effect upon the student? From the responses given, it is clear that Sierra had some impact on the lives of its students, but how much? Five years later, few students remember all of what they were taught in dorm class. Others are not able to identify anything special which they gained from the program that they could not have gained being freshmen in any university dormitory. Yet, all appear to have a sense of the uniqueness of the Sierra experience, and many attribute their growth, particularly on broad social-oriented issues, to their time there.

In a sense, I am left to interpret what ex-Sierrans have been trying to tell me these past months. As a participant in Sierra, I have been keenly aware of it being set apart from other portions of my otherwise conventional education. I know that the type of learning it offers can never be compared to that stemming from the Humanities Core course or from General Chemistry. The experiential, close-knit, process-it-yourself, think-and-write-it, feel-and-speak-it, believe-and-do-it curriculum of Sierra was like no other classroom most of us had ever had. It was a lecture session, encounter group, community assembly, family circle, and home base all rolled into one. No wonder it is difficult for Sierrans to say, in a few words, all of what Sierra was.

Characteristically, higher education in America has continued to take on the tones of detached pedagogy. Professors speak through remote microphones to audiences of several hundred; students learn from textbooks which hypnotize them with theories related abstractly, or not at all, to everyday life, using references to little known academicians piled 12 feet deep. It is to this kind of education — removed, austere, and usually bewildering — that Sierra is a response. Its community, values, human development, and relational growth set it apart from other curricula that feign relevance to a modern world.

The Sierra program was far from perfect; students have mentioned to me dismay at administrative oversights, poorly conducted modules, etc. However, the nature of the program, its hopes and thrusts, have remained salient; years later, students are able to recall the miracle of community, the late night dialogue, and the group-processed experience for which Sierra is famous.

There are two ways to finalize our impressions on the lasting impact of Sierra as a program. One is from the outside. Draper Kauffman, in his classic, *Teaching the future: A guide to future-oriented education* (1976), has noted three characteristics of an innovative curriculum: a) it teaches students the connection between chalkboard lessons and their own concerns and objectives; b) it involves active learning; and c) it involves a "democratization" of learning, with everyone, teachers and students, contributing as much as possible to the process of instruction and growth. When considered with respect to these three objectives, Sierra emerges shining.

The other way is from the inside. No year-long program can be expected to transform all its students' lives. Yet, the average response from ex-Sierrans is far from discouraging. To most, it was a notable time, something that stands out even from other meaningful memories of their university experience. The responses of one woman epitomize what I think the average student feels many years after Sierra:

L: So would you say that Sierra changed your life, or just gave you a new way to look at your life?

K: I think it added some flavor to my life. It added to it, gave it variety . . . . I think it really changed my life.

L: Was Sierra a really important part of your life — truly significant?

K: It was a significant part of my life — like a step.

EPILOGUE: THE NECESSITY FOR A VALUE STANCE

Earlier, I stated my belief that students in Sierra must be explicitly told what the value stance of the staff is, and must be given a variety of perspectives from which to examine moral questions. These two activities need not contradict one another; the instructors (psychologists and resident staff) can openly admit to the value assumptions they hold and still present a full span of alternative choices for consideration.

The question arises, however, as to the degree to which the instructors should take a public stance on their values. The controversy has moved into a polemic dialogue among those who state that instructors should not only make their own values explicit, but encourage students to adopt those they feel are vitally important.

I believe that indoctrination must be avoided at all costs; however, some values will inevitably be encouraged. They will be encouraged because "unbiased" instructors have a sense that some things are more right or more wrong than others — right or wrong for the individual, for relationships, and for society.

It is my belief that when they do feel strongly, they cannot remain silent.

The problem is a delicate one. Instructors lose much of their value to students if they become the sole judges of right and wrong, ardent despots over moral convictions. Education, as we have come to know it in this society, can only survive in an atmosphere of openness. On the other hand, refusing to wrestle with issues of right and wrong is ridiculous — especially when the topic of one's instruction is morality. Wilson (1975) states it this way:

> In moral education, we have (rightly) abandoned the idea that all we need is some authority telling us the answers, but (wrongly) fallen into talking as if there were no such things as true or correct answers, quite independently of whether "society," or pupils, or teachers think there to be. Over and above any "democratic" interplay of ideas, beliefs, "values," and so on, there stands the notion of what is actually reasonable or right; if it did not, we could not educate at all — we could only influence pupils' attitudes in various fashionable directions for which we had no final justification (p. 91).

Traditionally, there have been four reasons why college faculty do not want to tangle with the teaching of values: 1) An enlightenment view prevails which suggests that education provides individuals with knowledge and reason such that they will, therefore, choose the good life. 2) Maintaining objectivity is considered a prerequisite for seeking truth; it is feared that concern for values may distort truth. 3) All values are held to be relative; therefore, there are no universally valid standards by which to judge better from worse. 4) The division of labor is felt to be necessary in a complex society; therefore, the teaching of moral values should be left to the home and church. The goal of the university should be the development of intellect.

I disagree. The development of values cannot be left to chance. They are primary and, as Allport states, "the dominating force in life" toward which all activity is directed (Allport, 1961). They are the baseline measure of relationships and institutions, the declarative principles which ultimately unite communities or divide nations. It is not enough that students know how to condemn society; they must also know how to construct it.

Values are the building blocks of precepts that eventually domi-
nate legislation and public policy. Higher education cannot be
afraid to deal in values.

This is a function of education: the concept of developing
excellence in the student must include attention both to intellectual endeavor and to the development of value judgments.
Knowledge is inadequate without moral and social principles,
without ethical obligation or human accountability. We cannot
assume, in an age of secularism and changing family styles, that
home and church will continue as the sole means of moral
induction in society. Nor can we be tolerant and assume that all
values are equal. Some, like honesty, courage, modesty, and lib-
erality, have long found greater acceptance than others, such as
deceit or cruelty. Nor should the difficulty of locating absolute
values prevent the university from adopting a well-defined model
— one that is liberal in scope and filled with idealism.

To be more than just a catalog, the university must stand for
something. It must be a guiding force, not only in developing
the mind, but also in developing the conscience of society.
Ortega y Gasset (1944) frames it well:

> In the thick of life's urgencies and its passions, the university
> must assert itself as a "spiritual power," superior to the press,
> standing for serenity in the midst of frenzy, sharp seriousness
> in the face of frivolity and unashamed stupidity (p. 130, trans-
> lated from Spanish).

Not only is the instruction of values desirable, but it can be
initiated with a practical degree of effort: students can be given
a wide range of choices, taught to explore the impact of decisions, and encouraged to become involved in a variety of issues
requiring value judgments. They can be taught to isolate the
focus of an issue, to identify preliminary solutions and conflicts,
and to apply principles of personal value commitment to reach
a resolution of the issue, an answer to the question.

There is a fear of dogmatism on American campuses. Instruction of values must balance on the thin line dividing advocacy
from indoctrination, loyalty from blind partisanship, reverence
from idolatry. As Beck (1974) states:

> The problem of indoctrination is to be overcome not by retreat-
> ing from substantive theorizing, but rather by ensuring that

the development of ideas and principles takes place in an atmosphere such that students feel free to disagree, propose alternatives, change their minds, adopt idiosyncratic positions, and so on (p. 210).

Ours is an era which assumes that people have a sense of humanism. We take for granted that all know the nature of justice, the value of equal opportunity, the precious freedoms of speech and press. We assume that most people oppose oppression at heart, and have compassion for the impoverished and needy. Yet a tentative scan of any newspaper or magazine headline will demonstrate how presumptuous our assumptions are; the perpetual practice of man's inhumanity to man is a sufficient mandate for higher education's response. An education of values provides hope that people will not degenerate into machines, that society will persist in its pursuit of the integrity of the human spirit.

Programs such as Sierra carry great promise — particularly in an age when few who develop curricula are willing to grapple with issues of morality. But only as instructors and staff strive to be explicit in their own value orientation — and to ground themselves in values which carry the greatest promise for a free and just society — will their endeavors be fruitful. In order to achieve the greatest benefit for individuals and for society, educators must risk attempting to define what is good.

References

Allport, G. W. *Pattern and growth in personality.* New York: Holt, Rinehart & Winston, 1961.

Beck, C. *Educational philosophy and theory.* Boston: Little, Brown, 1974.

Broady, M. Sociology and moral education: The conditions of impartiality. In G. Collier, P. Tomlinson, & J. Wilson (Eds.), *Values and moral development in higher education.* New York: Wiley, 1974.

Kauffman, D. L., Jr. *Teaching the future: A guide to future-oriented education.* Palm Springs, CA: ETC Publications, 1976.

Ortega y Gasset, J. *El libro de las misiones.* Buenos Aires, Argentina: Editora Espasa-Calpe, 1944.

Raths, L. E., Harmin, M., & Simon, S. B. *Values and teaching: Working with values in the classroom.* Columbus, OH: Merrill, 1966.

Rest, J. R. Developmental psychology as a guide to value education: A review of "Kohlbergian" programs. *Review of Educational Research,* 1974, *44*(2), 241-259.

Wilson, J. Establishing a dialectic in moral education. In M. J. Taylor (Ed.), *Progress and problems in moral education.* Windsor, Birkshire, England: NFER Publishing, 1975, 87-92.

SECTION IV.

IMPLICATIONS OF THE SIERRA PROJECT

This final section provides the reader with a commentary on the Sierra Project from a number of different perspectives. Chapter 12 brings us back to the origins of the project — to the role and responsibility of higher education in shaping the development of character. The chapter then summarizes and interprets the principal findings from each of our four approaches to evaluation.

The Epilogue was written after the rest of the book had been completed. My purpose in writing it was to share a little of the "behind-the-scenes" experience of developing and administering the Sierra Project. The project was not simply what has been reported in the first 12 chapters of this book: namely, an orderly identification of the role of higher education in character development, the implementation of a psychological intervention and research study, and the report of the evaluation. It was also a stimulating interaction of a large number of people with varied skills and interests who participated in an intriguing, challenging, fallible, and often frustrating attempt to deal with significant issues of human development.

Chapter 12

REFLECTIONS ON THE SIERRA PROJECT
AND IMPLICATIONS FOR FUTURE RESEARCH

John M. Whiteley

This book began with the observation that universities tradi-tionally organize their curricula around academic disciplines and goals promoting academic development. A consequence of this traditional organization is to leave the primary influences over personal growth in college students to random events or to the power of the peer culture. We have argued that the college years provide educators with a unique opportunity to influence students' thinking on issues of morality because, for the first time in their lives, residential students are physically autono-mous from parents and siblings while actively pursuing psycho-logical autonomy. The circumstances of freshmen's physical and psychological autonomy are coupled with the demands of the developmental tasks in their transition from late adolescence to early adulthood. There is perhaps no period in young peoples' lives when they are more open to new experiences and to alter-native ways of thinking about those experiences.

Given this opportunity to stimulate students personal psy-chological development within a framework of rigorous aca-demic accomplishment, the Sierra Project has sought to study and influence the character development of university freshmen. This concluding chapter restates our original conception of the Sierra Project, reviews what we actually did and learned, and describes promising avenues for future research.

Many factors, both environmental and personal, contributed to the progress of the Sierra Project in ways which were both gratifying and sometimes wholly unexpected. The freshman year

271

itself turned out to be a far greater catalyst for change than any of us anticipated, and the university proved far more hospitable to the Sierra Project than I thought it would be. After scrutinizing our proposals, the faculty committees responsible for approving academic courses and research on human subjects allowed us to proceed with this project. While the Sierra dorm class with its four units of credit was essentially a freshman year elective, many students were able to carry more than a full academic load of science, math, language, and English courses.

Freshmen chose to participate in the Sierra Project in numbers which exceeded our capacity of fifty students. In the exploratory year of 1975-76 (the Class of 1979), Sierra Hall was the first choice of housing for 138 students. For the next three years (the Classes of 1980, 1981, and 1982), Sierra Hall was sufficiently oversubscribed to allow us to create an equal balance of men and women and a diverse ethnic mix. The students' willingness to serve as research subjects was gratifying, though the student staff had to pursue some longitudinal subjects with alacrity and ingenuity. While attrition in the research sample did occur, our adoption of the collateral control group design reduced the effects of this attrition in the longitudinal study.

Finally, there was a far more dedicated and dependable contribution by student and professional staff than I had anticipated during project planning. The sophomore student staff who lived in Sierra Hall became our "early warning system" for potential problems with both the curriculum and the evaluation components. Because they were close to the students' day-to-day lives, the student staff also helped us determine what issues would be developmentally relevant at a particular time; their insights into the complexity of race roles and sex roles for freshmen were particularly valuable. The diversity of the professional staff, which ranged from psychologists to data analysts, contributed a combined level of expertise without which we would not have been able to proceed as we did. For instance, the hierarchical cluster analysis and multidimensional scaling suggested by Magaña (1979) and the collateral control group design suggested by Nelson (1976) were two useful contributions which data analysts made to the evaluation program.

As we conclude the freshman phase of the Sierra Project, we find that we have generated more new questions about the transition from late adolescence to early adulthood in the realm of character development and its vicissitudes than we had when we began. Perhaps, though, this is a normal situation for a complex naturalistic study. When the four planned years of curriculum delivery to freshmen were ended (and I moved my attention to scrutinizing students' development during their remaining three years of undergraduate study), a committed group of professional staff and students continued to offer the curriculum as a feature for future residents of Sierra—a most gratifying circumstance.

In the first section of this final chapter, the deficiencies of our research design will be noted as a context for interpreting our results. In the second section, the major findings from the Sierra Project will be reviewed and implications for future research drawn.

LIMITATIONS OF THE EVALUATION DESIGN

None of the four evaluation approaches reported in Chapters 8, 9, 10, and 11 have the breadth of coverage necessary to convey adequately the complexity of what was actually occurring during each freshman year: the day-to-day life of forty-four freshmen and six sophomore student staff in constant interaction with each other; the demands placed on freshmen by the academic curriculum, faculty, and staff of a major research-oriented university; and the problems encountered in the transition from late adolescence to early adulthood in this society. If each of the evaluation approaches reported had been implemented more intensively, we would have concluded our four years of research on freshmen knowing much more about one component or another of the Project. However, we felt that since the terrain of character development in college freshmen was relatively unexplored, it was a better allocation of our personnel, logistical, and financial resources to try several different evaluation approaches. Despite the drawbacks of such a widespread assessment plan, the great value of this multiplistic approach is that our four methods of evaluation, taken together, provide us with a mosaic which better reveals what occurred in the freshman years of the Sierra Project.

The two greatest drawbacks of our multiple-assessment design are both attributable to the typical limitations on financial resources of most educational researchers. With limited resources, choosing several approaches to evaluation, rather than choosing one to be completed in great depth, required sacrifice of some information. For instance, when planning the Survey Design, we chose not to administer the Washington University Sentence Completion Test of ego development and the Moral Judgment Interview to students in Control Group I (Lago) and Control Group II (Random Control) for two reasons. First, we did not have the staff and financial resources to administer and score these tests for such a large population; second, we did not have enough funds to pay control students to complete pre- and post-tests. We knew from the exploratory year with the Class of 1979 that it was difficult to get Sierra students to complete the post-tests even though Sierra students had some motivation to participate derived from a close relationship with the community and staff. Since the control groups were already being asked to complete the paper-and-pencil tests, and since they had neither a relationship with project and staff nor monetary payment sufficient to induce participation, we did not believe that we would get substantial enough participation in the WUSCT and MJI administrations to make the effort worthwhile over a span of four years. Further, we were concerned that if we did request that the control groups take the WUSCT and the MJI, they might choose to reduce their participation in the testing we had scheduled as part of our basic Survey Design.

However, in retrospect, there is no decision I regret more than the one not to collect the MJI and the WUSCT on the two control groups. While I realize that it was probably a prudent decision given our constraints, it deprived us of useful data about the longitudinal development of moral maturity and ego in college students who have not participated in a psychological intervention. A further consequence of not administering the MJI and the WUSCT was that it was not possible to examine the differential effects of the Sierra experience on moral maturity and ego development, important dimensions for character development. Thus, priority areas for future research include examining longitudinal growth on moral maturity and ego development, and assessing the impact on these measures of psychological interventions such as the Sierra Project.

The second major drawback of our multi-assessment design was our inability to exploit fully each of the methods used. With Magaña's research, we were not able to determine the influence of the nature of the sample or of the constellation of measures on cluster characteristics. We also could not determine whether individuals with particular cluster characteristics (in the Magaña study, clusters 2 and 4) would have changed as a consequence of natural growth over the course of the year, or whether they changed as a consequence of the intervention. Since all students in the sample Magaña studied participated in the intervention, it was not possible for her to answer this question.

We also did not develop fully the potential of the Intensive Design as implemented by Resnikoff and Jennings because in the early years of the program we had to devote our limited staff time to organizing the curriculum and collecting data for the general Survey Design. For that reason, we were unable to utilize the intensive case study design until the Class of 1982 entered Sierra. We also were unable to use Lee's retrospective participant-observer interviewing technique except with the Class of 1979. Training some students participating in the Sierra intervention to function as participant-observers during their freshman year could have provided a richer perspective on the inner life of Sierra Hall. This would have complemented both the Resnikoff and Jennings and the Lee interviews. We chose not to do this training in our project because of limited resources and also because we felt that the scarcity of previous systematic studies on psychological interventions such as the Sierra Project made it important for us to include all possible freshmen as subjects.

It is apparent from Resnikoff and Jennings' observations, and from the richness of the retrospective insights and commentary by Lee, that interviewing is a valuable exercise in the evaluation of interventions with college students. We recommend that researchers invest the time and resources required to train and supervise observers as a useful method for investigating the critical relationship between moral reasoning and ego development on the one hand and moral action on the other. We also recommend in-depth interviewing of students in the three years following their freshman year as a means of obtaining information about delayed effects of the intervention.

Further research will also allow us to more clearly delineate differences between the character development of experimental and control students as revealed through the Survey and the Intensive Designs. The Resnikoff and Jennings and Lee interviewing approaches, while identifying how the Sierra Project may have influenced individuals, lack the control of an experimental design. The interviewing techniques cannot establish cause-and-effect relationships, but the approach can facilitate the generation of hypotheses for future empirical testing.

A final limitation of our evaluation which we would like to note is in its inadequate measurement of race roles and sex roles. We had no valid and reliable measure for assessing the impact of the curriculum on race roles, despite the emergence of race-role analysis as an important component of the curriculum. We also felt that the Bem instrument was not a relevant measure of the effects of the sex-role curricular modules which we developed for Sierra. Future researchers may have to create their own measures in these areas.

REVIEW OF RESULTS AND IMPLICATIONS

This section of the chapter will summarize and assess the principal findings from the four evaluation approaches utilized in the Sierra Project as reported in Chapters 8, 9, 10, and 11. The results from each of the evaluation approaches provide four very different views of the project; each has particular strengths for revealing patterns of growth on dimensions of character development and identifying effects of the Sierra Project.

The Survey Design

The Survey Design, described in Chapter 8, consisted of the administration of a battery of psychological tests at the start and at the end of the Sierra Project students' freshman year. An identical test battery was administered to the Classes of 1980,

1981, 1982, making it possible to study cohort (class) differences and to replicate basic findings.

There were three groups of subjects for each year of study. The residents of Sierra Hall comprised the experimental group participating in the year-long, psychologically based educational intervention. Like Sierra Hall, Lago Hall (Control Group I) housed fifty freshman students composed of equal numbers of men and women. Control Group II, in contrast, was selected at random from the remainder of the university's freshman class without respect to living arrangement.

Since the presentation of our data was organized around five questions, this review of principal findings and their implications for future research will follow the same format.

1. Are there changes during the freshman year which appear common to all of the groups sampled?

Our major finding was that scores on a measure of moral reasoning (principled thinking) increased during the freshman year for all three groups studied. The increase was moderate in size; the range of moral reasoning scores for our entire sample was restricted (largely conventional Stage 3). It would, therefore, be valuable to study growth patterns of freshman classes with a broader range of scores at other types of universities and colleges in different geographical regions of the country.

A second finding concerns psychological sense of community. Entering students had high expectations for the level of psychological sense of community which they expected to encounter at the university during the freshman year. We found that they were disappointed, uniformly perceiving themselves to have experienced less community than they had expected. Furthermore, the freshmen viewed people in less positive terms at the end of their first year than at its beginning — reflecting undoubtedly the competitiveness of our university's freshman curriculum, the psychological distance from faculty and staff, and the perceived low level of community. Until we complete further study, we will not know how students formed their initial expectations for community and what aspects of the freshman year lowered them.

Given the strenuous academic demands, new interpersonal challenges, and abrupt physical autonomy from parents, siblings, and previous friends, a supportive environment during the freshman year would be helpful on a host of dimensions. Unfortunately, this supportive environment is, in general, not considered by students to be present. Since the importance of a sense of community in promoting personal growth has been cited in the literature on psychological development (and due to a gap of obvious significance between expected and perceived community), educators should devote far more attention to providing a supportive psychological environment if freshmen students are to develop themselves to the fullest.

2. Are there changes during the freshman year which are different for students in Sierra Hall (the experimental group) than for students in the two control groups?

Measures of self-esteem and of moral reasoning were the only two constructs on which significant differences occurred. Unfortunately, our data collection procedure did not include assessment of moral maturity (MJI) and ego development (WUSCT) in the two control groups, which would have been necessary for us to study further differences between the Sierra experimental group and the two control groups.

In examining sample attrition, we found that Sierra Hall residents took the post-test in greater numbers than did the members of the two control groups. (The Sierra residents obviously had a greater involvement in the assessment program than did the volunteer control group members, having agreed to complete both pre-testing and post-testing in order to participate in the Sierra program.) Post-test participants for the two control groups, therefore, are somewhat less representative of their original pre-tested groups. Members of the control groups took the post-test in fewer numbers, and it is not likely that this attrition was random. We have assumed that certain motivational factors distinguish those control group members who chose to complete post-testing, and that equivalent participation in testing by all three groups would have revealed even greater differences between groups. It may be that this measurement problem is inherent in research on students in naturalistic settings. Confirmation or refutation of this assumption will have to await further inquiry.

Despite these problems, when we observe the post-test results with regard to self-esteem, we find that scores on our measure of self-esteem for students in the two coed all freshman residence halls (Sierra and Lago) increased, while scores for students in Control Group II (the Random Control), who had a variety of living arrangments (at home, in apartments with other students, in university residence halls with upper classmen, in rented rooms, etc.), declined markedly. This was a finding quite unexpected; we need to explore further factors influencing the self-esteem of college freshmen.

To complicate our picture, when scores on self-esteem for all groups were combined, there were no significant changes over the course of the year; therefore, our discussion of this finding is quite speculative. The most compelling explanation is that freshmen living together as a group are more supportive of each other than students in other living arrangments; these students may also tend to compare themselves to each other, as peers, as a source of self-esteem. Freshmen living with upperclassmen, in contrast, must constantly observe and compare themselves to those with more well-developed academic competencies and social skills. Until we know more about the circumstances influencing students in Control Group II (the Random Control), however, we can only conjecture about what influenced their decline in self-esteem.

The single most important empirical finding of the Sierra Project concerned student growth in moral reasoning. While freshmen as a group showed a moderate increase in their scores on the principled thinking measure of moral reasoning, the group who resided in Sierra Hall (who participated in the psychological intervention) increased twice as much as did the two control groups—using the adjusted gain score as the standard of change. The absolute amount of change was not great: for Sierra Hall residents, there was an adjusted gain score increase of +6.2662. The corresponding increase for Control Group I (Lago) was +3.1606 and for Control Group II (Random Control) it was +1.2557. In comparing the raw score differences between pre-test scores and post-test scores (even though there are methodological limitations in doing so), the unadjusted mean change between pre-test scores and post-test scores for all classes combined was Sierra, +6.9675; Control Group I, +3.1862; and Control Group II, −.0087.

The Sierra group changed three percentage points more on principled thinking than did the two control groups. Although our design does not allow us to specify which components of the intervention contributed to making that difference, it is my feeling that certain key components contributed to the additional growth of Sierra residents, namely: (1) the psychological sense of community; (2) the presence of more mature role models in the residence hall (the sophomore student staff); (3) the assertion training module which developed students' skills in identifying the rights of oneself and others and learning to resolve conflicts fairly; (4) the empathy training module which increased students' perceptions of how other people experience situations; (5) the greater responsibility for their educational experiences which was demanded of students; (6) the structured exercises which required students to rethink a number of previously unexamined beliefs; and (7) the consideration of sex roles and race roles which stimulated more complex thinking about ways of relating to other people.

There is an additional explanation of why the Sierra residents changed more on principled thinking than did members of the control groups which is not related to the curricular intervention. Because Sierra residents volunteered to participate in the character development program, one might assume that they were more motivated for personal growth than the residents of Lago Hall (Control Group I) and members of the random control group. However, we have data from the exploratory class of 1979 that suggest this explanation is not tenable. In that year, the large number of students requesting the Sierra program allowed random assignment of students to both Sierra and Lago Hall, theoretically equalizing motivational factors. However, results from that year did not indicate any significant differences between the groups beyond those found within the Classes of 1980, 1981, and 1982, suggesting that total differences were not caused by the voluntary nature of enrollment in Sierra. However, since that first year was an exploratory one, and since we made subsequent adjustments in both the curricular and assessment programs, our observation can not be considered definitive.

In trying to place the moderate additional difference in growth in moral reasoning within a theoretical framework, we must consider why the psychological intervention produced the change in principled thinking it did. We have described elements of the curriculum which we feel contributed to student growth. We believe that these elements influenced students because of their provision for both psychological and moral education experiences. In Chapter 5, we reviewed the previous research on moral education for college students, dividing it into what were essentially two approaches: those with an emphasis on moral reasoning, and those with a much broader focus on psychological education. Magaña, Whiteley, and Nelson (1980) reviewed the research in a related area — the interaction between developing ego and developing moral reasoning — and concluded that the level of ego development effectively places a ceiling on the level of moral reasoning. Based on this information, we have come to believe that moral reasoning is fostered most effectively within the broader context of ego development. However, little research is available to guide us in making this choice since the topic is still a relatively new area for inquiry.

Because of this conclusion, a greater emphasis was placed on psychological rather than moral education. The scope of our curricular materials was broad because of our concern with promoting ego development as well as moral reasoning. But we believe, in hindsight, that Sierra students would have benefited from explicit moral reasoning exercises of the type reported by Boyd (1976) and Justice (1977). We did not emphasize these types of exercises because the wealth of activities we drew from in planning our curriculum gave us more than enough to fill our schedule of classes, we had not yet acquired a base of experience to guide us, and our sophomore student staff usually recommended against the moral reasoning exercises. When we did employ the exercises, the Sierra freshmen did not particularly like them. Perhaps their lack of interest in the exercises reflects a mismatch between the students' developmental stage (a very conventional Stage 3) and the issues most directly raised by our prepared moral reasoning exercises (primarily focused on promoting transition from conventional to post-conventional thinking).

Subsequent researchers must pay close attention to the actual developmental stage of the specific populations with which they work. With the Class of 1979, our exploratory sample, we learned that the students were not in transition from conventional to postconventional thinking, but at an earlier stage. With the Classes of 1980, 1981, and 1982, we planned the curriculum knowing that our students were in the very early stages of conventional thinking. They responded most enthusiastically to small group discussions of personal dilemmas led by the sophomore staff and to structured classroom exercises—such as assertion training—with the professional staff. Perhaps college students at higher stages of development would be more responsive to structured moral reasoning exercises. We certainly recommend that future researchers introduce focused moral reasoning exercises and study their differential effects on students thinking.

A fundamental judgment must be made when reviewing these results—whether raising the level of principled thinking by three percentage points is worth all the energy that went into the Sierra Project. One consideration in making such a judgment is whether or not the differential changes between the Sierra group and the two control groups hold up over time. If we find that they do, we must then investigate whether the differences in level of moral reasoning ultimately makes a difference in moral behavior. Changes in moral behavior would indeed be a worthwhile effect of the curriculum.

In summary—because of the relationship between moral reasoning and ego development—we believe that the most productive line of inquiry involves studying interventions which blend moral and psychological education. Further, the developmental stage of the population of participants is a critical factor in curriculum design. Our results imply that broadly focused psychological interventions can influence specific components of character such as moral reasoning.

3. What is the empirical interrelationship of the three different measures of character development for college students?

To answer this question, in the absence of an instrument which assessed "character" based on stages of development, we elected to adopt three proximate measures: ego development, moral maturity, and principled thinking. We chose to use an empirical definition of character development based on three psychological measures which had been the subject of previous intensive psychometric investigation: the Defining Issues Test, the Moral Judgment Interview, and the Washington University Sentence Completion Test for measuring ego development. Researchers can employ these measures with confidence that they are valid (measuring what they claim to measure), and reliable (measuring with consistency).

Since both our conceptual and empirical definitions of character development are based on the assumption that the three measures assess different aspects of character, it was necessary to do a correlation matrix to determine the extent of the relationship between the measures. While we believed that moral maturity, principled thinking, and ego development were related aspects of character, we did want to detect whether our instruments were simply measuring the same construct. If empirical investigation suggested that the same factor was being measured by more than one of our instruments, we could have consolidated our test battery by eliminating one of them. With our sample the empirical results from the correlation matrix indicated that the three instruments possessed a satisfactory degree of interrelationship to meet the purposes of our study. A sample more heterogeneous in age or developmental stage might produce a somewhat different pattern of interrelationships.

Until there is an instrument which assesses character from a developmental perspective, we have concluded that the use of the three proximate criteria of ego development, moral maturity, and principled thinking is a satisfactory approach from both a theoretical and an empirical viewpoint.

4. Within the Sierra Hall group, what changes occurred during the freshman year in terms of measures of character development?

There was a moderate improvement in the scores of Sierra freshmen on all three measures of character: ego development, moral maturity, and principled thinking. Since it was not possible to measure ego development and moral maturity systematically in the two control groups, an important direction for future researchers is identifying the differential effects of psychological interventions like the Sierra Project on these aspects of character. Studying the nature of character development on all three dimensions in college freshmen who are not involved in a special psychological intervention will also prove valuable.

Longitudinal study of moral maturity, ego development, and principled thinking during the college years remains an unexplored area. The period of transition from late adolescence to early adulthood provides society with an opportunity to influence the character of its next generation of leaders, citizens, and parents. The third volume of *Character Development in College Students* (Whiteley & Associates, in preparation), which follows the Sierra freshmen each year through graduation, will attempt to provide further insights into this growth period.

5. Are there patterns of developmental change during the freshman year which are related to the level of moral reasoning or ego development?

There were several basic analyses completed, all examining the distribution of scores at the various stages of moral reasoning and ego development and determining how those distributions shifted from pre-test to post-test for each group of subjects. Since the scores from the three instruments lend themselves to different statistical treatments, separate analyses were performed on individual measures. For example, the Defining Issues Test was scored for percent of principled thinking as well as for stages of moral reasoning, while the Moral Judgment Interview yielded only a single Moral Maturity Score (MMS), a composite score.

The most immediate avenue for future research is to repeat the same basic analyses on data collected over a time interval longer than one academic year. In completing this investigation, the following specific analyses are suggested:

1. a simple visual representation illustrating the percentage of thinking exhibited at each stage of moral reasoning from the DIT pre-test and post-test results;

2. a statistical analysis exploring the pre- to post-test changes in the percentage of principled thinking at each specific stage of moral reasoning. While we employed a multiple analysis of variance (MANOVA) as our statistical technique, we were not satisfied that it dealt satisfactorily with our data; analyzing the data presents problems because the

stages are not independent of each other — as scored, the percentages sum to 100; and

3. an analysis of results from administration of the DIT, MJI, and WUSCT exploring stage of development on one instrument as related to subsequent development on the other instruments.

We intend to complete these analyses on results for Sierra Project students of the Classes of 1980, 1981, 1982, across their four-year college experience (Whiteley & Associates, in preparation).

Differential Response from Initial Differences

In Chapter 9, Magaña reports results from statistical procedures for analyzing developmental data. These procedures enabled her to ascertain whether the Sierra Project intervention had a differential impact based on initial differences in the students' personality profiles. The combination of statistical procedures she employed (including standardizing the scores, computing a similarity matrix, and separating the students into subgroups using hierarchical cluster analysis and multidimensional scaling) appears to have promise for other developmental research.

Magaña's finding that individuals in the Sierra Project change differently according to their cluster membership is one which has significant implications for general longitudinal research. She pointed out that most longitudinal research attempts to describe one growth trend for all individuals, aggregating and thereby overlooking more information available about trends. We now know that we can successfully apply the statistical procedures of multidimensional scaling and hierarchical cluster analysis to developmental data in order to identify groups of subjects who will respond differently to psychological interventions. If her results (that a priori individual differences may to some extent govern the course of developmental change) are reproduced in other areas, then we may conclude that the typical longitudinal research design is obscuring considerable information about the influences of interventions on development.

The consequence of this procedure is that we are able to study what kinds of subjects respond under specific conditions to particular interventions; for example, what prior subject characteristics are associated with positive responses to differential counseling or psychotherapeutic techniques. As Magaña suggests, we may be able to "design varying types of educational environments and experiences which are capable of meeting the needs of different types of individuals."

Magaña has proposed areas for further inquiry based on design restrictions in her work. She suggests that we need to determine the influence of the nature of the sample and of the constellation of measures on cluster characteristics. We also need to determine whether individuals with particular cluster characteristics (in the Magaña study, clusters 2 and 4) would have changed as a consequence of natural growth over the course of the year, or whether they were changing as a consequence of the intervention. Since all students in the sample Magaña studied participated in the intervention, it was not possible for her to address this important question.

Intensive Interviewing

The in-depth interviewing approach described in Chapter 10 provides a prism for viewing the effects of the Sierra experience that is quite different from the other approaches reported. Resnikoff and Jennings sought to capture a sense of the way in which the myriad of planned and unplanned sub-interventions influenced the lives of Sierra freshmen. By intensively interviewing a small sample over the course of a full academic year, they hoped to use a phenomenological perspective to identify what kinds of individuals change, under what circumstances, and in what directions. Their procedure allows us to understand the impact of Sierra on individual students, and the process of change itself. The strength of this approach—and its distinctive contribution to understanding the Sierra experience —are the perspectives and insights of the subjects who specifically relate curricular, extracurricular, and other developmental experiences to their own growth.

Resnikoff and Jennings' interviewing revealed individual variation in students' attitudes and growth. Some students within Sierra grew to accept a broad range of differences in student ideas and behaviors, while others remained fixed in their original beliefs or grew more defensive about their differences.

Some of Resnikoff and Jennings' observations about student development verify our own. For instance, students interviewed spoke at length about what we have termed a psychological sense of community. Resnikoff and Jennings report a decline in this sense of community, citing several possible reasons — including roommate conflict and the development of sub-group identifications, particularly those based on racial identification. Because of the importance both we and the students attach to a sense of community, early ending of the "honeymoon" period — and the subsequent abatement of community spirit — should alert future researchers to the importance of documenting some of the sources of that decline. Further examination of the roles which sub-group identifications play in the adaptation to college and in the promotion of psychological growth — as well as their contribution to a sense of security and identity — may prove helpful in understanding the dynamics of a sense of community in freshmen.

The intensive interviewing approach further identified areas of particular student concern by observing that "the content discussed in class often provided an impetus to reaction and reflection." The emergence of self-disclosure as a student concern coincided with the introduction of curriculum modules on communication, conflict resolution, and assertion skills. By studying the link between the formal and the informal curriculum, the Resnikoff and Jennings approach made it possible to observe the importance of the self-disclosure issue and the strong student reaction centering around it. This knowledge encourages us to discover what factors made certain classes effective in stimulating student thinking about self-disclosure, and how self-disclosure served students in improving their interpersonal and intimate relationships. Although Resnikoff and Jennings observed that class content provided an impetus to student reaction and reflection, they could not "delineate which aspects of the administered curriculum had a specific effect on these individuals."

Resnikoff and Jennings' interviews also were able to chronicle growth on a number of developmentally relevant variables; particularly that students were achieving a sense of competence and were learning to feel free to express their opinions whether or not those opinions would meet with the approval of peers. This latter achievement has implications for broader research on character development. Moving from Stage 3 to Stage 4 in moral reasoning involves, among other things, developing a thinking system which is not based primarily on concordance with the opinions and approval of others. Resnikoff and Jennings, through their interview method, observed the same initial process of stage transition which was registered by the two measures of moral reasoning administered as part of the Survey Design (the MJI and the DIT).

As a method for examining planned and unplanned factors affecting the transition from late adolescence to early adulthood in a university environment, the intensive interviewing method provided valuable insights; it is highly recommended as an approach to data collection with similar populations of college students.

Retrospective Observation by a Participant

Loren Lee's work as a participant retrospective observer, described in Chapter 11, began in the summer of 1980, a year after the Class of 1979 had graduated. Although Lee had not been involved in the Sierra Project during the intervening years, we asked him to interview graduates of the Sierra experience to discover how they perceived that experience (and other experiences in their freshman year) as influencing moral growth. All the students Lee questioned had been residents with him during the exploratory year of the Sierra Project, in the academic year 1975-76.

Lee did not find general agreement among the students he interviewed about what constituted a higher plane of morality, nor did he find that students made a distinction between the content and the structure of moral reasoning. He reported that students maintained that the causative factors in moral growth were, in order of importance, the individual (and his/her personal choices), the environment, and maturation.

When students were asked to indicate what they considered to be the impact of Sierra on their own moral growth, their answers ranged from "none at all" to "important." Most of the individuals Lee questioned could not recall their moral values being modified by their Sierra experience. What they did recall as affecting them were: intimate heterosexual relationships; membership in a tight-knit, cohesive, social group; a job or other experience in the "real world"; academic study of a humanistic discipline; and, for a small but convinced group, experience with drugs.

Within the group indicating that the Sierra experience did help them change, students mentioned several ways Sierra affected their growth: they improved their self-images and gained an increased appreciation of openness and trust; their value systems became more liberal; they learned to question significant issues such as the value of education; and their sex-role behaviors changed in some cases. The causes to which they attributed their change were varied. Among the factors cited were living arrangements with many different types of students (such as found in virtually any residence hall), and an increased toleration of different values brought on by the open dialogue and challenge of value systems in the intensive small groups, the class discussions, the informal life of the community, and the interactions with staff. Lee concluded that the Sierra experience was "helpful," though not "crucial," to moral growth. The major factors encouraging change seemed to be the challenges to students' previously held values and the presence of a supportive environment in which to consider those challenges.

Those students who felt that their moral values had not been modified by their Sierra experience generally cited one or more of five reasons why the Sierra curriculum had not made a greater impact on their moral growth: the small proportion of time devoted to class; the narrow theoretical framework; the few relevant moral issues in discussion; an emphasis on conflict induction rather than conflict resolution; and the lack of models of "mature moral reasoning."

In commenting on the students' first perception that Sierra's class time was too limited to influence moral growth, I suspect that our definitions of Sierra differ. The students seem to be defining Sierra in terms of the weekly four hours of class meetings. The broader definition of the Sierra Project held by the staff included the interactions in the residence hall, the class presentation of curricular content designed to influence out-of-class thinking and behavior, and intensive small group discussions used to influence thinking about extracurricular involvements, issues of living together in Sierra, etc. This apparent difference in definition may explain part, if not all, of the differences between student comments and our own perception.

While the exact meaning of the students' second commentary on the narrowness of the framework was not sufficiently explained to make us confident that we are directly responsive to their meaning, it appears that they are really critiquing the theoretical assumptions of how growth in moral reasoning occurs according to the cognitive-developmental framework. We agree in part.

We believe that Kohlberg and his associates have identified accurately the structurally different stages of moral reasoning through which people's thinking may progress, provided they are exposed to the proper sequence of growth-producing conditions. While there is continuing research on whether Stage 6 is theoretically and empirically valid, the existence and documentation of the structural characteristics of pre-conventional, conventional, and post-conventional thinking are well established empirically. As a framework for understanding individual differences in reasoning about moral issues, the cognitive-developmental approach is, for us, a valid system of understanding and ordering the moral reasoning facet of human development.

Our experience with attempting to foster growth, however, has led us to the conclusion that this aspect of the cognitive-developmental framework is too narrow. Providing disequilibrating experiences calculated to require thinking one-half to one stage above the moral reasoning level of individuals in an intervention is an important approach, and is theoretically based on cognitive-developmental assumptions.

In retrospect, we believe we should have offered more disequilibrating experiences based on simulated moral dilemmas. But our findings lead us to conclude that fostering ego development is essential to providing for the growth of moral reasoning. Further, our experience with empathy and assertion training, as has been discussed earlier in this chapter, confirms that there are important approaches to raising the level of moral reasoning which are not based theoretically on the cognitive-developmental approach. Our research design did not allow us to assess the differential effects of components of the intervention, and further inquiry is needed in this area.

The students' third perception — that there was a scarcity of relevant moral issues under discussion — touches on one of our central concerns in presenting the curriculum. We made a conscious effort to teach neither the theory nor the measurements of moral reasoning, while at the same time presenting moral issues in class and fostering discussion of those moral issues in small groups. We found age-specific moral issues to be very influential. The classroom served as a vehicle for stimulating students with exercises such as "Alligator River"[1] or "Looking for Johanna."[2] Previous curriculum materials developed by Boyd (1976) and Justice (1977) provide relevant classroom materials for promoting late adolescent to early adult development in moral reasoning.

We know now that curricula must be closely related to the population's developmental level. For example, when using the "Lifeboat" exercise[3] with the class of 1979 (from which Lee drew his sample), we had not yet learned that our students were closely grouped around Stage 3. The issues presented by the Lifeboat exercise — the individual's right to life, and the bases on which decisions about that right should be made — particularly lend themselves to analysis and discussion at the level of the transition from Stage 4 conventional to Stage 5 post-conventional thinking. This early failure to match moral dilemma exercises with students' specific developmental level may be a principal reason why the students from the Class of 1979 reported to Lee that such exercises "missed the mark."

[1]From Simon, S. B., Howe, L. W., & Kirschenbaum, H. *Values clarification. A handbook of practical strategies for teachers and students.* New York: Hart Publishing Co., 1972, 291-292.

[2]From Goethals, G. W., & Klos, D. S. *Experiencing youth.* Boston: Little, Brown, 1970, 216-225.

[3]"Lifeboat" exercise, "The right to live: Who decides?" excerpted from the motion picture, *Abandon ship.* Learning Corporation of America, 711 Fifth Avenue, New York, NY, 10022.

The students' comments about the scarcity of relevant issues suggest that we should have broadened that portion of the curriculum still further in order to help translate concerns from the class and the small group discussions to situations of "everyday reality." Living in a college residence hall with other freshmen presents students with actual moral issues almost daily. We need to discover how to capitalize more on the natural emergence of moral issues in the residence hall setting. Lee mentioned several, including value choices in intimate relationships and value choices pertinent to academic dilemmas (such as cheating). These are powerful issues, universal to freshmen. Lee reported that moral issues arising naturally are discussed in "after-dinner conversation or in late-night marathon talks," but that these talks "often stop short of individual application." One of our research tasks is to find ways to make the informal curriculum function as a natural pathway to what Lee termed "individual application" and, consequently, student growth. We also need to find ways to present moral issues through classroom dilemmas so that they will be more than what Lee characterized as "thought-provoking psychological exercises" which fail to show freshmen how they can be translated into everyday reality.

The students' fourth perception of why the Sierra Project did not have a greater influence on their moral reasoning was its emphasis on conflict induction rather than on conflict resolution. From our viewpoint, we made a concerted effort to teach conflict resolution skills as part of the assertion training module. At the same time, based on the equilibration theory, we did try systematically to induce cognitive conflict on moral issues.

A pivotal developmental issue for freshman students was striking a balance between assimilation (translating experience into previously successful patterns of thinking) and accommodation (new and more complex ways of thinking). It had been our assumption in designing the psychological intervention that achieving the supportive environment associated with a high level of psychological sense of community would facilitate more successful accommodations and, therefore, a higher (more complex) level of reasoning.

Why students felt that greater assistance with conflict resolution would have increased the influence of Sierra should be investigated in relationship to the developmental level of the population. With a predominantly Stage 3 population, there is a disposition to avoid or minimize conflict rather than to resolve it. Students at a different developmental level might offer another perspective on the conflict induction-conflict resolution question.

The final student perception pertained to the lack of models of "mature moral reasoning." This appears to be an important area to consider for those who design new curricula. Our experience over the past four years indicates that freshmen respond very positively to panels of individuals of divergent lifestyles. These lifestyle panel participants reasoned about moral issues from different perspectives than did our freshmen. Likewise, the sophomore staff and the professional staff had different — and usually more complex — ways of thinking about moral issues. One student observation reported by Lee indicated that the staff should be required to be quite explicit about their own values. It would follow that those presenting models of moral reasoning should be quite explicit about their moral views and the reasoning behind them.

Finally, Lee's approach to evaluating the Sierra Project allowed him to comment on delayed effects. He interviewed graduates of the university who could reflect back over Sierra and their three subsequent years of study. The principal value of what he did in this area was to suggest potential avenues for future inquiry concerning effects of the freshman year psychological intervention which did not appear until later in the remaining three years of undergraduate study.

Our own longitudinal design is such that we are not prepared to address the question of delayed effects of the Sierra intervention until after the Class of 1982 has graduated. That research will be presented in Volume III (Whiteley and Associates, in preparation).

References

Boyd, D. R. *Education toward principled moral judgment: An analysis of an experimental course in undergraduate moral education applying Lawrence Kohlberg's theory of moral development.* Unpublished doctoral dissertation, Harvard University, 1976.

Justice, G. E. *Facilitating principled moral reasoning in college students: A cognitive-developmental approach.* Unpublished doctoral dissertation, Saint Louis University, 1977.

Magaña, H. A. *Individual differences on multiple assessments and their relationship to rate of development: Implications for developmental research and intervention.* Unpublished doctoral dissertation, University of California, Irvine, 1979.

Magaña, H. A., Whiteley, J. M., & Nelson, K. H. Sequencing of experiences in psychological interventions: Relationships among locus of control, moral reasoning and ego development. In V. L. Erickson & J. M. Whiteley (Eds.), *Developmental counseling and teaching.* Monterey, CA: Brooks/Cole, 1980.

Nelson, K. H. *Personal communication,* 1976.

Whiteley, J. M., & Associates. *Character development in college students* (Vol. III), in preparation.

EPILOGUE

John M. Whiteley

In reviewing what has gone before in this book, I have come to the conclusion that we have not yet captured and shared with the reader the full experience of participating in the Sierra Project. Our written portrayal up to now suggests that it was far neater, more orderly, better thought out from its inception than it actually was. We did try to anticipate problems and plan for contingencies, but we simply didn't begin to imagine the complexities of what we were getting into at almost every level of the Sierra Project. None of this unanticipated, complicated, sometimes frustrating experience appears in our sequential rendition of theories of character, relevant psychological constructs, setting and participants, evaluation plan, and review of results.

The planning and staffing stages of the Sierra Project resulted in issues that I had not anticipated. There were problems getting the diverse staff to work together (bridging the generation and experience gap) at a common level of understanding. This understanding of the project's goals and operations was a necessary prelude to our working effectively as a team.

The first major problem we encountered was that, despite a common commitment to the project, the initial staff seemed unable to work in harmony with one another. A number of factions developed, each certain that its members knew the best way for us to proceed; each had its own methods for inviting initial participants, for detailing the curriculum for the exploratory year, and for designing the components of the evaluation. Conflict reached the point that there was a movement to split into two projects before we had even been able to get one project under way.

The dilemma for me was based on our need for the expertise of each faction. The principal antagonists were the sophomore student staff and the initial contingent of graduate students, professional staff generally aligning themselves with one group or the other. The sophomore student staff, because they were closest to the entering freshmen in age, had the most realistic and accurate assessment of freshman reactions to what we were planning. The graduate student staff was conversant with the relevant literature from developmental and counseling psychology and had the training to lead discussion sections on issues of character development. Each group had skills and perspectives no other group of staff possessed; we clearly needed the collegial assistance of both sophomores and graduate students.

I assume in retrospect that we were all reacting to feeling underprepared and insecure as we anticipated the arrival of the first group of Sierra freshmen. The conflicts seemed to dissipate when the staff was organized into informal groups, working on either the curriculum or the evaluation. Staff members could choose which area to focus on, and were welcome to attend the meetings of the other planning group. Much to my relief, this organizational structure served to channel energies away from incessant conflict and into productive effort. Perhaps we also recognized that the freshmen would show up whether we were prepared for them or not, and so concluded that we had all better submerge our differences and get to work. The time and energy devoted to staff problems had certainly not been anticipated when we originally conceived the Project.

Initially, one of my approaches to encouraging a common understanding of the Sierra Project in its totality was to a give a lot of my personal time to the sophomore staff at the start of the year. One evening, I invited them to the clubhouse near my home for a steak dinner and a soak in the jacuzzi. (A jacuzzi is a small pool filled with hot bubbling water at 105° F, intended to relax those who sit in it.) We were sitting together in the jacuzzi when one of the sophomore staff blurted out, "Dr. Whiteley, are you comfortable doing this?" My immediate response, "Yes," really missed the mark. His question probably reflected his own discomfort at socializing in this way with a university official (at the time I was the Dean of Students). For them (and for me) it was a risky venture to try to collaborate as intensely as we were on developing and delivering the Sierra Project. I answered "Yes" at the time because it was my own turf; I frequently sat in the same jacuzzi with my own children and some of their friends. The memory serves to sharpen for me the difficulty of trying to "bridge the generation gap" and all that entails.

Once we got beyond the initial staff problems and achieved a satisfactory level of shared understanding and cohesiveness, we encountered more unexpected problems when we actually tried to teach freshmen in the naturalistic, non-academic setting. The formal Sierra class meetings occurred in the living room of the first "home away from home" most of these freshmen had ever had. On one occasion, our instructor showed up for class to find a major pillow fight in progress in the living room. The initial tone of the evening's class was obviously very different from what we had expected. The student staff reported another experience peculiar to teaching in the residence hall, a game frequently repeated over several years. In this game, some of the freshman women would hide in their closets or bathrooms before class was to start, so that the student staff would have to go find them and bring them, protesting, into class. There was a high level of affection, silliness and fun in these transactions; obviously, anyone who really didn't want to go to class could simply have hidden in a place which he or she knew was undiscoverable. For the instructor with a well-prepared class, however, there is an unexpected atmosphere when some students are pulled "reluctantly" into the classroom.

Another problem we did not plan for was the disconcerting amount of effort involved in trying to achieve community in a naturalistic, non-traditional class setting. In attempting to foster this sense of community, we had reviewed the relevant literature, obtaining some exercises which we hoped would prove helpful. One of these exercises was a two-day simulated society game (involving the freshmen, student staff, and classroom instructor) which we scheduled during a weekend retreat in the mountains early in the fall. We intended to give the students an opportunity to get to know each other via the activities of a structured exercise. However, it came to our attention after the retreat began that one of the students turned out to have an alcohol abuse problem the first evening we were in the mountains. He ran into a tree at such a speed as to require numerous stitches at a rural mountain hospital at 3:00 A.M. Because of the accident, the classroom instructor had to drive the student down the mountain to the hospital, returning to the retreat at dawn. After staying up all night and dealing with this emergency, she was not in any physical or emotional condition to want to promote community or put much spirit into the day's schedule.

Some of our unanticipated experiences were related to the developmental stage of the freshmen who participated in the Sierra Project, particularly those involving conflict with authority and the assumption of responsibility for shaping one's own education. Conflict with authority and the resolution of that conflict are frequently discussed in studies of the transition from late adolescence to early adulthood; I had anticipated that the issue of conflict with authority in Sierra Hall would be raised in some dramatic way by our freshmen. Since UCI does not consider itself bound to the types of residence hall rules which college students historically have found noxious, I had not expected any challenge to authority based on traditional residential or student-university issues. I had, however, expected some conflict on issues related to the curriculum; this expectation proved to be unfounded. At one point, the classroom instructor herself tried to raise issues concerning the structure of the class and its requirements in order to engage the students' participation and iron out any potential conflict. The students, instead of involving themselves in the issues, disagreeing, or even participating, simply responded that the instructor was "paid to decide that sort of thing." Once we learned that the developmental status of our students was very conventional, it helped to explain their failure to question or challenge our authority. Our instructional problem became how to get them to question authority at all.

The substantial exception to this absence of conflict with authority occurred one year when the student resident assistant indicated that he did not feel that his job required him to use his master key at virtually any time of the day or night to unlock the closet where the vacuum cleaner was kept. The student resident assistant that year was a very gentle, soft-spoken young man, as non-authoritarian as anyone I have ever met. Yet he became the focus of conflict and challenge for one student who tried to infect the rest of the residence hall. We named this conflict the "Chicken Little" incident, since the student who felt offended started going around the residence hall with the basic message that the sky was falling. The offended student felt that the RA was "terrible" because he would not agree to use his master key to help them at any time he was requested to do so. My reason for relating such a trivial incident is that we had expected there to be fundamental conflicts with authority and, at least with this group, there were not.

Getting students to accept some responsibility for their education turned out to be a very difficult task. We had expected that students might be somewhat passive about their learning —that the structured format of the high school setting, the necessarily simplified high school learning, and the reliance on authoritative textbooks which imply that the world is composed of issues having correct answers had not encouraged them to actively think for themselves. Therefore, we sought early in the year to make them actively involved in shaping their education by assigning them responsibility for planning a specific class session. The result of their first effort they billed as a "Talent-No-Talent Night," an entertainment session with no academic relevance. Had it been the Gong Show, it would have been our shortest class of the year. We learned not to try this activity again until the spring quarter, and then only with support and guidance. What struck us was the extraordinary difficulty the freshmen had in trying to control their own learning—in drawing on their own backgrounds, the assigned readings, and the experiences of others, then actively organizing that material.

I have chosen to wait until now to answer a question very frequently asked of me when I have spoken about the Sierra Project: given all of the work it entailed, would I do it again? By choosing to answer this question in the Epilogue, I wanted to demonstrate—by reference to the descriptions of theory, curriculum, and results—that the Sierra Project turned out to be a far more demanding, challenging, exhilarating, and personally educational odyssey than I had ever imagined it would be. I would unquestionably do it again. Encountering so many young people who are dedicated, interested in their university, and serious about the importance of the development of character in our society has been an opportunity and experience I will always treasure.

APPENDIX A

BACKGROUND DATA

REPORTING DEMOGRAPHIC CHARACTERISTICS AND GOALS OF SIERRA PROJECT PARTICIPANTS

TABLE A-1
POLITICAL ORIENTATION OF SIERRA FRESHMEN

	National Norms For Freshmen %	UCI Freshmen %	Sierra %	Control Group I (Lago) %	Control Group II %
		Class of 1979			
	n = 71,897	n = 772	n = 48	n = 51	n = 22
Far Left	1.6	2.80	2.33	2.56	4.76
Liberal	34.88	33.33	34.88	30.77	28.57
Independent[0]	51.10	46.60	23.26	35.90	19.05
Conservative	14.20	16.80	20.93	20.51	33.33
Far Right	0.50	0.40	2.33	0	0
Other*			16.28	10.26	14.29
		Class of 1980			
	n = 85,006	n = 752	n = 42	n = 40	n = 34
Far Left	1.70	1.30	2.38	2.50	2.94
Liberal	29.20	31.30	35.71	40.00	35.29
Independent[0]	52.60	48.50	19.05	17.50	11.76
Conservative	15.80	17.80	30.95	22.50	35.29
Far Right	0.70	1.10	0	2.50	0
Other*			11.90	15.00	14.70
		Class of 1981			
	n = 198,641	n = 921	n = 34	n = 34	n = 32
Far Left	**	**	2.94	2.94	0
Liberal	**	**	29.41	26.47	21.88
Independent[0]	**	**	26.47	35.29	12.50
Conservative	**	**	35.29	17.65	40.63
Far Right	**	**	0	0	3.13
Other*			5.88	17.64	21.88
		Class of 1982			
	n = 187,603	n = 856	n = 46	n = 33	n = 32
Far Left	1.30	1.50	2.17	0	0
Liberal	26.70	27.80	32.61	48.48	28.13
Independent[0]	54.00	52.00	43.48	21.21	12.50
Conservative	17.40	18.10	10.87	24.24	50.00
Far Right	0.60	0.60	0	0	0
Other*			10.87	6.06	9.38

[0]This position was labeled "middle-of-the-road" on the ACE questionnaire and "independent" on the Sierra Background Questionnaire.
*On Sierra Background Questionnaire, this category represents both "political" and "other" responses.
**This question was not included in the ACE questionnaire this year.
　Sources: Sierra Project Background Questionnaire and ACE Cooperative Institutional Research Program.

TABLE A-2
ESTIMATED PARENTAL INCOME: NATIONAL AND UCI
FRESHMEN[1]

	Class of 1979		Class of 1980	
	National Norms % n = 71,897	UCI Freshmen % n = 772	National Norms % n = 85,006	UCI Freshmen % n = 752
less than $ 3,000	1.8	2.4	1.9	1.7
$ 3,000 to $ 3,999	1.1	0.8	1.3	1.0
$ 4,000 to $ 5,999	2.4	1.0	2.5	3.0
$ 6,000 to $ 7,999	3.1	1.4	3.1	3.0
$ 8,000 to $ 9,999	4.3	3.4	4.2	3.8
$10,000 to $12,499	9.7	6.5	8.6	8.1
$12,500 to $14,999	11.3	8.4	10.3	9.7
$15,000 to $19,999	18.0	14.6	17.2	14.7
$20,000 to $24,999	15.5	20.7	15.6	16.0
$25,000 to $29,999	9.2	11.0	9.6	12.8
$30,000 to $34,999	7.2	10.9	7.7	7.5
$35,000 to $39,999	4.5	4.8	4.9	4.8
$40,000 to $49,999	4.2	6.4	4.8	4.9
$50,000 or more	7.6	7.6	8.3	8.9

	Class of 1981		Class of 1982	
	National Norms % n = 198,641	UCI Freshmen % n = 921	National Norms % n = 187,603	UCI Freshmen % n = 856
less than $ 3,000	1.6	3.0	1.5	1.8
$ 3,000 to $ 3,999	1.1	1.3	1.0	1.8
$ 4,000 to $ 5,999	2.2	2.8	1.8	2.8
$ 6,000 to $ 7,999	2.8	3.4	2.4	2.2
$ 8,000 to $ 9,999	3.5	3.7	2.9	3.8
$10,000 to $12,499	7.6	7.0	6.2	6.7
$12,500 to $14,999	8.8	7.9	7.1	5.3
$15,000 to $19,999	16.5	11.4	13.9	11.8
$20,000 to $24,999	16.1	17.0	16.2	15.5
$25,000 to $29,999	10.5	10.7	11.5	12.2
$30,000 to $34,999	8.7	10.8	10.3	10.0
$35,000 to $39,999	5.4	5.8	6.3	5.7
$40,000 to $49,999	5.4	4.8	6.8	8.2
$50,000 or more	9.7	10.4	12.0	12.2

[1]Parental income data was not collected from Sierra, Lago, or Control groups.
Source: ACE Cooperative Institutional Research Program.

TABLE A-3
FATHER'S OCCUPATION
NATIONAL AND UC IRVINE NORMS

	Class of 1979		Class of 1980	
	National Norms % n = 71,897	**UCI Freshmen** % n = 772	**National Norms** % n = 85,006	**UCI Freshmen** % n = 752
Artist (or Performer)	0.8	1.5	1.0	0.5
Businessman	31.4	30.9	34.6	32.2
Clergy or Religious Worker	0.7	0.4	0.7	0.4
Educator (College Teacher)	3.9	4.5	1.3	0.8
Doctor (M.D. or D.D.S.)	1.8	2.0	3.9	6.7
Educator (Secondary)	2.1	2.5	3.2	3.4
Educator (Elementary)	0.6	0.3	0.6	0.3
Engineer	10.4	20.4	10.6	17.3
Farmer or Forester	2.9	1.2	4.6	0.7
Health Professional (non M.D.)	1.3	2.2	1.6	1.6
Lawyer	2.4	2.9	2.4	1.7
Military Career	1.6	2.1	1.9	1.5
Research Scientist	1.1	1.7	1.2	1.3
Skilled Worker	13.0	7.4	8.2	6.7
Semi-Skilled Worker	6.1*	2.4*	4.1	2.3
Laborer (unskilled)			2.3	3.2
Unemployed	1.8	2.4	1.5	1.5
Other Occupation	18.0	17.8	16.3	17.9

TABLE A-3 Continued

	Class of 1981		Class of 1982	
	National Norms % n = 198,641	UCI Freshmen % n = 921	National Norms % n = 187,603	UCI Freshmen % n = 856
Artist (or Performer)	1.1	0.7	1.0	1.1
Businessman	34.4	30.1	35.0	32.0
Clergy or Religious Worker	0.8	0.5	0.9	0.4
Educator (College Teacher)	1.4	1.0	1.5	0.7
Doctor (M.D. or D.D.S.)	3.7	4.0	4.1	4.9
Educator (Secondary)	3.2	4.4	3.5	2.0
Educator (Elementary)	0.6	0.1	0.6	0.6
Engineer	10.8	19.9	10.9	17.1
Farmer or Forester	3.2	0.8	3.0	1.5
Health Professional (non M.D.)	1.6	1.4	1.6	1.2
Lawyer	2.5	2.4	2.5	2.9
Military Career	2.0	2.2	1.9	3.4
Research Scientist	0.9	1.7	1.2	0.9
Skilled Worker	8.6	6.2	8.2	6.0
Semi-Skilled Worker	4.1	3.5	3.6	2.2
Laborer (unskilled)	2.3	2.3	2.0	1.5
Unemployed	1.4	1.3	1.5	2.7
Other Occupation	17.4	17.4	17.1	18.9

Source: ACE Cooperative Institutional Research Program
*Semi-skilled and unskilled workers are grouped together in this year.

TABLE A-4
FATHER'S OCCUPATION FOR SIERRA PROJECT FRESHMAN

	Class of 1979			Class of 1980		
	Sierra % n = 45	Control Group I % n = 39	Control Group II % n = 23	Sierra % n = 43	Control Group I % n = 39	Control Group II % n = 34
Executive	20.00	12.50	18.18	23.26	28.21	35.29
Manager	17.78	27.50	18.18	23.26	20.51	11.76
Administrative	17.78	35.00	27.27	13.95	17.95	23.53
Clerical	15.56	7.50	9.09	2.33	0	0
Skilled Worker	6.67	7.50	4.55	20.93	15.38	14.71
Semi-Skilled Worker	0	2.50	0	9.30	5.13	0
Unskilled Worker	11.11	2.50	4.55	2.33	0	2.94
Unemployed	2.22	0	0	0	2.56	2.94
Housewife	0	0	0	0	0	0
Deceased	6.67	2.50	9.09	4.65	2.56	0
Retired	2.22	2.50	9.09	0	7.69	8.82
Student	0	0	0	0	0	0

TABLE A-4 CONTINUED

		Class of 1981			Class of 1982	
	Sierra % n = 35	Control Group I % n = 35	Control Group II % n = 32	Sierra % n = 43	Control Group I % n = 32	Control Group II % n = 33
Executive	11.43	31.43	21.88	20.93	31.25	21.21
Manager	31.43	31.43	46.88	18.60	28.13	39.39
Administrative	11.43	20.00	9.38	9.30	28.13	18.18
Clerical	8.57	2.86	9.38	9.30	9.38	3.03
Skilled Worker	17.14	5.71	6.25	11.63	0	6.06
Semi-Skilled Worker	17.14	0	3.13	13.95	0	0
Unskilled Worker	0	0	0	4.65	0	3.03
Unemployed	0	0	3.13	0	0	3.03
Housewife	0	0	0	0	0	0
Deceased	0	8.57	0	6.98	3.13	3.03
Retired	2.86	0	0	4.65	0	3.03
Student	0	0	0	0	0	0

Source: Sierra Project Background Questionnaire

TABLE A-5
FATHER'S EDUCATION
NATIONAL AND UC IRVINE NORMS

	Class of 1979		Class of 1980	
	National Norms % n = 71,897	UCI Freshmen % n = 772	National Norms % n = 85,006	UCI Freshmen % n = 752
Grammar School or Less	3.7	2.1	4.2	5.3
Some High School	7.8	4.1	7.8	6.2
High School Graduate	22.9	11.6	22.9	15.6
Post-Secondary Other Than College	4.1	3.7	4.1	3.9
Some College	14.2	16.3	13.5	15.1
College Degree	24.6	27.6	24.9	24.4
Some Graduate School	3.3	4.0	3.5	5.1
Graduate Degree	19.4	30.5	19.0	24.3

	Class of 1981		Class of 1982	
	National Norms % n = 198,641	UCI Freshmen % n = 921	National Norms % n = 187,603	UCI Freshmen % n = 856
Grammar School or Less	3.8	4.2	3.5	5.1
Some High School	7.3	6.3	6.7	6.0
High School Graduate	22.8	11.4	21.3	12.2
Post-Secondary Other Than College	4.0	2.9	4.1	3.4
Some College	13.9	16.1	13.9	17.4
College Degree	25.0	27.8	25.3	25.5
Some Graduate School	3.4	4.8	3.7	4.0
Graduate Degree	19.9	26.4	21.6	26.4

Source: ACE Cooperative Institutional Research Program

TABLE A-6
FATHER'S EDUCATION FOR SIERRA PROJECT FRESHMEN

	Sierra %	Control Group I %	Control Group II %
Class of 1979			
	n = 45	**n = 41**	**n = 22**
Less than 12 years	15.56	17.07	4.55
12 years	15.56	14.63	31.82
13 to 16 years	40.00	34.15	31.82
17 to 18 years	11.11	17.07	9.09
19 to 20 years	13.33	17.08	22.73
More than 20 years	4.44	0	0
Class of 1980			
	n = 43	**n = 40**	**n = 34**
Less than 12 years	13.98	12.50	11.76
12 years	23.30	17.50	14.70
13 to 16 years	39.61	27.50	38.22
17 to 18 years	4.66	22.50	11.76
19 to 20 years	18.64	20.00	23.52
More than 20 years	0	0	26.09
Class of 1981			
	n = 34	**n = 34**	**n = 32**
Less than 12 years	14.70	5.88	9.38
12 years	23.52	11.76	3.13
13 to 16 years	38.32	26.46	43.75
17 to 18 years	5.78	23.52	21.88
19 years or more*	17.64	32.34	21.88
Class of 1982			
	n = 46	**n = 32**	**n = 33**
Less than 12 years	15.22	3.13	0
12 years	28.26	9.39	12.12
13 to 16 years	30.43	53.13	54.55
17 to 18 years	17.39	9.39	12.12
19 years or more*	8.70	25.00	21.21

Source: Sierra Project Background Questionnaire
*For the Class of 1981 and 1982 this category replaced the "19-20" and "more than 20" categories.

TABLE A-7
MOTHER'S OCCUPATION
NATIONAL AND UC IRVINE NORMS

	Class of 1979		Class of 1980	
	National Norms % n = 71,897	UCI Freshmen % n = 772	National Norms % n = 85,006	UCI Freshmen % n = 752
Artist (or Performer)	0.9	1.3	1.6	1.2
Business Woman	7.8	10.0	6.5	6.7
Business (clerical)	*	*	9.7	10.8
Clergy or Religious Worker	0.1	0.0	0.1	0.1
Educator (college teacher)	0.7	1.2	0.5	0.8
Doctor (M.D. or D.D.S.)	0.3	0.8	0.3	0.1
Educator (secondary)	2.5	3.9	3.5	3.2
Educator (elementary)	4.7	4.6	6.7	6.7
Engineer	0.0	0.3	0.1	0.0
Farmer or Forester	0.2	0.0	0.2	0.3
Health Professional (non M.D.)	1.4	2.6	1.7	2.5
Homemaker full-time	*	*	36.6	33.2
Lawyer	0.2	0.1	0.1	0.0
Military Career	0.0	0.1	0.0	0.0
Nurse	*	*	6.4	6.3
Research Scientst	0.1	0.3	0.1	0.4
Skilled Worker	0.5	1.1	1.4	2.0
Semi-Skilled Worker	2.1**	1.3**	2.5	2.8
Laborer (unskilled)			1.5	0.9
Unemployed	8.2	10.1	7.4	8.0
Other	70.3	62.2	13.3	14.0

TABLE A-7 (CONTINUED)

	Class of 1981		Class of 1982	
	National Norms % n = 198,641	UCI Freshmen % n = 921	National Norms % n = 187,603	UCI Freshmen % n = 856
Artist (or Performer)	1.7	0.7	1.6	2.0
Business Woman	7.1	8.7	7.9	9.2
Business (clerical)	9.6	7.9	10.3	10.8
Clergy or Religious Worker	0.1	0.0	0.1	0.0
Educator (college teacher)	0.4	0.5	0.4	0.4
Doctor (M.D. or D.D.S.)	0.3	0.3	0.3	0.1
Educator (secondary)	3.4	3.6	3.7	2.3
Educator (elementary)	6.9	7.6	7.0	7.6
Engineer	0.1	0.3	0.1	0.1
Farmer or Forester	0.2	0.1	0.2	0.1
Health Professional (non M.D.)	1.8	2.2	1.7	1.8
Homemaker full-time	33.8	33.2	32.5	28.2
Lawyer	0.1	0.2	0.2	0.4
Military Career	*	*	*	*
Nurse	6.5	6.5	1.2	1.6
Research Scientst	0.1	0.5	6.4	7.5
Skilled Worker	1.4	2.0	1.6	0.7
Semi-Skilled Worker	2.6	2.0	2.4	2.6
Social/Welfare Worker	1.2	1.2	0.2	0.5
Laborer (unskilled)	1.5	1.0	1.5	1.5
Unemployed	7.5	9.1	7.2	9.2
Other	13.8	12.2	13.8	13.5

*Category was not included in the questionnaire for that year.
**Semi-skilled and unskilled laborers are grouped together in this year.
Source: ACE Cooperative Institutional Research Program.

TABLE A-8

MOTHER'S OCCUPATION FOR SIERRA PROJECT FRESHMEN

	Class of 1979			Class of 1980		
	Sierra % n = 45	Control Group I % n = 40	Control Group II % n = 22	Sierra % n = 44	Control Group I % n = 40	Control Group II % n = 35
Executive	0	2.50	0	2.27	2.50	0
Manager	8.89	27.50	27.27	13.64	7.50	8.57
Administrator	4.44	7.50	9.09	9.09	0	5.71
Clerical	20.00	15.00	31.82	18.18	15.00	22.86
Skilled Worker	0	2.50	0	2.27	5.00	0
Semi-Skilled Worker	2.22	2.50	4.55	2.27	5.00	2.89
Unskilled Worker	4.44	2.50	0	0	0	0
Unemployed	4.44	0	0	4.55	2.50	0
Housewife	55.56	40.00	27.27	47.73	60.00	60.00
Deceased	0	0	0	0	0	0
Retired	0	0	0	0	0	0
Student	0	0	0	0	2.50	0

TABLE A-8 (CONTINUED)

	Class of 1981			Class of 1982		
	Sierra %	Control Group I %	Control Group II %	Sierra %	Control Group I %	Control Group II %
	n = 35	n = 35	n = 32	n = 44	n = 34	n = 32
Executive	0	0	3.13	4.55	5.88	3.13
Manager	14.29	14.29	9.38	13.64	20.59	6.25
Administrator	5.71	8.57	6.25	4.55	5.88	3.13
Clerical	17.14	8.57	15.63	9.09	11.76	18.75
Skilled Worker	8.57	22.86	6.25	11.36	8.82	3.13
Semi-Skilled Worker	0	2.86	9.38	11.36	8.82	3.13
Unskilled Worker	5.71	0	0	6.82	0	0
Unemployed	0	2.86	6.25	6.82	0	0
Housewife	45.71	40.00	43.75	22.73	38.24	62.50
Deceased	0	0	0	6.82	0	0
Retired	2.86	0	0	2.27	0	0
Student	0	0	0	0	0	0

Source: Sierra Project Background Questionnaire

TABLE A-9
MOTHER'S EDUCATION
NATIONAL AND UC IRVINE NORMS

	Class of 1979		Class of 1980	
	National Norms % n = 71,897	UCI Freshmen % n = 772	National Norms % n = 85,006	UCI Freshmen % n = 752
Grammar School or Less	2.4	1.0	2.5	5.6
Some High School	6.4	4.4	6.3	5.4
High School Graduate	37.4	26.0	36.3	27.4
Post-Secondary Other Than College	7.8	6.3	8.1	7.9
Some College	16.7	26.2	16.6	21.0
College Degree	19.8	22.0	20.8	22.7
Some Graduate School	2.9	4.6	2.9	3.5
Graduate Degree	6.5	9.5	6.5	6.5

	Class of 1981		Class of 1982	
	National Norms % n = 198,641	UCI Freshmen % n = 921	National Norms % n = 187,603	UCI Freshmen % n = 856
Grammar School or Less	2.3	4.3	2.2	4.7
Some High School	6.0	5.5	5.6	6.3
High School Graduate	36.8	25.8	35.0	24.9
Post-Secondary Other Than College	7.6	6.2	7.6	7.3
Some College	16.8	24.4	17.1	23.0
College Degree	20.4	20.9	21.0	20.2
Some Graduate School	2.9	4.0	3.3	2.8
Graduate Degree	7.2	9.0	8.2	10.7

Source: ACE Cooperative Institutional Research Program

TABLE A-10
MOTHER'S EDUCATION FOR SIERRA PROJECT FRESHMEN

	Sierra %	Control Group I %	Control Group II %
		Class of 1979	
	n = 46	**n = 41**	**n = 22**
Less than 12 years	17.39	12.20	0
12 years	34.78	24.39	31.82
13 to 16 years	41.31	43.91	40.91
17 to 18 years	6.52	9.76	9.10
19 to 20 years	0	9.76	18.18
More than 20 years	0	0	0
		Class of 1980	
	n = 44	**n = 39**	**N = 35**
Less than 12 years	11.35	15.36	8.58
12 years	24.97	15.36	31.46
13 to 16 years	47.67	56.32	57.20
17 to 18 years	11.35	7.68	2.86
19 to 20 years	4.54	2.56	0
More than 20 years	0	2.56	0
		Class of 1981	
	n = 34	**n = 35**	**n = 32**
Less than 12 years	11.76	8.58	15.63
12 years	29.40	28.60	12.50
13 to 16 years	38.22	42.91	59.38
17 to 18 years	11.76	17.16	6.25
19 years or more*	8.82	2.85	6.25
		Class of 1982	
	n = 46	**n = 34**	**n = 33**
Less than 12 years	23.91	8.82	0
12 years	26.09	8.82	27.27
13 to 16 years	41.30	67.65	60.61
17 to 18 years	6.52	8.82	9.09
19 years or more*	2.17	5.88	3.03

Source: Sierra Project Background Questionnaire

*For the Class of 1981 and 1982 this category replaced the "19-20" and "more than 20" categories.

TABLE A-11

VOCATIONAL CHOICE OF SIERRA PROJECT FRESHMEN[1]

	Class of 1979						Class of 1980					
	Sierra n = 48		Control Group I n = 51		Control Group II n = 22		Sierra n = 47		Control Group I n = 43		Control Group II n = 46	
	%		%		%		%		%		%	
Vocation	male n = 26	female n = 22	male n = 24	female n = 27	male n = 11	female n = 11	male n = 26	female n = 21	male n = 23	female n = 20	male n = 28	female n = 18
Art/design	0	0	0	11.1	0	0	0	4.8	4.3	5.0	0	5.6
Business	15.4	9.1	12.5	0	9.1	9.1	15.4	4.8	17.4	10.0	3.6	5.6
Engineering	3.8	0	0	3.7	9.1	9.1	3.8	4.8	8.7	0	14.3	0
Entertainment/sports	0	0	12.5	3.7	0	0	0	0	4.3	0	10.7	5.6
Government	0	0	0	3.7	9.1	0	3.8	4.8	0	0	3.6	0
Health	46.2	22.7	25.0	18.5	36.4	18.2	19.2	0	30.4	15.0	7.1	5.6
Journalism/publishing	3.8	4.5	4.2	0	0	9.1	0	9.5	4.3	10.0	0	0
Law	0	0	16.7	3.7	0	18.2	3.8	0	4.3	10.0	17.9	0
Politics	0	0	0	0	0	0	3.8	9.5	0	0	0	0
Natural Sci.	7.7	4.5	0	7.4	27.3	27.3	11.5	0	4.3	0	10.7	0
Behavioral Sci.-research orient.	0	4.5	0	3.7	0	0	7.7	9.5	4.3	10.0	3.6	5.6
Behavioral Sci.-practition. orient.	0	4.5	0	0	9.1	0	7.7	9.5	4.3	15.0	0	11.1
Teaching	0	27.3	0	11.1	0	0	0	28.6	0	10.0	0	11.1
Other	0	9.1	0	11.1	0	0	3.8	14.3	0	5.0	0	5.6
Data missing	23.1	13.6	29.2	22.2	0	9.1	19.2	0	13.0	10.0	28.6	44.4

TABLE A-11 (CONTINUED)¹

| | Class of 1981 | | | | | | Class of 1982 | | | | | |
| | Sierra n = 43 % | | Control Group I n = 42 % | | Control Group II n = 32 % | | Sierra n = 46 % | | Control Group I n = 34 % | | Control Group II n = 33 % | |
Vocation	male n = 20	female n = 23	male n = 20	female n = 22	male n = 14	female n = 18	male n = 22	female n = 24	male n = 16	female n = 18	male n = 15	female n = 18
Art/design	0	0	0	4.5	0	5.6	0	0	0	0	0	0
Business	5.0	8.7	5.0	4.5	7.1	11.1	0	4.2	18.8	5.6	13.3	5.6
Engineering	25.0	4.3	20.0	0	7.1	0	13.6	0	0	0	6.7	0
Entertainment/sports	0	4.3	0	9.1	0	5.6	0	0	6.3	11.1	0	5.6
Government	10.0	0	0	0	7.1	0	0	0	0	0	0	5.6
Health	10.0	13.0	15.0	4.5	28.6	22.2	22.7	25.0	12.5	33.3	26.7	22.2
Journalism/publishing	0	0	0	4.5	0	5.6	4.5	0	0	0	6.7	5.6
Law	5.0	13.0	5.0	9.1	7.1	0	9.1	20.8	6.3	11.1	0	0
Politics	0	0	0	4.5	0	0	4.5	0	0	0	6.7	0
Natural Sci.	0	0	20.0	13.6	14.3	5.6	18.2	0	6.3	0	6.7	5.6
Behavioral Sci.-research orient.	5.0	8.7	5.0	4.5	14.3	5.6	9.1	16.7	43.8	5.6	13.3	5.6
Behavioral Sci.-practition. orient.	0	26.1	5.0	13.6	0	11.1	9.1	20.8	0	11.1	13.3	11.1
Teaching	5.0	17.4	5.0	4.5	7.1	22.2	4.5	4.2	0	11.1	0	11.1
Other	0	0	0	0	7.1	0	4.5	8.3	6.3	11.1	6.7	22.2
Data missing	35.0	4.3	25.0	22.7	0	5.6	0	0	0	0	0	0

¹Figures shown are relative percentages.

TABLE A-12
CHOICE OF MAJOR OF SIERRA PROJECT FRESHMEN[1]

	Class of 1979						Class of 1980					
	Sierra n = 48 %		Control Group I n = 51 %		Control Group II n = 22 %		Sierra n = 47 %		Control Group I n = 43 %		Control Group II n = 46 %	
Major	male n = 26	female n = 22	male n = 24	female n = 27	male n = 11	female n = 11	male n = 26	female n = 21	male n = 23	female n = 20	male n = 28	female n = 18
Humanities & Fine Arts	7.7	9.1	4.2	11.1	0	9.1	0	19.0	8.7	25.0	0	11.1
Social Ecology	0	27.3	8.3	3.7	9.1	9.1	3.8	23.8	0	10.0	3.6	22.2
Social Sciences	7.7	18.2	25.0	14.8	0	9.1	23.1	4.8	8.7	15.0	7.1	5.6
Biol. Sciences	53.8	36.4	29.2	22.2	36.4	18.2	38.5	19.0	52.2	25.0	17.9	11.1
Physical Sciences (other nat. sci.)	7.7	0	8.3	7.4	27.3	27.3	11.5	4.8	13.0	5.0	10.7	5.6
Engineering	0	0	0	0	0	0	0	0	0	0	0	0
ICS	0	0	0	0	0	0	0	0	0	0	0	0
Other	15.4	0	8.3	3.7	27.3	18.2	7.7	9.5	0	5.0	10.7	0
Undecided	0	9.1	0	18.5	0	9.1	0	19.0	8.7	10.0	35.7	11.1
Data Missing	7.7	0	16.7	18.5	0	0	15.4	0	8.7	5.0	14.3	33.3

TABLE A-12 (CONTINUED)

	Class of 1981						Class of 1982					
	Sierra (n = 43)		Control Group I (n = 42)		Control Group II (n = 32)		Sierra (n = 46)		Control Group I (n = 34)		Control Group II (n = 33)	
Major	male n = 20 %	female n = 23 %	male n = 20 %	female n = 22 %	male n = 14 %	female n = 18 %	male n = 22 %	female n = 24 %	male n = 16 %	female n = 18 %	male n = 15 %	female n = 18 %
Humanities & Fine Arts	5.0	4.3	0	9.1	0	11.1		4.2H 4.2FA	0	16.7H 11.1FA	6.7	22.2H 5.6FA
Social Ecology	10.0	56.5	5.0	9.1	0	5.6	4.5	25.0	0	0	0	11.1
Social Sciences	0	13.0	5.0	4.5	21.4	16.7	27.7	16.7	18.8	5.6	20.0	11.1
Biol. Sciences	10.0	13.0	30.0	22.7	42.9	38.9	36.4	25.0	50.0	27.8	40.0	27.8
Physical Sciences (other nat. sci.)	25.0	4.3	30.0	0	21.4	16.7	4.5	4.2	0	0	6.7	0
Engineering	0	0	0	0	0	0	13.6	0	0	0	6.7	5.6
ICS	0	0	0	0	0	0	9.1	0	6.3	16.7	13.3	5.6
Other	5.0	4.3	5.0	13.6	7.1	5.6	4.5	0	0	0	0	0
Undecided	15.0	0	0	18.2	7.1	5.6	0	20.8	25.0	22.2	6.7	11.1
Data missing	30.0	4.3	25.0	22.7	0	0	0	0	0	0	0	0

[1]Figures shown are relative percentages.

NAME INDEX

SUBJECT INDEX

Accommodation, 45; relation to assimilation, 45-46; role in Sierra Project, 46

Alienation: results in Survey Design, 135-136, 141. *See also* Keniston Alienation Scale Analysis of covariance, 142

Assertion training, 56-58; as curriculum module, 106; in moral reasoning; 58; with Stage 2 individuals, 59-60; with Stage 3 individuals, 60-61; role in Stage 3 transition, 56, 62-65; with Stage 4 individuals, 61-62; role in Sierra Project, 56, 58, 62-65

Assimilation, 45; relation to accommodation, 45-46; role in Sierra Project, 45-46

Attitude toward People: results in Survey Design, 138, 142. *See also* People in General Scale

Attrition: effect on evaluation, 120-121; in control populations, 118; in testing, 278

Background questionnaire, 114

Bem Sex-Role Inventory: as instrument in Survey Design, 113-114; results in Survey Design, 138-139; results in Personality Profile Analysis, 175, 177, 185

Carkhuff Empathy Scale, 115

Carkhuff Gross Rating of Facilitative Functioning, 115

Character: historical definitions, 9-11; conceptual and empirical definitions, 282-283; Sierra Project definition, 13-14; developmental model of, 13; measurement of: 14; in Sierra Project, 17-35, 98-101, 282-283; relation between measures of, 98-101, 282-283; relation between measures of, in Sierra Project, 282-283; *See also* Defining Issues Test, Moral Judgment Interview, Washington University Sentence Completion Test, Moral Reasoning, Ego Development

Character development: historical definitions, 11-12; core curriculum, 107; Sierra Project definition, 9-15, 14; in higher education: 4, 7; past role of, 5; six obstacles, 3-4; measurement of, 151-153; results in Sierra Hall, 283-284. *See also* Moral Reasoning, Ego development

Character education: in Sierra Project, 14-15; measurement of, 15

College Experience Questionnaire, 114

College Self-Expression Scale, 115

Community: *See* Psychological Sense of Community Control groups: collateral control, 119-121; make-up of, in Sierra Project, 118-119

Counseling psychology: assertion training in, 40; contributions to developmental education, 40; empathy in, 40; influence on Sierra curriculum, 40; psychological sense of community in, 40; social perspective-taking in, 40. *See also* Assertion training, Empathy, Psychological sense of community, Social perspective-taking

Curriculum: as moral education, 281; as psychological education, 281;